Labour Law in South Korea

Labour Law in South Korea

Hakchun Lee
Bongsoo Jung

This book was originally published as a monograph in the International Encyclopaedia of Laws/Labour Law and Industrial Relations.

Founding Editor: Roger Blanpain
General Editor: Frank Hendrickx
Volume Editor: Frank Hendrickx

Wolters Kluwer

Published by:
Kluwer Law International B.V.
PO Box 316
2400 AH Alphen aan den Rijn
The Netherlands
E-mail: international-sales@wolterskluwer.com
Website: lrus.wolterskluwer.com

Sold and distributed in North, Central and South America by:
Wolters Kluwer Legal & Regulatory U.S.
7201 McKinney Circle
Frederick, MD 21704
United States of America
Email: customer.service@wolterskluwer.com

Sold and distributed in all other countries by:
Air Business Subscriptions
Rockwood House
Haywards Heath
West Sussex
RH16 3DH
United Kingdom
Email: international-customerservice@wolterskluwer.com

Printed on acid-free paper

ISBN 978-94-035-1681-3

e-Book: ISBN 978-94-035-1682-0
web-PDF: ISBN 978-94-035-1683-7

Printed in the United Kingdom.

The Authors

Professor Lee was born in March 1954. He graduated from Dong-A University with both his Bachelor's and Master's degrees in law, he then pursued his doctorate at Bielefeld University, receiving his PhD in 1994 as a Doctor of Law. He then worked in senior offices within the Ministry of Education for the central government and was then invited to be a professor of Law at Dong-A University. He subsequently founded the International Society of Labour and Policy, which involved Korean, Chinese and other East Asian scholars. He was elected as Vice-president of the Korean Comparative Law Association and went on to become President of that society. He is currently the President of the Kim-hae Foreign Workers Support Centre (since 2007), and is President of the Job Centre for Immigrant Wives (as of 2010). He is a ministerial level member of the Migrant Wives' Committee as of 2010. He has created the *Asian Journal of Employment and Industry*, which Professor Blanpain joined as co-editor. He has translated the German scholar Hans Brox's *German Labour Law* (14th edition) for the first time into Korean. He established the Department of International Legal Affairs as a graduate school and International Studies in graduate school. He obtained a national research grant from central government to focus on the international arbitration of FTA legal disputes. To enhance this project, he established International Arbitration Department at the Graduate School.

His new research fields are the International Futures Trading College and the Alternative School of North Korean Youth Refugees.

Dr Bongsoo Jung was born in May 1967. He had worked in the human resources field in a Korean foreign-invested company for seven years and then he passed the Korean labour attorney's exam in 2003. He founded the KangNam Labour Law Firm in 2005 and has been working as the representative labour attorney at this firm since then. Korea's foreigners' monthly journal, *10 Magazine*, selected this labour law firm as one of the '10 Lawyers in Seoul for English-speaking Foreigners' in 2017. Dr Jung has published a bilingual book, *The Korean Labour Law Bible* in 2005 (since then, its fifth edition was published in 2016); a bilingual case book, *Korean Labour Law:*

Disputes and Resolutions in 2009 (since then, its third edition was published in 2014); and bilingual work manuals, *The Workforce Restructuring Manual* in 2018, *The Practical Guide for Foreign Employment and Immigration* and the *Manual for Lawful Dismissal* in 2019. Dr Jung together with the KangNam Labour Law Firm has published *A Bilingual Code of Korean Labour Law* in 2015 and quarterly periodicals, *Labour Cases* since 2007 (volume 46 was published in June 2019). He has posted his writings and publications on a cell-phone based application or app; its key word at an i-phone app store or android phone playstore is ‘Korean labour law’. Dr Jung obtained a master’s degree in labour law at the Korean University graduate school in 2014, and a doctorate degree in labour law at Ajou University graduate school in 2018.

Table of Contents

List of Abbreviations

AEPA	Act on Age Discrimination Prohibition in Employment and the Employment Promotion of the Elderly
BEPA	The Basic Employment Policy Act
DWPA	Act on the Protection, etc., of Dispatched Workers
EEWRA	Act on Equal Employment and Support for Work-Family Reconciliation
EIA	The Employment Insurance Act
EPRDA	Act on Employment Promotion and Vocational Rehabilitation for Disabled Persons
ESA	The Employment Security Act
FWEA	Act on Foreign Workers' Employment, etc.
FPWPA	Act on the Protection, etc., of Fixed-term and Part-time Workers
IACIA	Industrial Accident Compensation Insurance Act
ILO	International Labour Organization
ISHA	Industrial Safety and Health Act
LDAA	Labour Dispute Adjustment Act
LLC	Local Labour Committee
LRCA	Labour Relations Commission Act
LSA	The Labour Standards Act
MWA	Minimum Wage Act
NLC	National Labour Committee
POTUA	Act on the Establishment, Operation, etc., of Public Officials' Trade Unions
SLC	Special Labour Committee
SME	Small and Medium Enterprises
TULRAA	Trade Union and Labour Relations Adjustment Act
WCGA	Wage Claim Guarantee Act
WPCA	Act on the Promotion of Worker Participation and Cooperation
WRBSA	Worker Retirement Benefit Security Act
WVSDA	Workers' Vocational Skills Development Act

Preface

The first edition of Korean labour law was written by Kim Chi-seon in 1980 and this book is the third edition, by Hakchun Lee and Bongsoo Jung. As of the date of publication there are approximately 2.3 million foreign residents in Korea, some working and some not. However, many of them struggle, often needlessly, simply as a result of not knowing their rights and the details of the law as it pertains to their situation.

While there are numerous laws, amendments and presidential decrees which are pertinent to this matter the absence of appropriate translation services means that migrant workers are often unaware of those rights to which they are entitled. As a result, it is often those foreign workers who are most vulnerable that lack vital information regarding the laws which protect them during the time in Korea. This is simply because they lack the access to the laws themselves. With regard to this matter, if the free movement of the labour force is to be ensured through foreign trade agreements with nations such as the US and China, it is important that guest workers are aware of these laws. With regard to this the need for an appropriate translation service becomes clear.

Even as the author of this book, the greatest challenge was one of simple translation. As domestic scholars struggle with the process of translation and foreign scholars are excluded simply on the basis of language the flow of information has been a slow one. As a result the process of compiling this work has been slow and I would like to thank Professor Nicholas Bibby for his help. Without this, this book would have been difficult to publish. Furthermore I am indebted to Professor Zoon-Ki ko, for his admirable assistance in the translation process. Since 2018, this book has been updated by Bongsoo Jung, labour attorney, who represents the KangNam Labour Law Firm. His thorough update of the book following revisions of Korean labour laws has made it possible for this book to be revived as the most recently updated labour law guide. My hope is that as a result of this book, foreign scholars and legal practitioners, as well as those who have thus far lacked access to their rights while working in Korea, will have a greater understanding of the laws which pertain to this issue.

General Introduction

Chapter 1. General Remarks

§1. Definitions of Labour Law

1. Understanding of the labour laws is the most basic requirement of efficient human resource management. Human resources and labour managers implement their tasks on the basis of their knowledge of the labour laws.

Labour law can be defined as 'those laws which govern the relationship between employers and those workers who provide them with labour in a position of subordination' within the capitalist system. Labour law does not apply to independent labour which is done freely according to an individual's own plans and goals. Thus, subordinate labour relations are the main issue in defining labour law.[1] In determining whether to give the protection of labour law, the reality of the situation takes precedence over the form of the contract.[2]

2. Under the capitalist system, in reality, the relationship between employer and employee is neither free nor equal.[3] In other words, the employee is bound by the commands and orders of the employer and has little voice in matters concerning labour conditions. Labour law is a body of legal norms which aims to redress any evils arising from these subordinate labour relations and offers protection to workers in response to their unequal and subordinate position in relation to their employers. Therefore, the spirit of labour law may be defined as 'the law for the protection of employees'.[4]

§2. The Historical Development of Korean Labour Law

3. Korean labour law has been influenced by a unique mixture of foreign legal systems, particularly those of Japan, Germany and the United States.

1. For instance, the work done by a worker will be covered by labour law if s/he is employed by a company to do it, whereas the same work will not be covered by labour law if s/he merely works under contract with a customer.
2. Chi Sun Kim, Kluwer Law International, The Hague London Boston, *South Korea*, p. 15.
3. But civil law accounts for the supply and demand of labour on the basis of a naive conception, namely, that of a contract of employment which is concluded between two free and equal parties.
4. Chi Sun Kim, *op. cit.*, p. 15.

4. For instance, major components of Korean labour laws were borrowed from those of its neighbouring country, Japan,[5] which, in turn had followed the model of advanced capitalist countries immediately after the war. Provisions concerning collective bargaining agreements set out in the Trade Union and Labour Relations Adjustment Act (1997) – hereinafter TULRAA – were significantly influenced by German collective agreement laws, whereas the unfair labour practices provisions of the current TULRAA used the American Wagner Act as a template.

5. The legislation forming new, modern labour law was established in Korea after it was liberated from Japanese colonial rule. The Korean Constitution, which was adopted in 1948, declares a guarantee of workers' fundamental rights and establishes the premise that working conditions should accord with human dignity. In order to bring these constitutional principles into practice, the government enacted three major pieces of legislation: the Labour Standards Act (LSA), the Trade Union Act, and the Labour Dispute Adjustment Act in 1953. Since its origins, Korean labour law has gone though many changes and amendments, and as even a basic framework for industrial relations it is still in the process of formation.

§3. An Overview of the Korean Labour Law System

6. Korean labour law was traditionally understood to be comprised of two major branches: individual labour relations law and collective labour relations law. However, an increasing number of scholars have begun to recognize a third branch: labour market law. These three branches have their legislative grounding in the Constitution promulgated in 1948. As for labour and employment relations in the public sector, it should be noted that special regulations apply.

§4. The Constitution

7. The Korean Constitution guarantees fundamental social rights in Articles 32 to 34.

8. Article 34, commonly called the 'right to live' provision, proclaims the principle of the welfare state.[6]

Articles 32 to 33 deal directly with labour and employment relations, as will be seen below.

5. The government enacted three major labour laws, namely the Labour Standard Act, the Trade Union Act, and the Labour Dispute Adjustment Act in 1953. It is remarkable that these laws were made in the middle of Korean War, which was an unexpected time to observe such laws at all.
6. Article 34:
    1. All citizens shall be entitled to a life worthy of human beings.
    2. The State shall have the duty to endeavour to promote social security and welfare.
    3. The State shall endeavour to promote the welfare and rights of women.
    4. The State shall have the duty to implement policies for enhancing the welfare of senior citizens and the young.

9. These provisions on fundamental social rights were influenced significantly by Germany's Weimar Constitution.[7]

§5. Labour Market Law

10. The term 'labour market' pertains to the market in which employers and workers exchange labour for income. Article 32, paragraphs 1 and 2 of Constitution, which states that 'All people shall have the right to work' and that 'All people shall have the duty to work', expresses a basic government policy that people who earn their living by their work should have the opportunity to obtain suitable work in the labour market.

11. This right to work can be said to generate two political obligations: first, the state should intervene in the labour market so as to enable workers to obtain suitable job opportunities. Second, the state bears a political obligation to guarantee the livelihood of those workers who cannot obtain such opportunities.

12. These two paragraphs of the Constitution form the basis of labour market law. Corresponding to this first legislative mandate, various statutes were enacted as is seen below:

- the Basic Employment Policy Act (1993),[8] BEPA, which proclaims the general principles of labour market policies;
- the Employment Security Act (1994),[9] ESA, which regulates employment placement services, recruitment and labour supply businesses;
- the Workers' Vocational Skills Development Act[10] (WVSDA) of 1997;

5. Citizens who are incapable of earning a livelihood due to a physical disability, disease, old age or for other reasons shall be protected by the State under the conditions as prescribed by Act.
6. The State shall endeavour to prevent disasters and to protect citizens from harm therefrom.

7. These social rights provisions in the Constitution provided an important political and legislative basis for the development of social policy in Korea.
8. The BEPA was enacted to formulate and implement a comprehensive employment policy for the State; in addition it aimed to contribute to employment security, the improvement of the economic and social status of workers and a balanced development of the national economy and society, by helping individual nationals develop and display their abilities to the maximum, and by attaining enhanced efficiency in the labour market as well as ensuring a balance in the demand and supply of manpower (BEPA, Article 1).
9. The ESA strives for the employment security of every worker, and to contribute to the development of the national economy, by giving him or her an opportunity to find employment in which he or she may develop and display his or her own abilities, and, in turn, supporting the expansion of the work force required for the nation's industry.
10. The WVSDA aims to secure the employment of workers, raise their social and economic status, and improve the productivity of enterprises, thus contributing to social and economic development by promoting and supporting employees' skills development throughout their lives.

- the Act on Equal Employment and Support for Work-Family Reconciliation (EEWRA)[11] (amended from the Act on Equal Employment of 1987);
- the Act on Employment Promotion and Vocational Rehabilitation for Disabled Persons (EPRDA)[12] of 1990;
- the Act on Age Discrimination Prohibition in Employment and the Employment Promotion of the Elderly (AEPA)[13] of 1991;
- corresponding to the second mandate, the Employment Insurance Act[14] (EIA) of 1993 was enacted;
- to balance the supply and demand of manpower and achieve the development of the national economy by systematically introducing and managing foreign workers, the Act on Foreign Workers' Employment, Etc. (FWEA) (2003) was enacted.

§6. Individual Labour Relations Law

13. The term 'individual labour relations' denotes relationships between individual employers and workers relating to the initiation, development and termination of employment contracts. Individual labour relations law is a shorthand expression for the legal regulation of individual employment relations. Under current law, individual employment relations can be characterized as dealing with the conclusion, continuation and termination of labour contracts between individual workers and their employers.[15]

14. Individual labour law has its basis in Article 32, Section 3 of the 1987 Constitution, which provides that standards of working conditions shall be determined by law at a level guaranteeing human dignity.

11. The purpose of this Act is to realize gender equality in employment in compliance with the idea of equality as stated in the Constitution of the Republic of Korea by ensuring equal opportunities and treatment for men and women in employment, while protecting maternity and promoting women's employment, as well as to contribute to the improvement of the quality of life for all workers by providing support for the reconciliation of work and family life.
12. The purpose of this Act is to contribute to the employment promotion and vocational rehabilitation of disabled persons so that they may live decent lives through work suited to their abilities.
13. The purpose of this Act is to prohibit employment discrimination based on age without a reasonable reason, and to contribute to the security of employment for the elderly and the development of the national economy by supporting and promoting employment suited to their abilities.
14. The purpose of this Act is, through the enforcement of employment insurance, to seek to prevent unemployment, promote employment and develop and improve workers' vocational skills; to strengthen the nation's vocational guidance and job placement capacity and to stabilize the livelihood of workers and promote their job-seeking activities by granting them the necessary benefits when they are out of work, thereby contributing to the economic and social development of the nation.
15. Kazuo Sugeno, *Japanese Employment and Labour Law*, Carolina Academic Press/University of Tokyo Press, 2002, 74.

15. The LSA[16] (1997) is the foremost law regulating individual labour relations law and the most important and comprehensive piece of protective labour legislation; it establishes minimum standards for working conditions. In addition the government enacted a series of legislation to protect employees. Individual labour law embraces the Minimum Wage Act (MWA)[17] (1986), the Occupational Safety and Health Act[18] (1990), the Industrial Accident Compensation Insurance Act (IACIA)[19] (1994), the Act on the Protection, etc. of Dispatched Workers (DWPA)[20] (1998), the Act on the Prevention of Pneumoconiosis and Protection, etc. of Pneumoconiosis Workers[21] (1984), the Wage Claim Guarantee Act (WCGA)[22] (1998), the Worker Retirement Benefit Security Act (WRBSA)[23] (2005), the Act on the Protection, etc. of Fixed-term and Part-time Employees (FPWPA)[24] (2006), the Act on the Employment Improvement, etc., of Construction Workers[25] (1996), and others.

16. The purpose of the LSA is to set the standards for the conditions of labour in conformity with the Constitution, thereby securing and improving the living standards of workers and achieving a well-balanced development of the national economy.
17. The purpose of this Act is to stabilize workers' lives and improve the quality of the labour force by guaranteeing them a minimum level of wages and thereby contributing to the sound development of the national economy.
18. The purpose of this Act is to maintain and promote the safety and health of workers by preventing industrial accidents and diseases through establishing standards on occupational safety and health and clarifying where the responsibility for such lies, and by creating a comfortable work environment.
19. The purpose of this Act is to compensate workers rapidly and fairly for any work-related accidents by carrying out industrial accident compensation insurance activities, to establish and operate insurance facilities to promote the rehabilitation of victims of accidents and their speedy return to society, and to contribute to the protection of workers by preventing accidents and carrying out other projects for promoting workers' welfare.
20. The purpose of this Act is to enhance the flexibility of the supply and demand of manpower by managing workers' dispatch undertakings properly and establishing the criteria for the working conditions of dispatched workers, thereby contributing to their employment security and the promotions of their welfare.
21. The purpose of this Act is to contribute to the protection of workers' health, and the promotion of their welfare, by strengthening measures for the prevention of pneumoconiosis and issues related to health management for workers engaged in work in dusty conditions, and by providing for matters concerning the payment of compensation benefits to workers suffering from pneumoconiosis or to their bereaved family members.
22. The purpose of this Act is to contribute to the stabilization of workers' livelihoods by measures to guarantee the payment of overdue wages, etc., to workers who have retired, having wages or other payment still due as a result of the company being unable to continue its business, or when its business is unstable due to economic fluctuations, changes in industrial structure, etc.
23. The purpose of this Act is to contribute to securing workers' stable livelihoods in their old age by stipulating those matters needed to establish and operate a retirement benefit scheme for workers.
24. The purpose of this Act is to promote the sound development of the labour market by redressing undue discrimination against fixed-term and part-time employees and strengthening the protection of their working conditions.
25. The purpose of this Act is to improve the employment conditions of construction workers, to promote their welfare and to contribute to the development of the construction industry by assisting and promoting their employment security and the development and improvement of their vocational skills and by conducting welfare programmes such as providing construction workers with retirement mutual-aid benefits.

§7. Collective Labour Relations Law

16. Collective labour relations refers essentially to the organization, formation and management of labour unions composed of groups of workers, and the nature of collective bargaining between such groups and their respective employers or employer associations.

17. Collective labour relations are mainly regulated by Korea's Constitution as well as the TULRAA[26] (1997).

18. Collective labour law has its basis in Article 33 of the Constitution which guarantees to workers the right to organize, bargain and act collectively. Since these rights are recognized as an element of workers' fundamental human rights, they may not be violated nor may they be infringed by either the state or by employers.

19. The right to organize embraces:

- the right to form labour organizations whose principal goal is to sustain and advance working conditions;
- the right to operate those organizations and, therefore, the right to bargain collectively, as this protects workers' collective negotiations with their employers. Through collective bargaining, workers seek to conclude an agreement with their employers or those organizations that will determine their terms and conditions of employment and the rules governing their labour relations. The right to collective action includes two types of rights: first a principle of recognizing the right to engage in industrial dispute and then, more broadly, the right to engage in other union activity.

20. Only such public officials as are designated by the Act shall have the right of association, collective bargaining and collective action. The right of collective action by workers employed in important defence industries may be either restricted or denied under the conditions as prescribed by an Act (Article 33 paragraph 3 of Korean Constitution).

21. Any legislative or administrative act which denies this constitutional guarantee would be deemed unconstitutional and declared null and void by the courts. Furthermore, any agreement which infringes the fundamental rights of workers as guaranteed by the Constitution shall be deemed null and void, since such constitutional guarantees are a part of maintaining the public order.[27] Consequently, workers have a cause of action against an employer who infringes upon their rights in

26. The purpose of this Act is to maintain and improve working conditions and to improve the economic and social status of workers by securing the workers' rights of association, collective bargaining and collective action pursuant to the Constitution, and to contribute to the maintenance of industrial peace and to the development of the national economy by preventing and resolving labour disputes through the fair adjustment of labour relations.

27. For instance, yellow-dog contracts in which an employee promises to refrain from joining a union or to secede from a union as a condition of employment, or which allow for the dismissal of an

relation to union activity.[28] Workers are immune from any criminal or civil liability relating to their engagement in legitimate union activities.

22. Collective labour law serves to reinforce individual labour law with the same purpose of raising workers' social and economic status. Collective labour law is a term referring to that body of rules which governs the collective relationship between employers and the trade union or workers.

23. The TULRAA establishes the requirements for qualified unions, it prevents the unfair labour practice system which prohibits employers from undertaking anti-union activities, and gives collective bargaining agreements normative effect.

24. The Labour Relations Commission Act (LRCA) was enacted in 1997. The purpose of this Act was to contribute to the security and development of labour relations by establishing the Labour Relations Commission and regulating matters in relation to the operation of the Commission in order to perform, in a prompt and fair manner, its functions of adjudication and adjustment in labour relations.

25. The Act on the Promotion of Worker Participation and Cooperation (WPCA) was enacted in 1997; it was passed in an effort to maintain industrial harmony and, as a result, to contribute to the development of the national economy by promoting the common interests of labour and management by encouraging mutual participation and cooperation in resolving disputes or addressing interests.

26. The Act on the Tripartite Commission for Economic and Social Development was enacted in 1999. The effect of this Act was to establish the Tripartite Commission for Economic and Social Development where workers, employers and the government could consult each other and discuss issues such as labour policies and related economic and social policies. Based on a spirit mutual trust and cooperation, the Commission answers questions posed by the president, and prescribes such matters as are necessary with regard to its organization and operation in a bid to promote industrial peace and to contribute to the balanced development of the national economy.

27. In the case of public servants, only those public officials who are designated by Act, shall have the right to freedom of association, collective bargaining and collective action (Article 33 paragraph 2 of Constitution). Article 5 of the TULRAA clarifies this further by stating that 'workers are free to organize a trade union or to join it, except for public servants or teachers who are subject to other enactments'. Therefore, employees in the national and local public service are subject to special regulations, by the Act on the Establishment, Operation, etc., of Public Officials'

---

employee because of union membership, are null and void. At the same time, the Trade Union Act prohibits them – together with discriminatory treatment of employees because of their union activities or membership refusal to engage in collective bargaining, or domination and interference with unions – as unfair labour practices (TULRAA, Article 81).

28. For instance, the dismissal of a worker for reasons of his/her undertaking legal union activities is deemed to be null and void as it violates the constitutional norm.

Trade Unions (2006). Employees of the police service, the prison service, the fire defence service and so on, are prohibited not only from going on strike, but also from organizing labour unions. All public employees, both in the national and local civil service, are prohibited from striking and any violation is punishable by criminal sanctions. The right to collective action by workers employed in important defence industries may be either restricted or denied under the conditions as prescribed by legislation (Article 33 paragraph 3 of the Constitution). To regulate matters concerning the organization of trade unions for teachers, the Act on the Establishment, Operation, etc., of Trade Unions for Teachers[29] was enacted in 1999.

§8. The Legal Nature and Basic Spirit of Labour Law

I. Legal Nature

28. Civil law is based upon a range of principles such as the sovereignty of ownership, the freedom to contract and the presumption of self-responsibility in accidents; this has induced greater economic and social inequality between people. Hence, labour laws have been constituted to reform this inequality. Since special laws are considered prior to general laws, labour laws originating from or modifying the principles of civil law are special laws within civil law and are generally applied before more general aspects of civil law.[30]

29. Labour law offers guardianship to protect workers which takes account of their unequal and subordinate position in relation to their employers. So, labour law cannot help but intervene in and modify the traditional principles of private law. Therefore, labour law has an obscure legal nature, for it is juxtaposed between private and public law.

30. Generally speaking, labour law in Korea is thought to have an imperative nature both in individual and collective labour law. Even with regard to individual labour relations, a typical example of private legal relations, labour law regulates them with legal force.[31] In the realm of collective labour relations, the TULRAA

29. The purpose of this Act is to stipulate matters concerning the organization of trade unions for teachers in conformity with the provisions of Article 5 of the TULRAA and to regulate special such provisions as may be necessary for the TULRAA to be applied to teachers, notwithstanding Article 66 (1) of the State Public Officials Act and Article 55 of the Private Schools Act.

30. Chi Sun Kim, Kluwer Law International, The Hague, London, Boston, South Korea, p.17.

31. Usually, labour law regulates it with punitive provisions and administrative supervision. For example, the LSA provides minimum standards for working conditions. Any labour contract – whether the agreement was made individually or collectively – which sets lower standards is null and void; and employers may be punished by fines or imprisonment for violating the LSA. Article 15 (Labour Contracts Contrary to this Act):

    1. A labour contract which establishes working conditions which do not meet the standards provided for in this Act shall be null and void to that extent.
    2. Those conditions invalidated in accordance with the provisions of paragraph (1) shall be governed by the standards provided in this Act.

acknowledges the superiority of collective bargaining by giving normative legal effect to collective agreements, which means that any works rule or individual labour contract contrary to the provision of a collective agreement is made null and void.[32]

Also, any agreement which infringes the fundamental rights of workers guaranteed by the Constitution shall also be considered null and void.[33]

II. Basic Spirit of Labour Law

A. *The Protection of Workers*

31. Labour law arose from the necessity to protect factory workers, and its application has been gradually extended to workers in general. Therefore, the primary and the most important mission of labour law is the protection of workers.[34] So, 'human dignity' as provided for in Article 32, paragraph 3 of the Constitution[35] should be the ultimate standard in both enacting and interpreting positive labour law.

B. *The Consideration of the Public Interest*

32. Article 37, paragraph 2 of the Constitution provides that the freedoms and rights of citizens may be restricted by an Act only when deemed necessary for national security, the maintenance of law and order or for public welfare. And even when such a restriction is imposed, no essential aspect of any freedom or right shall

---

32. Article 33 (Validity of Terms and Conditions)

    1. Any part of the rules of employment or contract of employment which violates the standards concerning working conditions and other treatment of workers as specified by collective agreement shall be null and void.
    2. Matters which are not stipulated by a contract of employment, and which have been invalidated by paragraph (1), shall be governed by the terms and conditions of collective agreement.

33. For instance, yellow-dog contracts in which an employee promises to refrain from joining a union or to secede from a union as a condition of employment, or which allow the dismissal of an employee because of union membership, are null and void. At the same time, the TULRAA prohibits them – together with discriminatory treatment of employees because of their union activities or membership, refusal to engage in collective bargaining, or domination of, or interference with, union activities – as unfair labour practices (TULRAA, Article 81).
34. The purpose of the LSA is to set the standards for the conditions of labour in conformity with the constitution, thereby securing and improving the living standards of workers and achieving a well-balanced development of the national economy (Article 1 of the LSA).
35. Standards of working conditions shall be determined by Act in such a way as to guarantee human dignity (Article 32, paragraph 3 of the Constitution).

be violated. Therefore, in interpreting labour law any courts or other authorities concerned should make a careful examination of the question of balancing the protection of workers with the public interest.[36]

C. Respect for Labour–Capital Autonomy

33. Acknowledgement of the autonomy between labour and capital is of great significance in establishing good labour relations. In essence the principle enshrines the notion that negotiations between workers and management should be both the initial and primary means of resolving disputes. Article 33 of the TULRAA grants a normative effect to that part of a collective agreement which lays down the standards of labour conditions,[37] while Articles 47 and 48 of the TULRAA provide for the resolution of labour disputes by means of labour–capital autonomy.[38] As for the reason why labour–capital autonomy is approved, we may note that the problems arising from labour relations mainly concern economic interests and therefore resolution through the efforts of the parties is most desirable. However, respect for labour–capital autonomy cannot be infinitely approved. Especially when it affects the national life, it may have its own limitations.

34. Besides institutional guarantees of autonomy, a cooperative relationship between employer and employee is essential to the realization of labour–capital autonomy. Today, the relation between labour and capital is changing from a relation of social opponents to that of a social partnership. To keep industrial peace and

---

36. However, as long as they do not weaken the competitive strength of the national economy and do not disturb the balance of the national economic order, favourable labour conditions should be provided, as they contribute to the improvement of workers' economic and social status (Chi Sun Kim, *op. cit.*, p. 18).
37. Article 33 of TULRAA:

    1. Any part of the rules of employment or a contract of employment which violates the standards concerning working conditions and other treatment of workers as specified in a collective agreement shall be null and void.
    2. Matters which are not stipulated by a contract of employment, and which have been invalidated by paragraph (1), shall be governed by the terms and conditions of the collective agreement.

38. Article 47 (Efforts towards Voluntary Adjustment)

    No provisions of this Act shall be construed as to prevent the parties in a labour relationship from taking part in deciding labour-related matters including, but not limited to, working conditions, or from making every effort to resolve disputes or differences arising from labour relations, through labour-management consultation or through collective bargaining.

    Article 48 (The Obligations of the Parties)

    The parties in a labour relationship shall stipulate in their collective agreement the procedures and methods for labour-management consultation or other collective bargaining means needed to maintain reasonable labour relations, and shall make every effort to resolve labour disputes by themselves when such disputes arise.

contribute to the development of the national economy by promoting the common interests of labour and management through their participation and cooperation, the Act on the Promotion of Worker Participation and Cooperation (1997) was enacted.

§9. Enforcement Mechanisms for Labour Law

35. Korea has no courts specially designated for labour litigation. All labour and employment related lawsuits must be filed in ordinary courts. Korea has a three-tiered court system: district courts, high courts and the Supreme Court.

36. The Ministry of Employment and Labour is responsible for the administration of labour law and labour policy. Within the Ministry of Employment and Labour several bureaux are in charge of the administration and implementation of labour laws. Local government authorities often establish labour offices. A labour office aims to provide consultation, conciliation, and other administrative support for the resolution of individual and collective labour disputes.

37. The Labour Relations Commission (comprising the Central Labour Relations Commission, the Regional Labour Relations Commissions and the Special Labour Relations Commission) deal with the work of judging, deciding, resolving, approving, confirming or redressing discrimination, and other matters, in accordance with the TULRAA, the LSA, among others. The Commission is an independent administrative committee comprised of an equal number of representatives of employers, workers and the public interest who serve as commissioners.

Chapter 2. The Sources of Labour Law

§1. The Constitution

38. A principal characteristic of Korean labour law is that its basic principles and the rights those underpin are established within the Korean Constitution. As was stated above, Articles 32 to 33 of Constitution deal directly with labour and employment relations. To stay within the spirit of the Constitution, any interpretation of legislation needs to factor in, primarily, the fair and favourable treatment of workers.

§2. Legislation

39. Excluding the Acts enacted by the Japanese, which served to oppress the labour movement of Koreans, the modern history of labour legislation began following the 1945 Liberation with the help of the American Military Government. Most major labour legislation was enacted during the Korean War[39] and was amended or supplemented in the early 1960s and in the 1990s.[40] The legislation which created a new, modern system of labour law in Korea was developed by the government. Since its enactment, these laws have seen many amendments and are still in the process of formation.

40. The labour market laws are as follows:

- the Basic Employment Policy Act (1993)[41] (BEPA);
- the Employment Security Act (1994)[42] (ESA);
- the Workers' Vocational Skills Development Act (1997)[43] (WVSDA);
- the Act on Equal Employment and Support for Work-Family Reconciliation (amended from the Act on Equal Employment)[44] (EEWRA) (1987);

39. The legislation enacted during war time (1953) includes the Trade Union Act, the Labour Dispute Adjustment Act (LDAA), the Labour Committee Act, and the LSA, which may be termed the four major labour laws.
40. Chi Sun Kim, *op. cit.*, p. 20.
41. The BEPA aims to formulate and implement a comprehensive employment policy for the state and to contribute to employment security, the improvement of the economic and social status of workers and a balanced development of the national economy and society by helping individual nationals develop and display their abilities to the maximum and by attaining enhanced efficiency in the labor market and a balance in the demand and supply of manpower (BEPA, Article 1).
42. The ESA was enacted to strive for the employment security of every worker, and to contribute to the development of the national economy, by giving each worker an opportunity to find employment in which he or she may develop and display his or her own abilities, and supporting an expansion of the workforce as required for the nation's industry.
43. This WVSDA was enacted to secure the employment of workers, raise their social and economic status, and improve the productivity of enterprises, thus contributing to social and economic development by promoting and supporting employees' skills development throughout their working lives.
44. The purpose of this Act is to realize gender equality in employment in compliance with the idea of equality in the Constitution of the Republic of Korea by ensuring equal opportunities and treatment for men and women in terms of employment, while protecting maternity and promoting women's

- the Act on Employment Promotion and Vocational Rehabilitation for Disabled Persons[45] (EPRDA) (1990);
- the Act on Age Discrimination Prohibition in Employment and the Employment Promotion of the Elderly (AEPA)[46] (1991);
- the Employment Insurance Act (1993)[47] (EIA);
- the Act on Foreign Workers' Employment, etc. (FWEA) (2003); this law was revised in 2009, to encourage, invite and regulate foreign workers and their professional activities. These workers are deemed to be non-Korean citizens based in Korea and in receipt of a salary, or someone intending to participate in such work in the future.

41. The individual labour relations laws are as follows:

- the Labour Standards Act[48] (1997) (LSA);
- the Minimum Wage Act[49] (1986) (MWA);
- the Occupational Safety and Health Act[50] (1990);
- the Industrial Accident Compensation Insurance Act[51] (IACIA) (1994);
- the Act on the Prevention of Pneumoconiosis and Protection, etc., of Pneumoconiosis Workers[52] (1984):

---

employment, as well as to contribute to the improvement of workers' quality of life by providing support for the reconciliation of their working and family life.

45. The purpose of this Act is to contribute to the employment promotion and vocational rehabilitation of disabled persons so that they may live decent lives through work suited to their abilities.
46. The purpose of this Act is to prohibit employment discrimination based on age without a reasonable reason, and to contribute to the security of employment for the elderly and the development of the national economy by supporting and promoting employment suited to their abilities.
47. The purpose of this Act is, through the enforcement of employment insurance, to seek to prevent unemployment, promote employment and develop and improve workers' vocational skills; to strengthen the nation's vocational guidance and job placement capacity and to stabilize the livelihood of workers and promote their job-seeking activities by granting them the necessary benefits when they are out of work, thereby contributing to the economic and social development of the nation.
48. The purpose of the LSA is to set the standards for the conditions of labour in conformity with the constitution, thereby securing and improving the living standards of workers and achieving a well-balanced development of the national economy.
49. The purposes of this Act are to stabilize workers' lives and to improve the quality of labour force by guaranteeing them a minimum level of wages and thereby contributing to the sound development of the national economy.
50. The purpose of this Act is to maintain and promote the safety and health of workers by preventing industrial accidents and diseases through establishing standards on occupational safety and health and clarifying where the responsibility for such lies, and by creating a comfortable work environment.
51. The purposes of this Act are to compensate workers rapidly and fairly for any work-related accidents by means of industrial accident compensation insurance activities, to establish and operate insurance facilities to promote the rehabilitation of accident victims and their return to society, and to contribute to the protection of workers by preventing accidents and carrying out other projects for the promotion of workers' welfare.
52. The purpose of this Act is to contribute to the protection of workers' health and the promotion of their welfare by strengthening the prevention of pneumoconiosis and systems of health management

- the Wage Claim Guarantee Act[53] (WCGA) (1998);
- the Worker Retirement Benefit Security Act[54] (WRBSA) (2005);
- the Act on the Protection, etc., of Fixed-term and Part-time Employees[55] (FPWPA) (2006);
- the Act on the Protection, etc., of Dispatched Workers (DWPA) (1998); the law was revised in 2010, it aims to establish the criteria under which dispatched workers may be employed. A dispatched worker is one who is engaged under contract to one employer but works for another. However, this role is distinct from that of a sub-contractor which is dealt with in other legislation;
- the Act on the Employment Improvement, etc., for Construction Workers[56] (1996).

42. The collective labour relations laws are as follows:

- the TULRAA;[57]
- the Labour Relations Commission Act[58] (LRCAA) (1997);
- the Act on the Promotion of Worker Participation and Cooperation[59] (WPCA) (1997);

for workers engaged in working in dusty environments, and by providing for matters concerning the payment of conpensation benefits to workers suffering from pneumoconiosis or their bereaved family members.

53. The purpose of this Act is to contribute to the stabilization of workers' livelihood by coming up with measures to guarantee the payment of overdue wages, etc., to workers who have retired, having wages, etc. unpaid because the company cannot continue its business, or its business is unstable due to economic fluctuation, changes in industrial structure, etc.
54. The purpose of this Act is to contribute towards securing workers' a stable livelihood in their old age by stipulating matters necessary to establish and operate a retirement benefit scheme for workers.
55. The purpose of this Act is to promote a sound development of the labour market by redressing undue discrimination against fixed-term and part-time employees and strengthening the protection of their working conditions.
56. The purpose of this Act is to improve the employment situation of construction workers, to promote their welfare and to contribute to the development of the construction industry, by assisting and promoting their employment security and the development and improvement of their vocational skills, and by conducting welfare programmes such as providing construction workers with retirement mutual-aid benefits.
57. The purpose of this Act is to maintain and improve working conditions and to improve the economic and social status of workers by securing those workers' rights of association, collective bargaining and collective action pursuant to the Constitution, and to contribute to the maintenance of industrial peace and to the development of the national economy by preventing and resolving labour disputes through the fair adjustment of labour relations.
58. The purposes of this Act is to contribute to the security and development of labour relations by establishing the Labour Relations Commission and regulating matters pertaining to the operation of the Commission in order to perform, in a prompt and fair manner, its functions of adjudication and adjustment in relation to labour relations.
59. The purpose of this Act is to keep industrial peace and to contribute to the development of the national economy by promoting the common interests of labour and management through their participation and cooperation.

- the Act on the Establishment, Operation, etc., of Public Officials' Trade Unions[60] (POTUA) (2006);
- the Act on the Tripartite Commission for Economic and Social Development[61] (1999);
- the Act on the Establishment, Operation, etc., of Trade Unions for Teachers[62] (1999).

43. Individual labour-relations law, which controls labour-contract relations between individual employers and workers, is a form of individual contract law. By contrast, collective labour-relations law regulates the formation of organizations, collective consultations and exchanges between those organizations, and their collective activities. In individual labour-relations law, there are many labour-protection statutes which regulate the content of contracted relations in detail. By contrast, collective labour-relations law contains a small number of statutes which are primarily designed to create the legal framework for promoting the sound development of an autonomous relationship between unions and industry. The main aim of collective labour-relations law is thus to provide an arena in which management and labour can deal with one another on an equal basis.[63]

§3. Custom and Practice

44. There are cases where positive labour laws cannot provide a resolution to a problem arising from a dispute between labour and capital. Although theorists are divided as to whether custom and practice can be used as a source of law in such cases, it is generally accepted that such aspects of custom and practice, which do not contradict positive law or public order, may be regarded as a source of law.[64] Custom and practice is of special importance as a source of labour law, for it is widely acknowledged and respected in the field of labour relations. Furthermore, it is assumed that custom and practice can be put to practical use in establishing positive labour laws.[65]

60. The purpose of this Act is to stipulate matters concerning the organization of trade unions for public officials.
61. The purpose of this Act is to establish the Tripartite Commission for Economic and Social Development where workers, employers and the government consult on labour policies and related economic and social policies, etc. based on mutual trust and cooperation, to have the Commission answer questions posed by the president, and to prescribe necessary matters regarding the organization and its operation in a bid to promote industrial peace and to contribute to the balanced development of the national economy.
62. The purpose of this Act is to stipulate matters concerning the organization of trade unions for teachers in conformity with the proviso of Article 5 of the TULRAA and to regulate special provisions necessary for the TULRAA to be applied to teachers, notwithstanding Article 66 (1) of the State Public Officials Act and Article 55 of the Private School Act.
63. Kazuo Sugeno, *op. cit.*, p. 494.
64. Chi Sun Kim, *op. cit.*, p. 21.
65. *Ibid.*

§4. AUTONOMOUS REGULATIONS

45. Autonomous regulations include collective agreements, work rules and union bylaws.

46. The supreme aim of labour law is improving the economic and social position of workers through improved working conditions. As a result, acknowledging collective agreements as a source of labour law is quite normal within a modern system of labour laws,[66] through which we can expect voluntary order between union and employer. Moreover, considering the ever-changing nature of the relationship between labour and capital, every positive labour law is assumed to required to be supplemented by autonomous regulations. In any case, these autonomous regulations are established mainly according to the balance of power between unions and employers.[67]

47. The TULRAA provides that any part, or parts, of either rules of employment or contracts of employment which violate the standards concerning working conditions and other issues relating to the treatment of workers as specified in collective agreement shall be null and void (Article 33, paragraph 1). The TULRAA provides that matters which are not stipulated by a contract of employment, and those which have been invalidated by paragraph (1), shall be governed by the terms and conditions of collective agreements (Article 33, paragraph 2). As this is the most important autonomous legal norm between the parties, no one can make a judgment without giving it due regard.

48. A collective agreement binds only the parties and their members in principle, but the TULRAA admits that this legally binding force can go beyond this limitation under certain conditions. If a collective agreement is applied to at least half of the ordinary number of workers performing the same kind of job and employed in a single business or workplace, it shall also apply to other workers performing the same kind of job and employed in the same business or workplace (Article 35).

49. Furthermore, if more than two-thirds of the workers performing the same kind of job and employed in the same area are subject to the application of one collective agreement, the administrative authorities may, with the resolution of the Labour Relations Commission, and upon the request of one or both parties to the collective agreement or by its own authority, make a decision that such a collective agreement shall apply to other workers performing the same kind of job and employed in the same area, as well as to their employers. The administrative authorities shall notify, without delay, the decision made under paragraph (1) (Article 36) to all those involved.

66. Article 33 of TULRAA grants a normative effect to that part of a collective agreement which lays down the standards of labour conditions.
67. Chi Sun Kim, *op. cit.*, p. 21.

50. Work rules also acquire the nature of legal norms in relation to the labour contract as far as working conditions are concerned. If a labour contract includes employment conditions that are below the standards stipulated within the work rules, such non-conformity shall be null and void. In this case, the invalidated provisions shall be governed by the standards provided for in the work rules (Article 97 of the LSA). However, the work rules shall not conflict with laws or decrees or the collective agreement(s) applicable to the workplace concerned. The Minister of Employment and Labour has the authority to order an amendment to any work rule which is deemed to conflict with laws or decrees or collective agreements (Article 96 of the LSA). The LSA also provides that an employer who employs more than 10 employees continuously shall prepare work rules and report them to the Minister of Employment and Labour (Article 93 of the LSA). Therefore, the role of the labour contract in industrial relations is a very limited one in Korea.[68]

51. Union bylaws also acquire the nature of a legal norm in order to guarantee an autonomous and democratic operation of the organization. Article 33 of TULRAA provides that, 'The trade union shall include the following matters in its bylaws:[69] Union bylaws shall not conflict with the Labour-related Laws; the administrative authorities may, with the resolution of the Labour Relations Commission, order the correction of the union bylaws which are in conflict with the labour-related laws' (Article 21, paragraph 1).[70]

§5. Administrative Interpretation and Case Law

52. In order to achieve a unified and efficient supervision and enforcement of labour protection laws, a great number of administrative interpretations are issued

68. Chi Sun Kim, *op. cit.*, p. 22.
69.
    1. name of a trade union;
    2. purposes and activities;
    3. location of main office/headquarters;
    4. matters relevant to union members (matters regarding its constituent organizations in the case of a trade union in the form of an associated organization);
    5. name of the associated organization which it belongs to;
    6. matters on a council of delegates if such a council of delegates has been established;
    7. matters concerning meetings;
    8. matters concerning representatives or officials;
    9. matters concerning accounting, including union dues and others;
    10. matters concerning modification of the union bylaws;
    11. matters concerning dissolution;
    12. matters concerning disclosure of the result of a vote on industrial action, the keeping of and access to voters' roll and ballot papers;
    13. matters concerning impeachment of representative or officials for violation of the bylaws;
    14. matters concerning election of officials and delegates; and
    15. matters concerning discipline and control.

70. In the case of orders for correction, a trade union shall implement such orders within 30 days, except that the period may be extended for a reasonable cause (Article 21, paragraph 3).

by a central administrative agency and communicated to the relevant government office on the scene. Administrative interpretations[71] are not positive law and do not have a legal binding force before the courts. In Korea, although there is an argument as to whether or not an administrative interpretation is a source of labour law, it certainly has an important affect upon labour administration as well as upon the judgments of the bench.[72]

53. Article 103 of the Constitution provides that judges shall rule independently, according to their conscience but in conformity with the Constitution and legal statutes. A judge is bound only by the Constitution and the law. Therefore, neither the notion of *stare decisis* nor that of case law is known in Korea. Under the Korean legal system, a case is not a legal source. In practice, however, case law is important because legislation tends to be rather abstract, prescribing only fundamental rules, and so case law is necessary to fill out the legislative provisions when new cases arise. Besides, it is very hard to change a judicial decision by the Supreme Court, because it requires a collegiate judgment of the whole membership.[73]

§6. International Sources

54. Article 6, Section 1 of the Constitution provides that treaties duly concluded and promulgated in accordance with the Constitution and with the generally recognized rules of international law shall have the same effect as the domestic laws of the Republic of Korea. In labour law, it is generally accepted that ratified conventions of the ILO[74] have a legal effect as a legal source of labour law.[75]

§7. Conflicts in the Sources of Labour Laws and the Order of Priority

55. The constitution is prior to all other laws. Labour laws originating from the principles of civil law are generally applied before the civil law. Principles of civil law (absolute principle of ownership, principle of freedom to contract, principle of self-responsibility in accidents) induced greater social inequality among people.

71. Administrative interpretation exists when the Ministry of Employment and Labour or the Ministry of Justice express their official opinions on the outline of labour administration or the interpretation of labour law to a subordinate office in the form of notes; or when the Ministry of Employment and Labour instructs on an interpretive standard of labour – especially the LSA in response to a question from its subordinate offices.
72. Chi Sun Kim, *op. cit.*, p. 22.
73. Up to now, especially in labour law, with its short history and the instability of legislation, very little case law has been established in Korea. But case law is expected to play a very important role in future (Chi Sun Kim, *op. cit.*, p. 22).
74. The movement for the international unification of labor legislation, which began as early as the end of the 19th century, finally gave birth to ILO conventions (Chi Sun Kim, *op. cit.*, p. 22).
75. Chi Sun Kim, *op. cit.*, p. 23.

Labour laws have been constituted to reform the inequality. Higher laws are preferred to lower laws (principle of priority of higher laws). Special laws are preferred to general laws (principle of priority on special laws).When two laws are applicable to a same situation, the law that has been most recently revised is preferred (principle of priority of most recent laws). Labour laws promoting better working conditions are preferred over the principle of priority on higher laws (principle of priority of better laws).

Chapter 3. The Law of the Labour Market

§1. The Concept of the Labour Market

56. The term 'labour market' pertains to the market in which employers and workers exchange income for labour. The concept of the labour market, in a narrow sense, may be understood as a system that serves as an intermediary between job-offering employers and job-seeking workers, thereby adjusting work force supply and demand. The concept, in a broad sense, is a system that determines wages and working conditions either in individual enterprises or an entire industry, and that trains, recruits, and adjusts a workforce, according to demand and availability.[76]

57. This chapter briefly deals with the major aspects of labour market, i.e. the systems to match job offers and job applications, and the systems to train, provide and adjust a work force for industry. Above all, the central theme is the positive employment policy that has been developed for the sake of the preservation and stability of employment, pursuant to the constitutional concept of a guaranteed right to work.

I. The Right to Work and Job Security

58. Generally speaking, the constitutions of the capitalist states stipulate the right to work in its limited meaning, so to speak, as a kind of political programme.[77] In addition, since the right to work is an abstract right, when the government fails to furnish the people with the opportunity for work, the government is not liable in terms of legal responsibilities, although frequently it faces political ones.

59. The Korean Constitution declares the right to work as a fundamental human right of all people.[78] This is interpreted as meaning that the government is under a political obligation to try and provide jobs for all those who have both the wish and the ability to work. As a result, the obligation to work[79] is interpreted as meaning

76. Kazuo Sugeno, *op. cit.*, p. 31.
77. The notion of the 'right to work' admits two different interpretations. The first is that in its literal meaning and is insisted upon from a communist standpoint. According to the Constitution of the USSR, 'the people shall have the right to work – the right to get a job guarantees that remuneration corresponding to the quantity and quality of labour shall be paid'. The other option is limited in meaning and is derived from a capitalist standpoint. According to the Weimar Constitution, 'All German people shall be given the opportunity to acquire subsistence commodities by economic labour. To those who are not given the opportunity to work, necessary living expenses shall be paid.' Guaranteeing the right to work in its literal meaning cannot be realized without direct or indirect conflict with the freedom of choice of occupation. Therefore, the constitutions of the capitalist states stipulate the right to work in its limited meaning (Chi Sun Kim, *op. cit.*, p. 67).
78. Constitution, Article 32, paragraph 1.
79. Constitution, Article 32, paragraph 2.

that to those who are able to work but do not want to the government has no responsibility to ensure the 'decent human life' guaranteed by the Constitution.[80] In detail, the government should take all necessary measures to secure jobs, such as public employment agencies, public undertakings to provide work for the unemployed, training schemes to improve workers' chances of getting better jobs, unemployment insurance scheme, and so forth.[81] All of these measures are put into effect by several laws including the BEPA (1993), the ESA (1994), the WVSDA (1997), the EPRDA (1990), the AEPA (1991) and the EIA (1993), among others.

II. The Legal Regulation of the Labour Market

60. The Constitution states that 'All citizens shall enjoy the freedom of occupation (Article 15)'.[82] In Korea, a basic principle governing the legal regulation of the labour market is that workers and employers have freedom under civil law with respect to contracting and the choice of an occupation. So there is a limit to legal regulation.

61. Also, the Constitution states that 'All people shall have the right to work' and 'All people shall have the duty to work' (Article 32 paragraphs 1 and 2). Because of the right to work, the nation has a political obligation to make an effort to ensure the employment of workers and to relieve unemployment. Therefore, legal regulation can produce legislation which conflicts with the employer's freedom, with respect to hiring contained in the former principle. In such cases, even if the constitutional right-to-work provision has the effect of authorizing such legislation, it would be constitutionally permissible only if it were enacted for this purpose and were both necessary and reasonable.[83]

62. Under current laws regulating the labour market, employers have rights with regard to whom and how many people they hire as part of their constitutionally guaranteed freedom in doing business, which stems from their constitutionally endowed freedom to choose one's occupation.

63. The employer can decide freely how many workers to employ and also determine the method of recruitment.

64. Although an employer is free to recruit workers based upon any criteria, which need not be publicized, the question arises as to whether such a freedom of hiring is unrestricted when the selection is made on account of a worker's beliefs, creed, sex or for other discriminatory reasons. It is not illegal to do so, because a refusal to hire an individual, in and on itself, on the basis of their beliefs or creed

80. Constitution, Article 34, paragaph 1.
81. Chi Sun Kim, *op. cit.*, p. 67.
82. The guarantee of free choice of an occupation in Article 15 of the Constitution applies to both workers and employers, which, for employers, means business freedom.
83. Kazuo Sugeno, *op. cit.*, p. 31.

is not unlawful. The freedom of hiring applies to the extent that no statutory or other special restrictions exist.[84] Such restrictions can be found in some current legislation. Discriminatory arrangements against union members, such as yellow-dog contracts requiring a person to renounce union membership, are prohibited as a form of unfair labour practice;[85] discrimination based on sex is another example. The current EEWRA prohibits discriminatory treatment against women in recruitment.

65. Apart from these restrictions, the Korean legal system has maintained its position in preserving the employer's freedom to hire freely and this position has been supported by the judiciary. The fact that once employed, a regular worker cannot be dismissed unless there is some compelling reason, such as serious misconduct, seems to influence significantly the court's interpretation of employers' freedom to hire as they wish.[86]

66. Legal regulations in the labour market were developed to promote employment and prevent unemployment. These reflect policies that: (1) support the efforts of firms to continue employing workers if at all possible, while dealing with economic fluctuations and structural changes in an industry and (2) to promote the employment of those who, because of structural reasons, are in an unfavourable position in the labour market.

67. The principal means of implementing those policies are, first, to offer referral and training services to job applicants, and to support their job-seeking efforts by paying them various benefits and allowances, and, secondly, to maintain and promote hiring and employment by paying employers various types of subsidies and benefits for doing so. The latter policy of the economic inducement for employers for providing employment security measures has developed into a prominent policy. In recent years, it has become an outstanding feature of legal regulation within the labour market. As will be seen below, these objectives are established within various kinds of laws.[87]

§2. Contents of Laws

I. The BEPA

A. The Purpose of the BEPA

68. The BEPA (1993) proclaims the general principles of labour market policies. The Act sets forth its immediate purpose as: (1) formulating and implementing the employment policy that should be comprehensively undertaken by the state and (2) contributing to employment security, improvement in the economic and social

84. Takashi Araki, *Labour and Employment Law in Japan*, The Japan Institute of Labour, 2002, p.62.
85. Article 81 of the TULRAA.
86. Takashi Araki, *op. cit.*, p. 62.
87. Kazuo Sugeno, *op. cit.*, p. 59.

status of workers and the balanced development of both the national economy and society by helping individuals develop and display their abilities to the maximum and attaining enhanced efficiency in the labour market as well as a balance in the demand and supply of manpower (Article 1).

B. The Basic Principles of the BEPA

69. The BEPA[88] sets forth the basic principles its operation as follows:

1. The State shall recognize any worker's freedom of occupation and their right to work, in addition it acknowledges the employer's independence of employment management. The Act further encourages the motives of workers who are willing to develop their abilities and, thirdly, supports employers so that they may pursue initiatives which enhance the security of employment (Article 2).

C. The Respective Duties of Workers, Employers, the State and Other Agents

70. The law requires the state to formulate comprehensively and implement any policies necessary to the accomplishment of the purposes of this Act (Article 4). In addition, the state is required to establish and operate the employment security agency (Article 7) and to establish and implement a system for the development of vocational skills (Article 11). Under Article 12, it requires that the state should support vocational guidance for students and others. Four articles later (Article 16) the Act mandates that there is a particular duty of care to support the employment promotion for the elderly, the disabled, the long-term unemployed, and so on. Promoting employment options for women is covered in Article 17 and doing so for young people is covered in the subsequent article. The employment security of daily workers, and those similarly employed is covered in the same article (Article 18-2), as is the provision of a level of work, which provides a minimum income and provides services to the community.[89] The implementation of employment promotion training is covered by Article 20 and the establishment and operation of the employment promotion facility follows it in Article 21.

71. Also, the law requires the Minister of Employment and Labour to formulate and implement a basic plan for employment policy (Article 5), to collect and employment information and make it available publicly (Article 8). In addition, the

88. The BEPA aims to formulate and implement a comprehensive employment policy for the state and to contribute to employment security, the improvement of the economic and social status of workers and the balanced development of the national economy and society by helping individual nationals develop and display their abilities to the maximum and attain enhanced efficiency in the labour market and balance in the demand for, and supply of, manpower (BEPA, Article 1).

89. Article 18-3 (Support for the Creation of Social Service Jobs) The State may provide the necessary support to a non-profit corporation or non-profit organization which creates jobs in public service areas like health, social welfare and education, which are publicly necessary but are not provided sufficiently in the market due to lack of profitability, etc.

minister is required to make a survey and study on occupations (Article 9), as well as presenting information on demand and supply trends in manpower (Article 10), finally the remaining responsibilities of the Minister shall be to implement a support plan for securing manpower through small and medium size enterprises, usually known as SMEs (Article 24). In addition there is a responsibility to implement activities which provide measures against unemployment (Article 28), finally, there is an obligation to establish and operate the employment promotion facility (Article 21).

72. In terms of the mandates placed upon employers, they relate in large part to the economic development of both society as a whole and the individual worker. Their first requirement is to increase skill levels and make efforts toward the development of the vocational ability of their workers (Article 3) and to conduct such vocational training for their hired workers as may be necessary (Article 13). Further, they should make efforts toward improvements in employment management, an enhancement of employment security and the promotion of employment equality of their workers (Article 3). Furthermore employers should not discriminate on the grounds of gender, religion, age, social status, birthplace, alma mater, marriage, pregnancy, medical history, etc. in employment (Article 19).

73. The law requires workers to choose an occupation suited to their aptitude and ability and develop the abilities necessary for that occupation constantly throughout their vocational life additionally they should make all reasonable efforts to achieve self-development through their occupation (Article 2, paragraph 1). The law requires trade unions to actively cooperate with the efforts of their members in the development of vocational skills and with employers for their endeavours towards the development of such skills, the improvement in employment management, the enhancement of employment security and the promotion of employment equality among workers (Article 2, paragraph 31).

II. The ESA

A. *The Purpose of the ESA*

74. The ESA 1994 regulates the employment security office,[90] job placement services,[91] vocational guidance,[92] the furnishing of employment information services, recruitment more generally and labour supply businesses.

90. The term 'employment security office' means a local labour administrative agency carrying out employment security services, such as job placement, vocational guidance, etc.
91. The term 'job placement' means to help, upon request, both an employer with a position to offer and a job-seeker towards the conclusion of an employment contract.
92. The term 'vocational guidance' means the provision of a vocational aptitude test, the furnishing of employment information, vocational counselling, practical exercises, invitations, advice, or other guidance as to employment, which are rendered to facilitate a choice of job suitable to the ability and aptitude of a person who desires to find employment.

75. The ESA sets forth its primary purposes as, first to strive for the security of employment of every worker, and secondly to contribute to development of the national economy, by giving all employees an opportunity to find employment in which they may develop and display their abilities, which in turn supports an expansion of the workforce required for the industry in question.[93] The law requires the government to carry out any necessary tasks[94] of in order to accomplish the purpose of this Act.[95] Additionally the directors of local government may, if necessary, provide placement services, placement guidance, and services which provide \employment information for both an employer offering a job as well as the job seeker (Article 4.2).

76. By means of these measures, the ultimate goal of the law is to 'provide all workers with an appropriate opportunity for a job that conforms to their abilities and to provide industry with the necessary workforce, thereby establishing employment stability and contributing to economic and social development'.

B. The Common Rules of the ESA

77. The Act makes clear that the basic roles of job referral or job placement, vocational guidance, employment information services and recruitment services that act as intermediaries between those seeking employment and those seeking employees can be carried out in a variety of ways in the labour market.

78. The ESA establishes the following common rules for employment related services. First is the prohibition of discriminatory treatment. The law provides that 'no person shall be treated in a discriminatory manner with regards to job placement, vocational guidance, or any decision regarding employment relations, for reasons of sex, age, religion, physical conditions, social status, marriage, etc.'[96]

79. Second, there is the freedom to choose one's occupation; as a result job placement services and the like must respect the freedom of job seekers to choose their occupations.

---

93. Article 1.
94. 1.matters concerning a proper adjustment of demand and supply of workforce;2. matters concerning domestic and overseas placement services for job offerers and seekers;

    1. matters concerning vocational guidance for job seekers;
    2. matters concerning collection, arrangement, or furnishing of information on employment;
    3. matters concerning assistance in vocational training or reemployment for job seekers; and
    4. matters concerning guidance and inspection of the service of job placement, the service of furnishing of employment information, recruitment or supply of labour.

95. Article 3.
96. Article 2.

80. The third component is an explicit statement regarding working conditions. The law provides that 'upon filing an application for workers with the head of an employment security office, the person seeking an employee shall specify the contents of the work for which job seekers are to be employed, and the working conditions, and the head of the employment security office shall specify them to the job seekers'.[97]

81. Finally the Act sets out the basic rules for job placement services regarding the guarantee of the right to work. The head of the employment security office shall not refuse to accept an application for help filed by any potential employer, with some exceptions.[98] Also, the head of the employment security office shall make efforts to enable any job seeker to find employment suitable to his or her ability, and to enable any person or organization looking to recruit to find job seekers suitable for the position being offered.[99]

C. *The Tasks of Central and Local Government and the Employment Security Office*

82. The law requires that the government should carry out the necessary tasks[100] of in order to accomplish the purpose of this Act.[101] However, aspects of those services should be carried out by the head of the employment security office.[102] The designated individual in charge of such services is the head of the employment security office. Heads of local authorities must, if necessary, provide placement services, placement guidance, and services providing employment information to both potential employees and those seeking employment.[103]

83. The law requires the Employment Security Office to help the job seeker in receiving training for vocational skills development,[104] additionally they should implement vocational guidance for those who desire to find new employment, who

97. Article 2.
98. Articles 8, 9.
99. Article 11.
100.
  1. Matters concerning the proper adjustment of the demand and supply of the work force;
  2. Matters concerning domestic and overseas placement services for both job offerers and seekers;
  3. Matters concerning vocational guidance for job seekers;
  4. Matters concerning the collection, arrangement and furnishing of information relating to employment;
  5. Matters concerning assistance in vocational training or reemployment for job seekers;
  6. Matters concerning the guidance and inspection of the services of job placement, of the furnishing of employment information and recruitment or the supply of labour.

101. Article 3.
102. Article 5.
103. Article 4-2.
104. Article 13.

are handicapped either mentally or physically, and those who require any special guidance as regards employment.[105] Furthermore the office should furnish various types of employment information to potential employers or recruiters as well as job seekers[106] and finally they have a responsibility to make efforts to develop both recruitment and application opportunities.[107]

D. The Regulation of Private Employment-related Service Enterprises

84. The ESA recognizes the role of private employment-related services companies and approves of their co-existence with public services. Private employment-related services are divided into two categories, essentially based upon the cost to the user; a distinction is made between free placement services and fee charging placement services. The term 'free placement service' means a job placement service rendered without receiving any fee, whether that is a membership fee or any money or valuables, while the term 'fee charging placement service' means a job placement service other than the free job placement service, i.e. one that receives remuneration for the service provided.[108]

85. In turn free placement services are categorized as either domestic and overseas recruitment organizations. Any person who desires to conduct a domestic free placement service must report to their city mayor, county chiefs, or the head of their respective Gu Administrative Office (this option is limited to the heads of Gu Administrative Offices of Self-Governing Gus), and any person who wants to conduct an overseas free placement service needs to report to the Minister of Employment and Labour. Any person who wishes to conduct such a free placement service is designated as either a non-profit juristic person or a public interest organization by presidential decree.[109]

86. A similar distinction exists for fee-charging placement services where, again, permission is granted depending on whether the organization is placing employees domestically or from overseas. A person who wishes to conduct a domestic fee-charging placement service must register with the relevant city mayor, county chiefs or the head of the appropriate Gu Administrative Office, and anyone aiming to establish an overseas fee-charging placement service shall register with the Minister of Employment and Labour.[110] A person conducting such a fee-charging placement service after being registered may not receive any monies or other valuables unless the fee as has been predetermined and notified by the Minister of Employment and Labour.

105. Article 14.
106. Article 16.
107. Article 17.
108. Article 4.
109. Article 18.
110. Article 19.

87. There are additional regulations: (1) the prohibition of the lending of a title[111] (i.e. a company may not present itself as a charity or non-governmental organization); (2) the prohibition of prepayment – that is to say that a service must secure employment for the applicant before any payment is receive;[112] (3) a restriction on placement services securing work for minors (those aged less than 18);[113] and (4) a report on their furnishing of employment services[114] – in essence they must report to the Ministry of Employment and Labour the number of positions they have filled, etc.

E. Regulations Regarding Recruitment

88. The term 'recruitment' means that a person who desires to employ workers invites a person who desires to find employment to be in his or her employ or has another person invite them to do so.

89. Although employers are free in principle to decide how to recruit workers, some regulations delineate the permissible and impermissible methods of recruitment under the ESA. The most important ones have been the prohibitions on private fee-charging employment placement services and labour supply businesses. Employment placement services were not, in principle, monopolized by the state, that is to say by public employment security offices. The ESA provides the general prohibition on private fee-charging placement businesses and organizes private placement services as a coexisting player with their public counterparts in the supply-and-demand adjustment of the Korean labour market.

90. Any person who desires to employ workers, may recruit them freely by way of an advertisements in any medium, including newspapers, magazines, websites, or other publications, or distribution of papers, etc.[115] If it is deemed necessary for establishing a sound order of recruitment, the Minister of Employment and Labour may recommend improvements to the recruitment methods, etc.[116] Any person who desires to employ workers, and who is engaged in such recruitment, shall not receive any money, goods or interest from applicants in connection with such recruitment, regardless of any pretext thereof.[117]

F. The Regulation of Labour-supply Businesses

91. The term 'labour-supply business' denotes companies or organizations which act to facilitate or coordinate information between employers and potential

111. Article 21.
112. Article 21-2.
113. Article 21-3.
114. Article 23.
115. Article 28.
116. Article 31.
117. Article 32.

employees.[118] Labour-supply businesses, through which employers can obtain labour without concluding employment contracts directly with the workers, are strictly prohibited. The law is quite clear that no person shall carry on a labour-supply business without obtaining the permission of the Minister of Employment and Labour. Those who utilize workers supplied by an illegal labour supplier are subject to criminal penalties.[119]

92. The valid period for the permission of a labour-supply business shall be three years, and those who intend to continuously carry on a labour-supply business after the expiry of the valid period must receive a renewal permission as determined by the Ordinance of the Ministry of Employment and Labour.[120]

III. The WVSDA

A. *Basic Policies of the WVSDA*

93. This law seeks to secure the stable employment of workers, to raise their social and economic status, and in addition improve the productivity of enterprises; this approach is thus intended to contribute to social and economic development by promoting and supporting employees' skills development throughout their working lives.[121]

94. The law requires that the state and local governments formulate plans for the development of vocational ability that will give concrete form to the above policies.[122]

95. Employers are required to provide their workers with the necessary training and education, and endeavour to promote the development and enhancement of those workers' vocational ability by extending necessary aid in order to facilitate their taking of vocational training and the like. While respecting the independent efforts of employers, both central and local government are also obliged to endeavour to promote and enrich training and education as provided by employers and others. They are also required to carry out vocational training for workers and others who wish to change jobs.

118. However, this excludes worker dispatch businesses as prescribed in sub-paragraph 2 of Article 2 of the Act Relating to the Protection, etc., of Dispatched Workers.
119. Article 47.
120. Article 33.
121. Article 1.
122. Article 4.

B. Basic Principles of Vocational Skills Development Training

96. First, vocational skills development training shall be conducted in a systematic way throughout a worker's entire life, taking into account the worker's desires, aptitude and abilities. The aim here is promptly to respond to employment and industrial trends, advances in technology, changes in the structure of industry and the internationalization of economic activity.

97. Second, vocational skills development training shall be conducted in a way that respects the autonomy and creativity of the private sector and is based on labour–management participation and cooperation.

98. Third, vocational skills development training shall be conducted in such a way as to not discriminate against workers on the basis of their gender, age, physical condition, employment type, faith or social status, and to guarantee equal opportunities for all workers.

99. Fourth, vocational skills development training shall be considered important, especially for people referred to in any of the sub-paragraphs as below.[123]

100. Fifth, vocational skills development training shall be conducted in such a way as to ensure the close connection between school education prescribed by education-related laws and industrial sites.[124]

123.

1. the aged and the disabled;
2. eligible recipients under the National Basic Livelihood Security Act;
3. those who gave distinguished services to the state and their families, both bereaved and non-bereaved, under the Act on the Honourable Treatment and Support for Persons, etc. with Distinguished Service to the State;
4. those who gave distinguished services within the 18 May democratization movement, and their families, both bereaved and non-bereaved, under the Act for the Honourable Treatment and Support for Persons of Distinguished Services to 18 May democratization movement;
5. those who were or will be discharged from military service under the Act on Support for Discharged Soldiers;
6. female workers;
7. workers in small- and medium-sized enterprises (hereinafter referred to as 'small and medium enterprises') under the Framework Act on Small- and Medium-Sized Enterprises;
8. production workers in the manufacturing industry;
9. daily workers, part-time workers, workers who have signed a fixed-term contract and workers employed for a temporary project;
10. dispatched workers under the DWPA.

124. Article 3.

C. The Duties of the State, Employers and Workers

101. The state and local governments are required to devise the necessary measures to promote and support vocational skills development training, etc. voluntarily taken up by workers and vocational skills development activities conducted by employers, employers' groups, workers' groups, etc. in order to develop workers' vocational skills throughout their working lives.

102. An employer shall make efforts to conduct vocational skills development training for its workers. An employer shall make efforts to create conditions for vocational skills development training, such as expanding the participation of workers in vocational skills development training, granting workers leave for their vocational skills development and appointing a person in charge of human resources development – this refers to any individual who plans, operates and evaluates vocational skills development activities in terms of vocational skills development training facilities, companies and so forth.

103. Workers have an obligation to make efforts to develop their vocational skills according to their aptitudes and abilities and participate in vocational skills development activities, whether those are provided by the state, a local government, an employer, or another body.

104. A person who conducts vocational skills development training shall make efforts to ensure that workers receive such training as is suitable to their aptitude and ability. This should be achieved by providing counselling concerning training as well as guidance services pertaining to jobs, establishing the selection criteria for training, and other relevant activities.[125]

IV. The AEPA

A. The Purpose of the AEPA

105. In this Act, 'the aged' means persons whose age is equal to or above that of 55, and 'the semi-aged' means persons aged 50 or older but younger than 55.

106. With the ageing of Korea's population, promoting the employment of older persons has become an important political and economic concern in Korea. As a result, in 2007, the AEPA of 1990 was revised.

107. The AEPA sets forth its immediate purposes as:

– the prohibition of employment discrimination based on age without a reasonable reason;

125. Article 4.

- contributing to the employment security of older workers and, as a result, the development of the national economy through supporting and promoting their employment in situations suited to their abilities.

B. *Government Responsibilities and Employers' Obligations*

108. The law requires that the government shall devise and implement an anti-age discrimination policy with the aim of eliminating the practice of age discrimination in employment situations. In addition, there is an obligation to pursue such policies as may be needed in an effective and comprehensive manner, such as establishing and implementing employment promotion measures for older workers, vocational skills development training and so forth, with the aim of improving the understanding of employers and the general public about the employment of the older workers and enhancing their employment promotion prospects and job security.[126]

109. Additionally the law requires the Minister of Employment and Labour to establish what is termed the Basic Plan for the Employment Promotion of the elderly, in consultation with the heads of the central agencies concerned, every five years.

110. Furthermore the law requires that employers make efforts to eliminate employment discrimination based on age, provide employment opportunities for the elderly suited to their abilities by developing their vocational skills, improving relevant working conditions and jobs, and increasing the employment opportunities for older workers by extending mandatory retirement age.[127]

1. Age Discrimination Prohibition in Recruitment, Employment, etc.

111. The law requires employers not to discriminate against a worker or a potential worker on the basis of age unless there is reasonable justification. The areas encompassed are set out below:

- recruitment and employment;
- provision of money and valuables aside from wages, and benefits packages;
- education and training;
- disposition, change of position or promotion;
- retirement and dismissal;

126. Article 3.
127. Article 4.

112. If an application of a standard, aside from age *per se*, without a justifiable reason leads to particularly unfavourable circumstances for a certain age group, this is also considered to be age discrimination.[128]

113. Any person who has suffered age discrimination as a result of the violation of the age discrimination prohibition is entitled to file a petition to the National Human Rights Commission.

2. Governmental Support for the Employment of the Elderly

114. In terms of the promotion of older people, the law requires the Minister of Employment and Labour to support, implement and provide a number of elements.[129] First, the collection of job-related information,[130] secondly, vocational skills development training for the elderly,[131] in addition employment guidance for the employer,[132] further support for the employer in the improvement of the working environment, education and training for the aged,[133] the strengthening of placement services,[134] the operation of employment information centres for the elderly,[135] the designation of a talent bank for the elderly,[136] the designation of job centres for elderly people deemed to represent special manpower,[137] businesses to promote the employment of the elderly,[138] and other necessary measures.

3. The Employment Promotion and Security of the Elderly

115. The law provides for the employment promotion and security of older workers in various ways: among these it establishes an employer's responsibility to employ older people,[139] it requires the establishment an employer's execution plan

128. Article 4-4.
129. After investigating a petition by the National Human Rights Commission in cases where existence of age discrimination has been determined and a remedy has been recommended, etc. to the chief of the assigned institute, organization or inspection agency, the National Human Rights Commission shall notify the Minister of Employment and Labour as well of the nature of the remedy (Article 4-6).
130. The Minister of Employment and Labour shall collect information relating to job offers and job searches as it pertains to older workers in order to promote the employment for those workers, enlarge the available opportunities both in terms of jobs being offered and being sought. The Minister shall provide the related data to job applicants, employers and organizations concerned (Article 5).
131. Article 6.
132. Article 7.
133. Article 8.
134. Article 9.
135. Article 10.
136. Article 11.
137. Article 11-2.
138. Article 11-4.
139. The employer who employs above a given numbers of employees, as determined by presidential decree, shall strive to employ the elderly at above the standard employment rate (Article 12).

for their standard employment rate of older workers,[140] it further offers tax credits, etc. to promote the employment of older workers,[141] the selection, etc. of priority occupations and employment in those priority occupations[142] and requests for the employment of the elderly and the semi-elderly, etc.[143]

4. Mandatory Retirement Age for the Elderly

116. An employer shall set the retirement age at 60 years or older. If the retirement age is set at under 60 by an employer it will be deemed to be 60.[144] In a situation where a person has reached this retirement age but wishes to be reemployed, the employer shall strive to reemploy him or her in such an occupation as is suited to his or her working abilities.[145] The Minister of Employment and Labour may provide support as is necessary, such as the provision of subsidies to any employer who reemploys retired persons or takes other necessary measures to ensure the employment security of those who retired at the retirement age.[146] The Minister of Employment and Labour shall cooperate with and give support to enterprises engaged in the employment of older workers, such as counsel and advice relating to wages or management of those past the mandatory age of retirement.[147]

V. The EPRDA (1990)

A. The Purpose of the EPRDA[148]

117. With international pressure promoting the equality of disabled persons and to encourage their full participation in society, promoting the employment of disabled people has, in recent years, become an increasingly important topic. The primary law dealing with this topic is the 1990 Act on the Employment Promotion, etc., of the Disabled. The law was originally enacted as the Physically Disabled Persons Employment Promotion Law. However, through revision, it was expanded to become the present EPRDA.

118. The purpose of this Act is to contribute to the promotion of employment and the vocational rehabilitation of disabled people so that they may live decent lives by means of work suited to their ability.

140. Article 13.
141. Article 14.
142. Articles 15 to 16.
143. Article 17.
144. Article 19.
145. Article 21.
146. Article 21-1.
147. Article 22.
148. The purpose of this Act is to contribute to the promotion of employment and the vocational rehabilitation of disabled persons so that they may live decent lives through work suited to their abilities.

119. In this Act, the term 'disabled persons' means those people who, due to physical or mental disability, are subject to considerable restrictions in their vocational life over an extended period of time, and who correspond to the standards defined by presidential decree. The term 'employment promotion and vocational rehabilitation' means to enable the individuals concerned to become self-supporting by means of their vocational life, as a result of the measures provided in this Act, with respect to the vocational guidance, vocational adjustment training, vocational skills development training, mediation of employments, employment, adjustment guidance after employment, and so forth for disabled persons, they should become more independent.

B. *Basic Principles of the EPRDA*

120. The basic principles of the EPRDA are as follows.

121. The law requires that both central and local government continually promote the education, public understanding – through means of publicity – and the promotion of employment of disabled persons, in order to enhance an understanding among both employers and the general public of the issues relating to the employment promotion and vocational rehabilitation of people with disabilities.[149]

122. The law further requires employers to cooperate in government policies on the employment of disabled persons, to acknowledge and act upon their obligations to provide disabled persons with employment opportunities with an adequate evaluation of their abilities, while, concurrently, performing adequate employee management.[150] Finally the Act requires employers not to discriminate against workers on the basis of their disabilities, in all personnel management functions, for example, recruitment, promotion, and the transfer of positions.

123. The law also obliges people with disabilities to take advantage of such career-support opportunities as may be available and to enhance their vocational life on the basis of this support.[151] As a result the Act lays responsibilities on both parties in any employment situation.

C. *Concerning the Employment Promotion and Vocational Rehabilitation of Disabled Persons*

124. Such agencies as are mandated with the execution of vocational rehabilitation for disabled persons (hereinafter referred to as the 'executive agencies of rehabilitation') are mandated to provide a range of diverse projects for vocational

149. Article 3 paragraph 1.
150. Article 5.
151. Article 6 paragraph 1.

rehabilitation, and to directly furnish them to such persons. In doing so, their particular focus should be ensuring that those with severe disabilities can lead a life in which they support themselves in a meaningful way.[152]

125. The Minister of Employment and Labour and the Minister of Health, Welfare and Family Affairs shall, in order to enable people with disabilities to obtain jobs suited to their ability, provide vocational counsel, vocational aptitude tests, an evaluation of vocational skills, and, as a result, implement vocational guidance such as furnishing employment information and other necessary provisions.[153]

126. These ministers may, in such cases where it is deemed necessary to enable the disabled persons to make a working living suited to their wishes, aptitude, capabilities and so forth provide vocational adaptation training to enhance the skills needed by disabled persons for their vocational environments.[154]

127. Further the Minister of Employment and Labour shall provide vocational skills development training for disabled persons, in order that they may make a viable living suited to their wishes, aptitudes, capabilities,[155] etc. Furthermore the Minister of Employment and Labour shall take the role of mediator in determining which jobs are suited to particular disabled persons on the basis of relevant employment information and in consideration of the criteria just mentioned.[156]

D. The Obligation to Employ Disabled Persons, and Levies

128. While any employer has the freedom to decide how many employees to hire, this Act imposes certain restrictions. It requires that the employer hire a certain quota of persons, as defined by the Act, as a part of the workforce. Even with is stipulation, the employer is not compelled to contract workers who fall within

---

152. Executive agencies of rehabilitation shall be as follows:

    1. educational institutes for the handicapped as prescribed under sub-paragraph 3 of Article 2 of the Act on the Promotion of Education for the Handicapped;
    2. welfare centres for disabled persons under Article 58(12) of the Welfare of Disabled Persons Act;
    3. vocational rehabilitation facilities for disabled persons as determined under Article 58 (13) of the Welfare of Disabled Persons Act;
    4. welfare organizations for disabled persons as designated under Article 63 of the Welfare of Disabled Persons Act;
    5. vocational skills development training facilities as determined under sub-paragraph 3 of Article 2 of the Act on the Development of the Occupational Abilities of Workers;
    6. other agencies deemed capable of conducting vocational rehabilitation projects for disabled persons by the Minister of Employment and Labour, and which are determined by the Ordinance of the Ministry of Employment and Labour (Article 9).

153. Article 10 paragraph 1.
154. Article 11 paragraph 1.
155. Article 12 paragraph 1.
156. Article 15 paragraph 1.

those categories as defined by the Act. However, such employers as fail to meet such a ratio are obliged to pay monies into a government fund which, in turn, supports those employers who have exceeded the relevant requirement.

129. Both central and local government are required to employ at least 3 per cent of their workforce from the disabled community.[157] Any employer who employs more than 50 full-time workers (in cases involving the construction industry where a confirmation of workers' number is difficult determine this shall be decided on the basis of whether work contract amount is in excess of the amount prescribed and notified by the Minister of Employment and Labour) shall employ disabled people equivalent to more than the rate fixed by presidential decree, which shall be within the scope of 5 per cent of their total number of workers (hereinafter referred to as 'obligatory employment rate') and if there is any fraction of less than one person in this number, such a fraction shall be omitted.[158]

130. Any employer (excluding employers who employ between 50 and 100 employees full-time) which employs a number of disabled persons which is short of its obligatory employment ratio shall pay a levy for the employment of disabled persons (hereinafter referred to as the 'levy') to the Ministry of Employment and Labour each year.[159]

E. The Korean Employment Promotion Agency for the Disabled

131. The Korean Employment Promotion Agency for Disabled Persons (hereinafter referred to as the 'Agency') shall be established with the purpose of supporting disabled persons to become self-sufficient as a result of their vocational activities and provide professional support to the employment of disabled persons by their employers.[160]

132. Employers shall work to eliminate bias in the workplace against those with disabilities, create stable working conditions for them, and educate their workforce to improve their awareness of persons with disabilities. Mandatory education covers all businesses or workplaces employing more than 50 workers and shall consist of one hour per year. Employers shall keep records related to the education for three years.[161]

133. Education to improve workplace awareness of persons with disabilities shall include: (1) the definition of disability and types of disability; (2) human rights, prohibition of discrimination against, and provision of fair accommodation for persons in the workplace with disabilities; (3) laws and systems related to

157. Article 27 paragraph 1.
158. Article 28 paragraph 1.
159. Article 33 paragraph 1.
160. Article 43 paragraph 1.
161. Articles 5-2, 5-3, 86

employment promotion and vocational rehabilitation of persons with disabilities; and (4) other matters deemed necessary to improve workplace awareness of persons with disabilities. This education can be done collectively, as an inquiry or a meeting, or through remote education using the Internet or other communication network, or experiential education in consideration of the size and characteristics of the business.[162]

VI. The EEWRA (Amended from the Act on Equal Employment)

A. *Women in the Korean Labour Market*

134. In the past, under the traditional male-dominated Korean employment system, women were generally regarded as non-regular, peripheral or ancillary workers. Industries that utilized women often introduced a system of mandatory retirement for women once they married or required an earlier mandatory retirement. However, various socio-economic and technological changes, such as the increase in the size of the service sector, developments in microelectronics, the decrease in the working population resulting from a falling fertility rate, the alleviation of domestic chores by electrical appliances, and the increased numbers of female students in higher education, contributed to an increase of women in the labour market. This steady transition has brought to light the traditional discrimination that existed against women within the traditionally male-centred Korean employment system.[163]

B. *Purposes of the EEWRA*

135. Current Korean law takes two approaches to achieving equal employment opportunities for both sexes: a prohibition of, and redress for, discrimination based on sex, and, secondly, legal assistance to facilitate workers harmonize work and family life.

136. The former is mainly regulated by the LSA and the Act of Equal Employment (1987). The current EEWRA (2007) was amended from the Act on Equal Employment. With regard to the statutory prohibition of discrimination against women, the LSA is confined to wage discrimination, etc. As a result, Korea needed new legislation to prohibit discriminatory treatment against women other than that relating to unequal rates of pay.

162. Article 5-2
163. The purpose of this Act is to realize gender equality in employment, in compliance with the idea of equality enshrined within the Constitution of the Republic of Korea, by ensuring equal opportunity and treatment for men and women in employment, while protecting maternity and promoting women's employment, as well as to contribute to improving the quality of life for all people by providing support for the reconciliation of work and family life for workers. Takashi Araki, *op. cit.*, p. 104.

137. The EEWRA set forth as its immediate purpose:
- to realize gender equality in employment in compliance with the idea of equality as stated in in the Constitution by ensuring equal opportunities for and treatment of both men and women in the workplace;
- to protect maternity rights and promote women's employment;
- to contribute towards the improvement of people's quality of life by encouraging a more balanced approach between their working and non-working lives.

C. *Responsibilities of Central and Local Government, Workers' and Employers' Obligations, etc.*

138. The law requires both tiers of government:

- to promote people's interest and understanding to realize the purposes of this Act;
- to support skills development and employment promotion for women;
- to make whatever efforts are necessary to eliminate all elements undermining the realization of gender equality in employment.[164]

139. Once again the burden of the law falls evenly as it also requires workers to make efforts to create workplace culture where men and women are equally respected based on mutual understanding.

140. Further the law stipulates that employers should:

- make efforts to create a working environment where male and female workers can show their abilities, under equal conditions, by improving those practices and institutions which undermine the realization of gender equality in an employment setting;
- make efforts to alter those practices and institutions in the workplace which run contrary to the reconciliation of work and family life, and create working environments that enhance such a reconciliation.[165]

D. *Ensuring Equal Opportunity and Treatment, etc. for Men and Women in Employment*

141. An employer must not discriminate against men or women based on their gender in terms of recruitment or hiring. When recruiting or hiring female workers, an employer shall not present or demand certain physical conditions such as appearance, height, weight, unmarried status, or other conditions as determined by the Ordinance of the Ministry of Employment and Labour, which are not required to

164. Article 4 paragraph 1.
165. Article 5.

perform a certain job.[166] An employer shall not discriminate against men or women with respect to retirement age or retirement and dismissal. An employer shall not enter into a labour contract stipulating issues relating to marriage, pregnancy or childbirth in the case of a female worker and suggesting that any of these may be a legitimate cause for retirement.[167]

E. Skills Development and Employment Promotion for Women

142. The Employment Security Office shall take measures necessary for vocational guidance, such as offering employment information and survey and research materials on occupations in a bid to help women choose an appropriate job according to their aptitudes, competencies, experiences and skills, and to make smooth adaptations to those jobs.[168] Central and local government, as well as private employers shall offer equal access, to both men and women, to relevant vocational training.[169]

143. The Minister of Employment and Labour may provide non-profit corporations and organizations, which establish and operate facilities to promote women's employment, with a subsidy for all or part of their necessary costs. And the Minister of Employment and Labour may provide any employer who conducts a project for the promotion of employment among women, or an employer who intends to improve to working environment in the workplace – such as establishing a women workers' lounge, breast-feeding facilities and so forth – with a subsidy for all or part of the necessary costs.[170]

F. The Establishment, Submission, etc. of Implementation Plans on Affirmative Action Measures

144. The term 'affirmative action measures' relates to any methods which provide favourable treatment to a specific sex, temporarily, in order to get rid of existing discrimination between men and women or to promote the employment equality in employment.

145. The Minister of Employment and Labour may request that any employer failing any of the following sub-paragraphs and whose employment rates for female workers' ratio fall short of the employment criteria for that industry as provided for in terms of both industry and by scale in accordance with the Ordinance of the Ministry of Employment and Labour, establish and submit an implementation plan for an affirmative action measure to reduce discriminatory employment practice and

166. Article 7.
167. Article 11.
168. Article 15.
169. Article 16.
170. Article 17.

systems (hereinafter referred to as the 'implementation plan'). In this case, the relevant employer shall submit an implementation plan; relevant employers are:

- heads of public agencies and organizations as prescribed by presidential decree;
- employers of establishments hiring workers greater than that number prescribed by presidential decree.[171]

146. The Minister of Employment and Labour may request heads of related administrative agencies to take necessary measures for the correction or prevention of discrimination in cases where he/she admits that they are necessary for the efficient implementation of affirmative action measures. In these cases, the heads of such agencies shall comply with them unless they are able to demonstrate exceptional grounds.[172]

VII. The FWEA

A. The Purpose of the FWEA

147. On 16 August 2003, the Act on the Foreign Workers Employment, etc. was legislated, which stipulates introduction of the Employment Permit System for Foreign Workers and measures of illegal foreign workers legalizing. Accordingly, employers who have failed to hire native workers will be legally allowed to hire foreign workers.

148. This Act is to achieve a smooth supply and demand of manpower and a balanced development of the national economy by systematically introducing and managing foreign workers.[173] With the introduction of the Employment Permit System, small and medium businesses are able to minimize labour shortages and foreign workers will enjoy basic rights under labour relations laws fully applied to them.

149. In Korea, foreign worker in this Act refers to a person who does not have a Korean nationality and works or intends to work in business or workplace located in Korea with the purpose of earning wages: provided, that among foreigners who are granted the status of sojourn eligible for employment pursuant to Article 18 of the Immigration Control Act, the Presidential Decree may exclude some foreign workers in consideration of the employment sector, period of stay, etc.[174]

171. Article 17-3.
172. Article 17-6.
173. FWEA, Article 1.
174. Provided that this provision shall not apply to seamen who work on board any ship under the Seamen Act and do not have a Korean nationality and ship owners who employ or intend to employ the said seamen (Article 3).

150. Foreign workers are covered by labour-related laws in an identical manner to native employees during their period of employment, for example, the LSA, the MWA, the Industrial Safety and Health Act, etc. (ISHA).

B. Employment Procedures for Foreign Workers

151. The first issue to consider is an employers efforts to hire native workers. An employer who intends to hire a foreign worker should first submit an employment announcement seeking native workers to an employment security centre ('employment security office'). The head of the relevant employment security office shall, upon receiving the employment announcement seeking native workers for a vacant post or posts, provide counselling and support to the employer to provide adequate job requirements, and actively provide job placement services to ensure the preferential treatment of qualified native workers seeking to be hired.[175]

152. The next issue is the preparation of a roster of foreign job seekers. The Minister of Employment and Labour shall prepare a roster of foreign job seekers in consultation with the heads of the government agency with responsibility for labour administration in whatever is the country of origin of the potential foreign worker.[176]

153. After this the law considers the foreign worker employment permit. An employer who has applied for domestic workers and has been unable to hire workers regardless of the job introduction, needs to apply for permission to employ foreign workers to an employment security office under the conditions prescribed by the Ordinance of the Ministry of Employment and Labour.[177]

154. Fourth comes the conclusion of a labour contract. If an employer intends to employ a foreign worker it has selected, the employer must sign a labour contract with the foreign worker by use of the standard labour contract form as prescribed by the Ordinance of the Ministry of Employment and Labour.[178]

155. The next stage an employer needs to consider is the matter of the certificate for visa issuance. An employer who has signed a labour contract with a foreign worker may apply to the Minister of Justice for a certificate for visa issuance on behalf of the foreign worker concerned pursuant to the Immigration Control Act.[179]

156. Finally there is the matter of employment training for foreign workers. Foreign workers shall receive training ('the employment training for foreign workers'), as provided by organizations determined by Presidential Decree to learn matters as

175. Article 6.
176. Article 7 paragraph 1.
177. Article 8 paragraph 1.
178. Article 9 paragraph 1.
179. Article 10.

may be deemed necessary for their employment, within a period determined by the relevant Ordinance of the Ministry of Employment and Labour after they enter Korea. An employer must enable foreign workers to receive such training.[180]

C. *Employment Management of Foreign Workers*

157. The working period is set at maximum three years to prevent settlement of foreign workers in Korea. Considering that the working period is short three years) under the Employment Permit System, accompanying family are banned. Employers and foreign workers must sign a labour contract using the standard labour contract to clarify working conditions such as the wage and their working condition. Foreign workers are supposed to work at the workplace where they signed labour contract for the first time. But, in the case of inevitable circumstances such as close-down or suspension of business, legitimate withdrawal from the labour contract, workers can be replaced to other businesses through the Employment Security Centre. The introduction of the Employment Permit System for Foreigners lays an institutional grid that enables foreign workers to work legally in Korea. Accordingly, continuous and adamant crack-down and stricter punishment will be enforced against illegal workers and their employers.

1. Departure Guarantee Insurance and Trust

158. Any business or the relevant employer within a workplace hiring a foreign worker shall take out an insurance or trust (known as 'departure guarantee insurance') with the foreign worker(s) as the insured or beneficiaries, in order to provide severance pay to foreign workers due in the event of causes such as the departure, etc. of that worker. In this case, the employers shall pay or entrust the payment of the monthly premium or trust amount. If an employer takes out departure guarantee insurance, etc. pursuant to paragraph (1), the employer shall be deemed to have put in place a severance pay system pursuant to Article 8(1) of the WRBSA.[181]

2. Health Insurance

159. With reference to the National Health Insurance Act, any employer and any foreign workers employed by them shall be regarded, respectively, as the employer and the workplace-based policy holders as defined by the Act.[182]

180. Article 11.
181. Article 13.
182. Article 14.

3. Return Cost Insurance and Trust

160. A foreign worker shall take out return cost insurance or trust in order to finance the costs of returning to his or her home country. Other necessary matters concerning the subscription methods, contents, management and payment of the insurance and trust shall be prescribed by presidential decree.[183]

4. Measures Necessary for Return

161. An employer shall take necessary measures, such as paying money or other valuables such as wages, and so forth if foreign workers return to their home country due to the termination of the employment relationship, expiration of period of sojourn, or similar points of separation.[184]

5. Restrictions on Employment

162. A foreign worker may work for three years from the date of his or her entry,;this period can be extended one time up to two more years.[185] A foreigner who has left afterhaving been employed in Korea, shall not be reemployed pursuant to this Act, if six months have not passed since the date of his or her departure.[186]

6. Cancellation and Restrictions of the Foreign Worker Employment Permit

163. In the case of an employer falling under any of the following considerations, the Minister of Employment and Labour may issue an order to cancel its foreign worker employment permit, as prescribed in Article 8 under the conditions prescribed by the presidential decree:

- an employer violating the payment of wages or other labour conditions promised in a contract made before entry;
- in any situation where maintaining a labour contract has become difficult due to overdue wages or the employer's violation of other labour-related laws;
- if an employment permit was obtained by false or fraudulent means.

164. An employer subject to the cancellation of a foreign worker employment permit shall terminate any labour contract with the foreign worker concerned within 15 days of the date of receiving the order.[187] The Minister of Employment and

183. Article 15.
184. Article 16.
185. Article 18, 18-2.
186. Article 18.
187. Article 19.

Labour may restrict employers who fall under any of the following sub-paragraphs from employing foreign workers for three years from the date of the incident:[188]

- those who employ foreign workers without obtaining an employment permit;
- those whose employment permit has been cancelled pursuant to this Act;
- those who have been punished for violating this Act or the Immigration Control Act;
- those who are covered by reasons as determined by presidential decree.

VIII. The Protection of Foreign Workers

A. *Prohibition of Discrimination*

165. An employer shall not treat foreign workers in an unfair or discriminatory manner on the grounds of their status.[189] Foreign workers under the Employment Permit System shall have the status of worker from the beginning and have their basic rights protected equally as Koreans for the three working years according to labour relations laws such as the Labour Standards Act. It is possible to differentiate the wage level if it is due to gaps in productivity or experiences between Korean and foreign workers, but it is impossible to unfairly discriminate against foreign workers just because they are not Korean. The Ministry of Employment and Labour will step in to monitor businesses that hire foreign workers to prevent industrial accidents, wage dues, and etc.

B. *Subscription to Guarantee Insurance, etc.*

166. Any relevant business, or the employer of a workplace as prescribed by presidential decree in consideration of the size of the business size and industry-specific characteristics, shall take out guarantee insurance to protect their foreign workers against the possibility of overdue wages. Foreign workers employed in businesses or workplaces as determined by presidential decree in consideration of industry-specific characteristics shall take out casualty insurance to cover themselves in the instance of any illness or death.[190] The Presidential Decree shall determine other necessary matters concerning the subscription methods, contents, management and payment of the guarantee insurance and casualty insurance.

188. Article 20.
189. Article 22.
190. Article 23.

C. Support for Foreign Workers-related Organizations, etc.

167. The government may support any organization or group which offers foreign workers counselling, education and other services as prescribed by presidential decree with part of the necessary costs of providing the services appropriated within the limit of available budgets.[191]

D. Permission for Change of Business or Workplace

168. In the case of a foreign worker having difficulties continuing his or her normal employment relationship in a business or workplace due to situations falling under any of the following criteria, the foreign worker may apply to an employment security office for a transfer to other businesses or workplaces under the conditions prescribed by the Ordinance of the Ministry of Employment and Labour:[192]

- if an employer intends to cancel a labour contract during the contract period or to reject the renewal of a contract after its expiration for justifiable reasons;
- if it is deemed impossible to continue to work in a workplace because of a business shutdown, closure and other reasons not attributable to the foreign worker;
- if an employment permit is cancelled or any restriction is imposed on the employment of foreign workers;
- where there are other reasons as prescribed by presidential decree.

191. Article 24.
192. Article 25.

Part I. Individual Labour Relations

Chapter 1. Introduction

§1. THE CONCEPT OF LABOUR RELATIONS AND INDIVIDUAL LABOUR RELATIONS LAW

169. The term 'labour relations' implies a legal relationship between an employer and an employee established by a labour contract in which the employee promises to provide his or her labour to the employer while the employer ensures the payment of wages for that labour.[193]

170. Labour relations have the following characteristics. First, they may be considered relations involving subordination since the employee offers labour in accordance with the employer's instructions.[194] Secondly, labour relations are a kind of continuous legal relationship.[195] Thirdly, labour relations generally take the form of collective relations.[196]

171. Meanwhile individual labour relations law is a shorthand expression for the legal regulation of individual employment relations. Under current law, individual employment relations can be characterized as dealing with the conclusion, continuation and termination of labour contracts between individual workers and their employers.[197]

193. As a type of obligatory contract, labour relations are a kind of employment contract stipulated by the Civil Code (Articles 655–663). However, it is specially treated in the sense that several laws and ordinances protecting the employee are applied to it (Chi Sun Kim, *op. cit.*, p. 25).
194. Modern law does not approve the employer's legal superiority. Legally speaking, a labour relationship is established between two 'equal' persons. But in reality, the employer exercises power over labour which is inseparably related to the employee, and because the employer possesses the means of production, s/he can gain control of labour relations. In this respect, subordination forms the main characteristic of labour relations, in comparison with other contractual relations.
195. As it assumes a unified and organic enterprise management, the employee is expected to offer labour for a given period of time under the command of the employer. Therefore, customary practices, which have governed the enterprise for a long time, often apply to labour relations. But in applying them, we should consider the protection of the employee, for they are not always reasonable in content (Chi Sun Kim, *op. cit.*, p. 25).
196. Although the labour relationship itself is an individual one between the employer and the employee, the employee is closely connected to the enterprise as a member of its workforce. As a result, employees usually organize a union to form a collective relationship with the employer
197. Kazuo Sugeno, *op. cit.* p. 74.

§2. The Parties to the Labour Relationship

I. The Worker

172. In the realm of labour relations law, the concept of the worker is used in a variety of senses depending upon their purpose.[198] The LSA defines the term 'worker' (employee) as 'a person who offers work at a business or workplace to earn wages, regardless of the kind of job in which he or she is engaged' (Article 2 paragraph 1),[199] while the TULRAA defines it as 'a person who lives on wages, salary, or other equivalent forms of income earned in pursuit of any type of job' (Article 2). The main difference between the two is that the former assumes the relationship of a labour contract while the latter includes unemployed would-be workers.

II. The Employer

173. The concept of the employer in the LSA and the TULRAA has the same meaning.

174. However the term 'employer' is used in a variety of ways within legislation.[200] The LSA and the TULRAA define the term 'employer' as a business owner, or a person responsible for the management of a business or a person who works on behalf of a business owner with respect to matters relating to workers (Article 2 paragraph 1 of the LSA and Article 2 of the TULRAA).

---

198. The LSA: the term 'worker' in this Act means a person who offers work to a business or workplace to earn wages, regardless of kinds of job he/she is engaged in (Article 2).
The TULRAA: the term 'worker' means a person who lives on wages, salary, or other equivalent form of income earned in pursuit of any type of job (Article 2).
The BEPA: the term 'worker' in this Act means any person who is employed by an employer or who intends to seek a job (Article 2-2).
The WVSDA: worker means a person who is employed by an employer and a person who has the intention of being employed (Article 2).
199. The traditional distinction between blue-collar and white-collar workers, which was important in terms of social status, still exists in Korean society. However, legally, the distinction has been completely removed because labour law does not permit any difference in their treatment. The government and individual enterprises are making efforts to totally abolish the remaining differentiation (Chi Sun Kim, *op. cit.*, p. 27).
200. The LSA: the term 'employer' in this Act means a business owner, or a person responsible for the management of a business or a person who works on behalf of a business owner with respect to matters relating to workers (Article 2 of the LSA).
The TULRAA: the term 'employer' means a business owner, a person responsible for the management of a business, or a person who works on behalf of a business owner with respect to matters relating to workers in the business (Article 2).
The AEPA: 'Employer' means the person who carries on a business which hires workers (Article 2).
The EPRDA: the term 'employer' means a person who conducts or intends to conduct a business by employing workers (Article 2)
The Occupational Safety and Health Act: the term employer means a person who conducts a business using workers (Article 2).

175. In essence the term 'employer' means a person who has labour service at his or her disposal in a labour relationship.[201] In both the LSA and the TULRAA, the term 'employer' is defined rather widely to keep pace with actual developments: an employer is the owner or manager of an enterprise, or other person who acts on behalf of the owner or manager, so far as matters related to employees are concerned.[202]

176. An organization shall not be considered to be a trade union if either employers or their representatives are allowed to join, or if employees are prevented from joining,[203] etc.[204]

§3. The Structure of Individual Labour Relations Law

177. Under current labour law, individual labour relations are constructed on the basis of a contractual relationship. This contractual relationship is regulated by various provisions of the worker protection laws, individual contracts of employment, work rules established by employers, and collective agreements, etc. Therefore, norms regulating working conditions in Korea are as follows: minimum standards of working conditions fixed by mandatory laws, individual contracts of employment, work rules established by employers, and collective agreements between groups of employees and employers either singularly or cooperatively. The conspicuous feature of the norms regulating working conditions in Korea lies in enabling flexible modifications to cope with changing socio-economic circumstances with an eye on maintaining the security of employment.

§4. Worker Protection Laws

178. The individual employment relationship between an employer and a worker is regulated by a variety of worker protection laws including, but not restricted to, the LSA (1997), the MWA (1986), the EEWRA (1987), the Occupational Safety and Health Act (1990), the IACIA (1994), the DWPA (1998), the Act

---

201. Therefore, regardless of whether s/he is a natural person or a legal personality, whether s/he owns the enterprise or not, whether s/he personally runs the enterprise or not. The term 'employer' is one thing, the term 'entrepreneur' is another.
202. Therefore, so-called executive personnel and supervisors can be included in the category of employer as long as their role is to act on behalf of the owner of the enterprise in matters concerning workers. Their acts are regarded as having been done by the employer in the narrow sense, and liability for these actions is attributable to both the owner of the enterprise and the doer. However, at the same time, executive personnel or supervisors are also regarded as employees in other respects and are covered by the protective aspects of labour law – as long as they are not on the board of directors of their company.
203. Provided that a dismissed person shall not be regarded as a person who is not a worker, until a review decision is made by the National Labour Relations Commission when he/she has made an application to the Labour Relations Commission for remedies for unfair labour practices.
204. Article 2 of the TULRAA.

on the Prevention of Pneumoconiosis and Protection, etc., of Pneumoconiosis Workers (1984), the WCGA (1998), the WRBSA (2005), the FPWPA (2006) and the Act on the Employment Improvement, etc., of Construction Workers (1996),[205] among others.

179. This framework of laws establishes compulsory standards to protect workers, provide equal opportunity within individual labour relations, as well as creating both the authority and mechanisms to administer and supervise their enforcement. The most fundamental and important is the LSA. Some laws, such as the MWA, the Occupational Safety and Health Act, the WRBSA, and the IACIA were outgrowths of LSA provisions. Other laws have been further developed from regulations in the LSA.

§5. Concerning Collective Agreements, Work Rules and Employment Contracts

180. A collective agreement is an agreed set of rules established between a labour union and the relevant employer concerning wages, working hours, or other issues. Work rules are a set of regulations set forth by an employer for the purpose of establishing uniform rules and conditions of employment within the workplace. Employment contracts are those contracts which are entered into in order for a worker to offer work and for an employer to pay wages for that work. The LSA requires the employer to clearly communicate the working conditions to the worker when concluding such a contract.

181. Collective agreements, work rules and individual employment contracts must not conflict with laws or decrees. A labour contract which establishes working conditions which do not meet the standards provided for in this or any Act is null and void in that regard.[206] Equally, work rules shall not conflict with laws or decrees or with the collective agreements applicable to the workplace concerned.[207] Such conditions invalidated by a labour contract contrary in terms of the provisions of the LSA are governed by the standards provided for in the LSA. The Minister of Employment and Labour has the authority to order amendments to work rules which are deemed to conflict with any of laws, decrees or collective agreements.[208] Equally, if any provision of a collective agreement is determined to be unlawful, the administrative authorities may, with the resolution of the Labour Relations Commission, order for the amendment of such a collective agreement.[209]

205. The purpose of this Act is to improve the employment situation of construction workers, to promote their welfare and to contribute to the development of the construction industry, by assisting and promoting their employment security and the development and improvement of their vocational skills, and by conducting welfare programmes such as providing construction workers with retirement mutual-aid benefits.
206. Article 15 of the LSA.
207. Article 96 of the TULRAA.
208. Article 96 paragraph 1 of the TULRAA.
209. Article 31 of the TULRAA.

182. In individual labour relations, the predominant standard is the agreement of the individual parties. Aside from this, there are collective agreements and work rules. In the hierarchy of legal norms, these rank below the standards of labour-protection laws and mandated labour-contract principles. Pursuant to labour legislation, however, they are endowed with a normative effect which directly controls labour contracts.[210]

183. Because collective agreements have a normative effect on both individual employment contracts and work rules, any provision of an individual employment contract or of work rules which contravenes the standards of working conditions provided for in such a collective agreement is void and invalidated provisions of the individual contract and the work rules are governed by the provisions of the collective agreement.[211] Therefore, parts of the work rules or employment contract which violate the standards concerning working conditions and other matters relating to the treatment of workers as specified by collective agreement shall be deemed null and void. Moreover, matters, which are not stipulated by a contract of employment, and which have been invalidated by Article 33, paragraph 1, are governed by the terms and conditions of collective agreements.

184. Work rules have a normative effect on any individual employment contract. Any provision within an individual employment contract which contravenes the standards of working conditions provided for in the work rules are void and invalidated provisions, and such provisions of an individual contract are, instead, governed by the provisions of the work rules.[212]

185. Therefore, if a labour contract includes employment conditions which are below the standards stipulated in the rules of employment, such non conformity is null and void. In this case, the invalidated provisions are deemed to be governed by the standards provided for in the rules of employment.

§6. The LSA

I. Purpose

186. The LSA is the primary and most general norm that regulates individual labour relations. Pursuant to Article 32, paragraph 3 of the Korean Constitution, which lays down that 'standards of working conditions shall be determined by Act in such a way as to guarantee human dignity', the LSA is to stipulate the standards for conditions of employment in conformity with the Korean Constitution, thereby securing and improving the living standards of workers and achieving a well-balanced development of the national economy.[213] The LSA is a typical workers'

210. Kazuo Sugeno, *op. cit.*, p. 84.
211. Article 33 of the TULRAA.
212. Article 97 of the LSA.
213. Article 1 of the LSA.

protection law. The LSA, which regulates such issues as the fundamental principles of labour contracts, the workers' bill of rights, working hours, wages, and work rules, can be ranked as the fundamental law governing individual labour relations.[214] Therefore, working conditions, as set forth by employment contracts, work rules and collective agreements are inferior to those standards set forth by the LSA and are, as result, void and automatically replaced by the law's mandatory legal norms.[215]

187. The LSA prevents the employer from determining conditions of employment through an abuse of power, and endows the worker with certain rights at each stage of the conclusion, continuance or termination of labour relations. However, without the employer's voluntary fulfillment of his or her obligations, these abstract rights cannot attain their desired goals. Therefore, the LSA nullifies conditions of employment inferior to those stipulated within it, prepares the labour inspection system and inflicts punishment upon actions violating the Act.[216]

II. Scope of Application

188. The LSA, in principle, applies to all businesses or workplaces in which five or more workers are ordinarily employed,[217] regardless of whether they are private enterprises, public enterprises, other enterprises or state-run. The Act also applies to public bodies, including, Seoul Metropolitan Government, other metropolitan cities, the provinces, Shi, Kun, Ku, Eup, Myon, Dong, or other municipal equivalents.[218]

189. This Act, however, does not apply to any business or workplace which employs only relatives living together, or to workers hired for domestic work.[219] With respect to businesses or workplaces which ordinarily employ fewer than five workers, only part of the provisions of this Act may be made applicable as prescribed by presidential decree.[220]

III. Content

190. The LSA covers the following areas;

- general provisions;
- labour contracts;
- wages;

214. Kazuo Sugeno, *op. cit.*, p. 83.
215. Article 15 of the LSA.
216. Chi Sun Kim, *op. cit.*, p. 27.
217. In the application of this Act, the method of calculating the number of workers ordinarily employed shall be prescribed by Presidential Decree (Article 11 paragraph 3).
218. Article 12.
219. Article 11 paragraph 1.
220. Article 11 paragraph 2.

- working hours and rest hours;
- women and minors;
- safety and health;
- work rest;
- accident compensation;
- work rules;
- dormitory provisions;
- labour inspectors;
- penal provisions.

In total, there are 12 chapters and 116 articles, excluding additions.

IV. Characteristics and Basic Principles of the LSA

191. The LSA not only stipulates regulations on public law that deal with regardless of any opinion of both labour and management, but also specifies regulations on private law that requires compensation for damages resulting from an employer's violation of the LSA, which causes the worker to terminate his/her labour contact.

Chapter 1 of the LSA declares the following basic principles, which might be called 'the Workers' Charter'.

A. *Prohibition of Lowering Working Conditions*

192. The purpose of the LSA is to secure and elevate the minimum level of workers' living standards. The working conditions provided for in the LSA prescribe the minimum standards and as a result such parties as are relevant to employment relations shall not reduce working conditions under the pretext of bringing them into compliance with this Act.[221]

193. Therefore, a labour contract which establishes working conditions which does not meet the standards provided for in this Act shall be deemed null and void to that extent. Those conditions invalidated are governed by the standards provided for in this Act.[222]

194. However, this does not mean that labour conditions should be set at the level determined by the Act; rather, the employer should make efforts to establish better working conditions. This article, in and of itself, has a close correlation with Article 34, paragraph 1 of the Constitution, which lays down that 'All citizens shall be entitled to a decent human life'.[223]

---

221. Article 3.
222. Article 15.
223. Chi Sun Kim, *op. cit.*, p. 28.

B. Equality in Determining Working Conditions

195. Working conditions shall be determined based upon mutual agreement between employers and workers, on an equal footing.[224]

196. Although this is one of the fundamental principles of modern private law, the worker is not a match for the employer, since the employer has both economic and social power that the employee lacks.[225] For this reason, in order to ensure substantial equality between them and to enhance working conditions, the Constitution invests workers with the right to independent association, collective bargaining and to collective action.[226]

C. Faithful Fulfilment and Observance of Contractual Norms

197. Both employers and workers shall comply with collective agreements, work rules, and terms of labour contracts, and abide by them in good faith.[227] As to action violating these provisions, there are no punitive provisions nor administrative supervision. Therefore, these articles are interpreted as nothing more than instructive provisions.

D. Equal Treatment

198. The employer must not discriminate against workers on the basis of gender, nor give discriminatory treatment in relation to working conditions on the basis of nationality, creed, religion, or social status.[228] This article establishes the constitutional principle of 'equal treatment'[229] within the field of labour law.[230] The term 'working conditions' refers to the treatment of any worker, in its entirety, within a labour contract relationship. 'Discriminatory treatment' means placing a specified or particular group of workers in separate classification from that of other workers and subjecting them to differential treatment. Race is also included within 'nationality'. Further, 'creed' means a person's thoughts, beliefs, and other innermost ways of thinking, and includes religious, political and other beliefs. As far as discrimination based on social status is concerned, regardless of whether such status was acquired by birth or attained thereafter (e.g. as the result of a criminal conviction or bankruptcy), social status should be understood as referring to a social classification from

224. Article 4.
225. Chi Sun Kim, *op. cit.,* p. 29.
226. Article 33 paragraph 1 of the Constitution.
227. Article 5.
228. Article 6.
229. Constitution, Article 11.
230. In Korea, it has been traditional practice that female workers were discriminated against in regard to remuneration or other labour conditions (dismissal and promotion for instance), even if they had the same labour efficiency as male workers. Discrimination because of nationality, religion, or social status is not so serious in Korea.

which one cannot escape by an exercise of one's own will. 'Social status' does not refer, however, to the classification as either a temporary or part-time worker.

199. Examples of discriminatory treatment range from discrimination based on sex, unequal pay for equal work, discrimination due to retirement age (whether that be male or female), retirement on account of marriage, discrimination based on nationality, especially having a dual nationality or being a foreign national, unequal treatment on account of religion and social status. But the principle of equal treatment is not violated in cases where unequal treatment is effected by work, efficiency, technology, etc. where it is accounted for by different working conditions job type, or job characteristics. Discrimination against male or female on retirement age, violates Article 6 of the LSA. The employer is not allowed to discriminate against a female worker due to her marriage. The intent of preventing unequal treatment on account of nationality is to protect dual nationality holders and foreign nationals from possible discrimination. The employer shall prohibit unequal treatment on account of social class or privileged status. It is a violation of law if the worker is discriminated on account of his/her religious beliefs or against on account of his/her lack of religious affiliation. With the exception of purpose-based companies, it is not considered a violation of law if the worker is fired due to any behaviour that is not in favour of the religious or political purpose of his/her company.

200. Actions (e.g. the dismissal, transfer, or disciplinary punishment of a worker) violating this article are null and void, and punitive provisions apply to them.[231] However, this provision does not tackle discriminatory treatment before the formation of a labour contract (i.e. at the recruitment or hiring stage).

E. Prohibition of Forced Labour

201. No employer shall force workers to work against their own free will through the use of violence, intimidation, confinement or any other means which unlawfully restrict their mental or physical freedom.[232] This provision embodies the constitutional right of personal liberty[233] as it relates to the field of labour law. It is worth noting that opinion is divided as to what 'any other mental or physical coercion' means. However, if we make the assumption that the employer is placed in a dominant position, there is a prohibition against predetermination of penalties or damages for non-observance[234] (in essence monies cannot be taken on the basis that some infringement may take place in the future). Further there is a prohibition on

231. Article 114.
232. Article 7.
233. Constitution, Article 12 paragraph 1.
234. No employer shall enter into a contract by which a penalty or indemnity for possible damages incurred from breach of a labour contract is predetermined (Article 20).

offsetting wages against advances,[235] in addition there is a prohibition of compulsory savings[236] that can be included among them – so long as they restrain the free will of the employee.[237] A punitive provision[238] applies to acts violating this article.

F. Prohibition of Violence

202. No employer shall physically abuse a worker for the occurrence of accidents or for any other reason.[239]

G. Elimination of Intermediary Exploitation

203. Unless otherwise provided by law, no one shall intervene in the employment of another person either for the purpose of making a profit nor to gain benefit as an intermediary.[240]

H. Guarantee of the Exercise of Civil Rights

204. No employer shall reject a request from a worker to be granted time necessary to exercise their franchise or other civil rights, or to perform official duties during his working hours. However, the time requested may be changed, provided that such change does not impede the exercise of those rights or the performance of those civil duties.[241]

---

235. No employer shall offset wages against an advance or other credits given in advance on the condition of worker's labour (Article 21).
236. No employer shall enter into a contract with a worker, in addition to a labour contract, which stipulates compulsory savings or the management of savings (Article 22 paragraph 1).
237. Chi Sun Kim, *op. cit.*, p. 29.
238. Article 107.
239. Article 8.
240. Article 9.
241. Article 10.

Chapter 2. The Labour Contract (Including Fixed-term Contracts)

§1. The Meaning and Characteristics of Labour Contracts

I. The Meaning of the Term 'Labour Contract'

205. Any labour relationship comes into being following the agreement of a labour contract. The labour contract is defined in the LSA as a contract which is entered into in order for a worker to offer work and for an employer to pay wages for that work. Also, a labour contract can be considered to mean 'a contract to provide labour, to which the LSA applies'. In many cases, a 'labour contract' corresponds to, and looks much the same as, a 'contract of employment' under the Civil Code. However, the special feature of the Civil Code's 'contract of employment' is that it bestows equal rights and obligations on all parties to the contract.[242] However, since it is the aim of labour law to bridge the gap between reality and the civil law system, labour law offers the labour contract substantial regulations from its inception to its termination, thus modifying many of the major principles of civil law.[243]

II. Characteristics of Labour Contracts

206. Labour contracts have the following general characteristics:[244]

- a continuous personal relationship (i.e. person-to-person) aimed at creating a situation leading to the provision and use of labour power;
- the systematization of the character of the work to be performed (such systematized work creates the need for uniform working conditions, and other equitable treatment of workers, and requires working conditions to be dealt with on an aggregate basis);
- an uncluttered and flexible quality – labour contracts tend to be simple and most of their contents are supplied and determined by work rules and collective agreements and the for the employers to occupy a predominant position in the relationship (the so-called subordination of the worker).

III. Contractual Capacity and Restrictions on Employment

A. *Minors*

207. The Civil Code stipulates that 'minors under 19 years of age can only conclude any kind of contract with the permission of their parents or guardians; excepting for those contracts by which they merely receive certain rights or are exempted

242. Kazuo Sugeno, *op. cit.*, p. 74.
243. Chi Sun, Kim, *op. cit.*, p. 37.
244. Kazuo Sugeno, *op. cit.*, pp. 75–76.

from certain obligations'.[245] This principle also applies to any labour contract. However, the LSA provides two exceptional provisions in order to protect minors. The LSA provides that 'neither a parent nor guardian shall enter into a labour contract on behalf of a minor'.[246] In addition the LSA provides that the 'parent and/or guardian of a minor, or the Minister of Employment and Labour may terminate a labour contract, if a labour contract may be deemed disadvantageous to the minor'. If an employer makes a labour contract with a person under the age of 18, the employer must specify the working conditions in writing and issue the same pursuant to Article 17 (Statement of Working Conditions).[247]

208. A minor may claim his or her wages in his or her own right.[248] That is, the parent or guardian may not receive the minor's wages by proxy.[249] In the LSA, a minor worker means one who is 15 to 18 years of age. In consideration of the mental and physical impact that work may have on a minor, the LSA also provides extensive special protection for minors in respect of the kinds of work permissible for them to undertake, their hours of work, night work and other working conditions.[250] For example there is a prohibition of employment in situations considered hazardous and dangerous – whether in terms of morality or health,[251] in addition there is a prohibition against excessive working hours,[252] restrictions on night work and holiday work,[253] a prohibition of working inside a pit,[254] etc.

209. The LSA stipulates that 'a person under the age of 15 (including those under the age of 18 who are attending a middle school pursuant to the Elementary and Secondary Education Act) shall not be employed as a worker. However any person with an employment permit issued by the Minister of Employment and Labour may be employed as a worker (Article 64 paragraph 1).[255] The LSA further provides that 'for each minor under 18, an employer shall keep in the workplace a certificate proving his or her family relationships and the written consent of his or her parent or guardian'.[256]

B. Women

210. As far as contractual capacity is concerned there is no special provision concerning women. Discrimination in working conditions on the basis of gender is

245. Articles 5 and 4 of the Civil Code.
246. Article 67 paragraph 1.
247. Article 67.
248. Article 68.
249. These provisions exist because parents or guardians do not always act for the benefit of their wards.
250. Chi Sun Kim, *op. cit.*, p. 37.
251. Article 65 paragraph 1.
252. Article 69.
253. Article 70.
254. Article 72.
255. Article 64.
256. Article 66.

prohibited by the guarantee of equality of the sexes stated within Article 6 of the LSA. On the other hand, the Act also provides rather extensive protection to female workers in respect of the kind of work, the hours of work that may be required, working at night as well as other working conditions.[257] That is to say that there is a clear prohibition of employment in hazardous and dangerous conditions, whether that be in terms of either morality or health,[258] a prohibition against excessive over-time work,[259] restrictions on night work and holiday work,[260] a prohibition against working inside a pit,[261] a guarantee of menstruation leave,[262] legal protection for pregnant women,[263] a specification of time off for prenatal examinations[264] and nursing hours,[265] etc.

IV. General Theory

211. The labour protection laws within the developed nations generally started with regulations to protect minors and women against unduly burdensome working hours, working at night, and hazardous or harmful works. Modern Korean law recognizes the particular issues faced by women and children[266] and offers them certain specific protections as a result. The principle of protecting women and minors is also enshrined in the constitution of Korea (Constitution Article 32, paragraphs 4 and 5).

212. Within the LSA, minors are considered to be 'persons who are under 18 years of age'. It further specifies that those, 'persons who are under 15 years of age' are entitled to special protection as 'children'. 'Minors' as defined under the Civil Code (i.e. those people who are under the age of 19) are guaranteed special protection with regard to concluding contracts.[267]

A. *Restrictions on the Employment of Women and Minors*

1. Minimum Age and Employment Permit

213. A person under the age of 15 (including those under the age of 18 who are attending a middle school pursuant to the Elementary and Secondary Education Act) shall not be employed as a worker. However, a person with an employment permit

257. Chi Sun Kim, *op. cit.*, p. 38.
258. Article 65 paragraph 1.
259. Article 71.
260. Article 70.
261. Article 72.
262. Article 73.
263. Article 74.
264. Article 74-2.
265. Article 75.
266. They may be harmed physically or morally unless properly protected by law.
267. Kazuo Sugeno, *op. cit.*, p. 352.

issued by the Minister of Employment and Labour in accordance with the criteria as prescribed by presidential decree may be employed as a worker (Article 64 paragraph 1).

214. The employment permit may be issued at the request of the individual concerned only by designating the type of occupation in which he or she is engaged, provided that such employment will not impede his or her compulsory education.[268] If a person receives the employment permit prescribed in paragraph (1) by a false or other fraudulent pretence, the Minister of Employment and Labor shall cancel the permission (Article 64 paragraph 3).

2. Prohibitions on Employment

215. No employer shall employ a female in pregnancy or with less than one year after childbirth (hereinafter referred to as pregnant female) and those aged less than 18 for hazardous and dangerous work in terms of morality or health.

216. In addition, no employer shall employ a female aged 18 or older who is not pregnant for work that is hazardous and dangerous to their pregnancy or childbirth among the hazardous and dangerous works in terms of health. Such occupations shall be determined by presidential decree.[269]

3. Minor Certificate

217. For every minor under the age of 18 in employment, an employer shall keep, in the workplace, a certificate showing their family relationships as well as a written statement of consent from their parent or guardian.[270]

4. Restrictions on the Working Hours of Minors

218. The working hours for a person aged between 15 and 18 shall not exceed seven hours per day or 35 hours per week. However, these working hours may be extended – by up to an hour per day, or five hours per week, respectively – through an agreement between the parties concerned.[271]

268. Article 64.
269. Article 65.
270. Article 66.
271. Article 69.

5. Restrictions on Night Work and Holiday Work

219. When an employer wishes to have a female employee aged 18 or older work between the hours of 10 pm and 6 am or on a designated holiday, the employer must obtain the consent of the worker concerned. In addition, an employer should not have a pregnant female worker nor one who is aged under 18 to work between those hours, nor on a designated holiday. However, this need not apply in the following instances and when the employer has obtained the permission of the Minister of Employment and Labour:

- where there is a consent from the person aged less than 18;
- where there is a consent from a female with less than one year after childbirth;
- where the female in pregnancy makes a request.

220. An employer, before obtaining the permission of the Minister of Employment and Labour should have consulted, in good faith, with a workers' representative of either the business or the workplace concerned as to whether there may be night work or holiday work in relation to the implementation methods for those working practices as they relate to the protection of the workers' health and with particular regard to maternity protection.[272]

6. Restrictions on Overtime Work

221. An employer shall not have a female employee within her first post-natal year work overtime in excess of 2 hours per day, 6 hours per week, or 150 hours per year, even if such overtime has been agreed by means of a collective agreement.[273]

7. Prohibition of Work Inside a Mine

222. No employer shall employ a female or minor under the age of 18 for any work inside a pit, except where the work is temporarily needed to perform the business as determined by presidential decree such as health, medicine, news reporting, news coverage, etc.[274]

272. Article 70.
273. Article 71.
274. Article 72.

B. Maternity Protection

1. Menstruation Leave

223. An employer shall, upon receiving such a request from a female worker, grant her one-day menstruation leave per month.[275]

2. The Protection of Pregnant Women

224. With regardto the protection of pregnant women an employer must:

1. grant a pregnant female worker 90 days of maternity leave which may be taken before and after childbirth. In such an instance, 45 days, or more, shall be allocated to the period following childbirth;
2. at the request of a pregnant employee who has had a miscarriage or when the child is stillborn after 12 weeks of pregnancy, the employer shall grant her protective leave as prescribed by presidential decree, except where the miscarriage is caused by an artificially induced abourtion operation (excluding cases as prescribed in Article 14(1) of the Mother and Child Health Act);
3. of the leave as set set out in paragraphs one and two, the first 60 days' leave shall be with pay, excepting that maternity leave benefits, etc., are already paid pursuant to Article 18 of the EEWRA Reconciliation, under these circumstances the employer shall be relieved of the responsibility for payment equal to to the extent of that amount;
4. no employer shall require a pregnant worker to undertake overtime and, in the event that such a worker requests, the employer is required to offer her light duties;
5. after the end of the protective leave as designated in paragraph (1), the employer shall allow the female worker to return to the same work, or one with the same level of pay, as before the leave.[276]

3. Allowing Time Off for Prenatal Examination

225. If a pregnant employee makes a request to take time off from work to receive a prenatal health check, the employer shall allow her to do so. In addition, the employer shall not cut a worker's wages on the grounds that she needs to take that time off.[277]

275. Article 73.
276. Article 74.
277. Article 74-2.

4. Nursing Hours

226. A female worker who has an infant under the age of twelve months shall be allowed to take paid nursing recesses, twice per day for more than 30 minutes each.[278]

§2. OTHER PROVISIONS OF THE LSA

I. Apprenticeships

227. The freedom of the choice of occupation and the right to work, as guaranteed in the Constitution[279] take concrete shape only when the State can offer the opportunity of employment to all people through vocational training and when it can give a proper job congruent with that individual's ability.

228. The EIA of 1993 and the WVSDA of 1997 exist to further this purpose. The EIA implements vocational skills development projects to prevent the unemployment of the insured,[280] those once insured and other people willing to be employed ('the insured, etc.'), to further promote their employment, expand their employment opportunities, provide opportunities and support for them to develop and improve their vocational skills; in addition it provides other support for employment security and helps employers to secure a workforce.[281] Meanwhile, the WVSDA exists to secure the employment of workers, raise their social and economic status, and improve the productivity of enterprises, thus contributing to social and economic development by promoting and supporting employee skills development throughout their working lives. The LSA provides that 'no employer shall abuse workers in training, workers on probation or any other apprentice whose purpose is to acquire a technical skill, or assign them to domestic work or other work not related to the acquisition of technical skill'.[282]

229. In contrast with the WVSDA, the provisions of the LSA concerning apprenticeship aim mainly at remedying all sorts of evils which may occur during an apprenticeship. Hence, the two are quite different in their motives.[283]

278. Article 75.
279. Constitution, Articles 15 and 32.
280. The term 'the insured' refers to workers who are insured or deemed to be insured (Article 2).
281. Article 19.
282. Article 77.
283. Chi Sun Kim, *op. cit.*, p. 59.

II. Dormitory Provision

A. General Remarks

230. In order to avoid any infringement upon a worker's private life and at the same time guarantee a healthy and orderly collective life, the LSA lays down the following provisions.

B. Protection of Dormitory Life

231. An employer shall not interfere with the private life of a worker lodging in a dormitory annexed to a business. An employer shall not interfere with the election of staff required for the autonomous management of a dormitory.[284]

C. Preparation of and Amendment to Dormitory Rules

232. An employer who wants to board his workers in a dormitory annexed to a business shall prepare dormitory rules concerning the following matters:

- matters pertaining to rising in the morning retiring at night, as well as going-out and overnight stays:
- matters pertaining to events;
- matters pertaining to meals;
- matters pertaining to safety and health;
- matters pertaining to the maintenance of buildings and facilities.

D. Other Matters Applicable to All Boarders

233. An employer shall obtain the consent of the representative who represents a majority of the boarding members with regard to the preparation of and amendment to the dormitory rules. Both the employer and the boarding member shall comply with the dormitory rules.[285]

284. Article 98.
285. Article 99.

E. Measures for Safety and Health

234. An employer shall take measures necessary for the maintenance of the health, morals and lives of the members who are lodged in any dormitory annexed to the business. The standards for the measures to be taken shall be provided for by presidential decree.[286]

III. Work Rules (Rules of Employment)

A. Introduction

235. Work rules are a set of regulations set forth by an employer for the purpose of establishing uniform rules and conditions of employment within the work-place. As the enterprise or workshop itself is a small society made up of its own members, it also needs standing rules in order to maintain internal order, to establish the standards of labour conditions and to regulate the behavior of its members. Strictly speaking, these are matters that should be decided within individual labour contracts. However, since the labour relationship between both parties is considerably standardized nowadays, it is not only troublesome but unnecessary to arrange these matters with every individual worker. Work rules are the rules stipulating such matters as constituting the contents of the individual labour contract, which are established by the employer and apply uniformly to all workers in the enterprise for the convenience of the management of individual labour relations.[287]

236. On the understanding that workers cannot object to the application of work rules – as a result of their subordinate status the LSA lays down stipulations concerning the state's supervision and control of such rules, through which they may play a role in protecting workers.

B. Legal Nature of Work Rules

237. The legal nature of work rules is still a point of contention in Korea. Roughly speaking the various theories can be divided into two groups – one which regards the works rules as a contract between the employer and their workers and another which regards them as a legal norm. As stated above, work rules exist for the convenience of the employer in concluding contracts with a number of workers. In fact, work rules serve as a norm since they apply to all employees in an enterprise or workplace as aspects common to each labour contract. They are not a contract in and of themselves, since they are drawn up and amended unilaterally by the employer, despite the fact that labour law declares the equality of both parties in deciding conditions. Moreover, the work rules can hold good in spite of objections from a group of employees. However, legally speaking at least, the work rules are

286. Article 100.
287. Chi Sun Kim, *op. cit.*, p. 64.

not a legal norm because the employer has no right to establish a legal norm without authorization from the state. Therefore, the work rules require an employee's consent, in any from, in order to be accepted as the content of a labour contract. If an individual employee has concluded a labour contract without any clear objection to the work rules as a whole, s/he is regarded as having consented to them even if s/he does not sufficiently understand their meaning.[288]

C. Duty to Draw up and Submit Work Rules

238. The LSA mandates that any employer who continuously employs 10 or more workers must draw up work rules on the following matters, and file it with the Minister of Employment and Labour. If any amendments to the work rules occur, the same procedures shall be followed:

- matters pertaining to the starting and finishing time of work, recess hours, holidays, leave and shifts;
- matters pertaining to the determination of wages, calculation of wages, means of payment, closing of payment, time of payment and wage increases;
- matters pertaining to the calculation of family allowances and means of payment;
- matters pertaining to retirement;
- matters pertaining to retirement pay as prescribed in Article 8 of the WRBSA, bonuses and minimum wages;
- matters pertaining to meal allowances and the allocation of expenses for operational tools or necessities;
- matters pertaining to educational facilities for workers;
- matters pertaining to maternity protection for female workers, such as maternity leave, child-care leave, etc., and support for reconciliation between work and family life;
- matters pertaining to safety and health;
- matters pertaining to the improvement of the working environment in accordance with workers' characteristics, such as gender, age or physical attributes;
- matters pertaining to support in the instance of occupational or non-occupational accidents;
- matters pertaining to awards and punishments;
- matters pertaining to workplace harassment protion;
- other matters applicable to all workers of the business concerned.

D. Procedures for the Preparation of and Amendment to Work Rules

239. An employer shall seek the opinions of a trade union, if there is a trade union composed of the majority of the workers within the workplace concerned, or the consultation of the majority of workers if there is no trade union comprising a

288. *Ibid.*, p. 65.

majority, with regards to the preparation of and amendments to the work rules. However, if the work rules are to be modified in a manner unfavourable to workers, the employer has to obtain the workers' consent. When an employer submits the work rules, a written document containing the result of the consultation shall be attached.[289] The employer has to inform the workers of the works rules by displaying or posting them in places accessible to all workers.

E. Reasonable Modifications and Criteria for the Reasonableness of Work Rules

240. In Korea, as is the case in Japan, the Supreme Court took a different position and established a unique rule regarding unfavourable modifications to work rules. According to this rule, a 'reasonable modification' of the work rules has a binding effect on all workers, including those who opposed the modification. Despite severe criticism asserting that there was no legal ground for recognizing such a binding effect, the Supreme Court has adhered to this rule, which has accordingly become the established case law.[290]

241. Traditional contract theory dictates that a worker who refuses modifications to his or her working conditions should be discharged. However, under Korean court rulings, such a dismissal may well be regarded as an abuse of the right to dismiss. On the other hand, because the employment relationship is a continuous contractual relationship, modification and adjustment of working conditions are inevitable. In light of these circumstances, Korean courts have given unilaterally modified work rules a binding effect on the condition that the modification is reasonable. The implication of this rule is that courts give priority to employment security, and in exchange therefore, workers are expected to accept and be subject to reasonable changes in working conditions.[291]

242. The principal test for 'reasonableness' requires the courts to weigh the disadvantage caused to the worker created by the modification against the business necessity for changing the working conditions. Courts also take other matters surrounding the modification into consideration, such as whether compensatory measures to mitigate the disadvantages to the workers are or were being taken, whether similar treatment is common in other companies within the same industry, and whether the majority union or the majority of the workers agreed to the modification.[292]

289. Article 94.
290. Takashi Araki, *op. cit.*, p. 55.
291. *Ibid.*, p. 53.
292. *Ibid.*, p. 54.

F. Limitation on Punitive Provisions

243. If a punitive reduction in wages for a worker is stipulated in the work rules, the reduction amount for each infraction shall not exceed half of one day's average wages, and the total amount of reduction shall not exceed one-tenth of the total amount of wages during each period of wage payment.[293]

G. Observance of Collective Agreements

244. The work rules shall not conflict with laws or decrees or with collective agreements applicable to the workplace concerned. The Minister of Employment and Labour has the authority to order an amendment to any work rules which are deemed to be conflict with such laws, decrees or collective agreements.[294]

H. The Effects of Violation

245. If a labour contract includes employment conditions which are below the standards stipulated in the work rules, such nonconformity shall be null and void. In this case, the invalidated provisions shall be governed by the standards provided for in the work rules.[295] The LSA gives work rules an imperative and direct effect on individual labour contracts.

IV. Workplace Order and Discipline

A. Restrictions on and Grounds Relating to Dismissals and Other Disciplinary Measures

246. An employer can exercise the right to disciplinary action concerning an employee's violation of service regulations to maintain the company's order; provided, however, that it is only justified when the authorized organization of the collective agreement or work rules exercises it fairly. Most work rules stipulate various kinds of disciplinary punishment for violations of management rules and orders, which range through warnings, wage cuts, suspensions, demotion,[296] and discharge.

247. In Korea, where dismissals for a worker's misconduct are strictly limited under the law and judicial precedents, disciplinary measures, rather than discharges, are a more customary method for punishing workers for their misconduct.

293. Article 95.
294. Article 96.
295. Article 97.
296. 'Demotion' refers to removing a worker from a present to a lower position as a disciplinary measure. Legally speaking there are two types of demotions. One is implemented as an imposition of the employer's personnel management right. The other is an imposition of discipline.

It does not follow, however, that employers immediately resort to disciplinary action when there are grounds for discipline. It is more common for a Korean employer to take various informal measures to cope with a worker's misconduct, such as a reprimand from a supervisor not amounting to a disciplinary action, giving a low performance evaluation, or a relegation to a less important position.[297]

248. Although the question as to whether an employer has the right to discipline workers for violation of contractual obligations has always been a subject of debate, that is to say, there are opposing theories ('managerial right theory' or 'contract theory')[298] today, the majority's opinion is that an employer does have the right to establish and maintain order within their enterprise, and that the workers' duty to respect this order is ancillary to the employment contract. In order to impose disciplinary measures apart from ordinary contractual liability, explicit contractual grounds, that is to say an agreement concerning the employer's power to discipline, or work rules whose content are incorporated into an employment contract must exist.[299] As we have already seen, the leading theories find their legal foundation in the contract. Thus disciplinary punishments can only be imposed when they are agreed upon clearly in the work rules or in a collective agreement.

249. The LSA mandates the inclusion of sanctions or disciplinary provisions in the work rules if the employer wishes to regulate these matters.[300] Although this LSA provision applies only to establishments with 10 more employees,[301] in practice, almost all employers have disciplinary provisions in their work rules.

B. Types of Disciplinary Measure

250. As mentioned above, the LSA requires that work rules include provisions on matters pertaining to awards and punishments. There is, however, no particular regulation concerning the types of disciplinary measures. Common methods for disciplinary practice are as follows.

297. Takashi Araki, *op. cit.,* p. 149.
298. There have been opposing theories among scholars concerning this question. The 'managerial right theory' contends that the right to impose disciplinary measures is derived from the employer's inherent managerial rights, and thus, no contractual provision is required to discipline workers. While the 'contract theory' suggests the right to discipline workers only on the basis of an agreement between the parties which provides the employer with such authority. According to the contract theory, an employer may not impose disciplinary sanctions on workers in the absence of a specific provision in a contract or in the work rules (Takashi Araki, *op. cit.*, p. 151).
299. Takashi Araki, *op. cit.*, p. 152.
300. LSA, Article 93, no. 11.
301. LSA, Article 93.

C. Reprimands and Warnings

251. Both reprimands and warnings seek to admonish a worker for his or her misconduct and to deter similar behaviour in the future. While reprimands usually require the worker concerned to submit a written apology, warnings do not. Usually these admonitions themselves do not immediately cause any disadvantage for the worker. However, they remain on record and can be considered in awarding bonuses, promotions, etc. The accumulation of such sanctions may also lead to more severe disciplinary action.[302]

D. Wage Decreases (Pay Cuts) or Degradation and Suspensions

252. Using a wage decrease as a disciplinary measure may be considered to be the deduction of a certain amount of payment from a worker's wages that would otherwise have been paid for the work performed. The LSA's regulations provide that 'when a punitive reduction in wages for a worker is stipulated in the work rules, the reduction amount for each infraction shall not exceed half of one day's average wages, and the total amount of reduction shall not exceed one-tenth of the total amount of wages during each period of wage payment'.[303] Degradation means, for a given period, promotion is restricted or position is lowered. The suspension from office concerns suspending those employees who violate company regulations while retaining their status. Wages are also unpaid during the suspension period.

E. Disciplinary Discharge

253. The most grave form of discipline is a disciplinary discharge. This is normally imposed without notice and severance pay can be withheld either in whole or in part. A worker will face serious obstacles to reemployment by virtue of the fact that he or she has been subject to a disciplinary discharge.

F. Grounds for Disciplinary Measures

254. In practice, work rules usually have provisions concerning the grounds for disciplinary measures. In light of the disadvantage that the worker would incur, however, courts tend to interpret such broad provision narrowly. Disciplinary actions are normally taken for types of misconduct performed by a worker as follows:[304]

- violation of the main duty to work: violation of job-related orders, neglecting their duties, etc.;

302. Takashi Araki, *op. cit.*, p. 153.
303. Article 95.
304. Takashi Araki, *op. cit.*, pp. 154–157.

– violation of ancillary duties: falsification of one's past record, misconduct in one's private life, dual employment, etc;
– a disturbance of the order necessary for the safe running on an enterprise.

G. The Appropriateness of Disciplinary Measures

255. Even when the grounds mentioned above for discipline are valid, a disciplinary action can be nullified when it is found to be an abuse of rights from the perspectives of proportionality or due process and the principle of legality.

H. Proportionality

256. Disciplinary punishment must be proportionate to the gravity of the act of misconduct. Disciplinary measures must not be excessive in comparison to those which have been imposed in similar acts in prior cases at the same company. Courts have held many disciplinary measures to be an abuse of the right to impose discipline on this rationale.[305]

I. Due Process and the Principle of Legality

257. Since disciplinary actions are a form of punishment, due process is required. Where prior consultation with a union or other procedures is required by a collective agreement or a provision in the work rules, disciplinary measures without the requisite procedure may be nullified as an abuse of rights. Even when no such provision prescribing procedures exist, the worker concerned must have an opportunity to explain and defend his or her actions.[306] Deciding whether certain behaviour is a violation or not and the method of punishment shall be regulated by the law beforehand. The worker is not to be punished twice for the same violation.

V. Labour Inspection

A. Introduction

258. Articles 107–116 of the LSA lay down punitive provisions ranging from fines to imprisonment in order to ensure their effectiveness. However, this kind of sanction is only an *ex post facto* measure, which is not effective in some fields of protective labour law (overdue wages and overtime work, for example). The labour inspection system plays an especially important role in Korea.[307]

305. *Ibid.*, p. 158.
306. *Ibid.*
307. Chi Sun Kim, *op. cit.*, p. 66.

B. Supervisory Authorities

259. The Ministry of Employment and Labour and its subordinate offices shall have labour inspectors to ensure the standards are enforced in terms of employee's conditions of labour.[308]

C. Authority of Labour Inspectors

260. In order to be able to carry out their duties, labour inspectors are appointed from those who have specialized qualifications and are given guaranteed security in their jobs. Also, they are required to keep secret any information acquired in the course of performing their official duties, even after their retirement.[309] The labour inspector has the following functions:[310]

- a labour inspector has the authority to inspect a workplace, a dormitory or other annexed buildings, to request presentation of books and documents, and to question both either an employer or their workers;
- a labour inspector who is a medical doctor or a medical doctor designated by a labour inspector has the authority to conduct medical examinations of workers who appear to suffer from a disease which precludes his/her continuous employment;
- a labour inspector or a medical doctor designated by a labour inspector shall present his identification card and a letter of order for medical examination issued by the Minister of Employment and Labour before performing his or her duty;
- with regard to a letter of order for inspection or medical examination, the date, place and scope shall be clearly stated therein;
- a labour inspector shall have the authority to perform the official duties of a judicial police officer in accordance with the Act Relating to Persons to Perform Duties of the Judicial Police and Scope of those Duties with regard to the crimes in violation of this Act or other laws or decrees pertaining to labour affairs.

D. Reports to Supervisory Authorities

261. If any violation of the provisions of this Act or any Presidential Decree that has been promulgated pursuant thereto occurs at a workplace, a worker may notify the Minister of Employment and Labour or a labour inspector of the violation. No employer shall dismiss or unfairly treat the worker concerned for giving such a notification.[311]

308. Article 101.
309. LSA, Article 103.
310. Article 102.
311. Article 104.

E. The Limits of Judicial Police Duty

262. Public prosecutors and labour inspectors shall be wholly in charge of the inspection, the request for and the presentation of documents, all questioning and the conduct of any other investigation, in accordance with this Act and other laws or decrees pertaining to labour affairs. However, this shall not apply to an investigation into an offence or a crime committed by a labour inspector in the course of performing his or her official duties.[312]

F. Delegation of Authority

263. The authority of the Minister of Employment and Labor under this Act may be delegated, in part, to the head of a local employment and labour office as prescribed by the Presidential Decree (Article 106).

VI. Non-regular Workers

A. Introduction

264. The typical Korean labour relationship is that of a regular worker working under a system of long-term employment, yet, these are surrounded by a variety of atypical labour relationships. Under the long-term employment system, an employer cannot engage in unrestrained numerical adjustment of its workforce. To compensate for the rigidity in numerical flexibility, Korean employers have utilized non-regular and contingent workers.

265. The employment relations of non-regular workers take on diverse employment forms. Legally, they can be divided into:

- workers hired under fixed-term contracts;
- part-time (or temporary) workers; and
- extra-company workers, comprised of workers under contract work arrangements and dispatch workers.[313]

266. The term 'fixed-term employee' refers to an employee who has signed a labour contract whose period is fixed ('fixed-term labour contract').[314] The term 'part-time worker' refers to a part-time employee whose contractual working hours per week are shorter than those of a full-time worker engaged in the same kind of job in the same workplace.[315]

312. Article 105.
313. Takashi Araki, *op. cit.*, p. 33.
314. Article 2 no. 1.
315. FPWPA, Article 2, no. 2: LSA, Article 2, paragraph 1, no. 8

267. Enterprises receive and employ workers who are furnished by other enterprises, and use those workers to perform work in their own enterprises. One of the methods of using non-company workers is to use dispatch worker. 'Dispatch worker' means a person who is employed by a sending employer and subject to worker dispatch.

B. The FPWPA

1. Legal Regulations Relating to Fixed-term Contracts and Part-time Workers

268. Theoretically, a fixed-term employment contract terminates automatically upon expiration of the time period specified therein. Since the termination is not a dismissal, the law on the abuse of the right to dismiss does not apply directly. Because Korea has enjoyed long-term economic growth, many fixed-term workers had had their contracts renewed repeatedly. As a result, they had been employed for many years and their employment relations had become indistinguishable from those of regular workers. However, when a company refuses to renew the contracts of fixed-term workers in response to a business slump, the question of social protection for those workers arises. When a reduction of their workforce is required, Korean employers have often turned to refusing the renewal of fixed-term contracts since dismissals of regular workers are severely restricted. Fixed-term contracts have functioned as shock absorbers to protect regular workers against fluctuating economic circumstances.[316]

269. In Korea, legal restrictions on the employment period of fixed-term employees, and the renewal of their contracts, as well as on overtime work for part-time employees mean that discriminatory treatment exists. The legal restriction on fixed-term contracts is that the term may not exceed two years. In the case of repeated fixed-term labour contracts, the sum of the periods of such contracts may not exceed two years. This serves to avoid unduly long periods of obligatory servitude of a worker to an employer. Since there is a restriction on the renewal of fixed-term contracts, if an employer hires a fixed-term employee for more than two years, the fixed-term employee shall be considered to be a worker who has made a labour contract with no fixed term.[317]

270. The FPWPA defines a part-timer as an employee whose contractual working hours per week are shorter than those of a full-time worker engaged in the same kind of job in the same workplace.[318] In Korea, there are so-called 'quasi-part-timers' who are hired under the contractual status of a part-timer and are treated differently from regular workers despite the fact that their working hours are almost as long as those of regular, full-time workers.

---

316. Takashi Araki, *op. cit.*, p. 34.
317. Article 4 paragraph 2.
318. LSA, Article 2, no. 8.

271. Like ordinary workers, part-timers are covered by all labour laws except in certain matters for which special regulations are provided, namely employment insurance, health insurance, employee pension insurance and income tax. Therefore, if a part-time worker is employed under an open-ended contract, the 'abuse of the right to dismiss rule' applies to that worker. However, part-timers are significantly different from regular workers with respect to their treatment in employment relations.[319]

2. The Purpose of This Act and the Scope of Its Application

272. Against the background of an increase in the numbers and diversification in the roles, of part-time workers and the growth of their social importance, the need to establish satisfactory forms of work becomes a matter of importance. This resulted in the FPWPA which was enacted in December 2006. In the light of the important role played by part-time workers in the Korean economy, and to make use of their abilities and promote their welfare, this law was designed for 'short-time workers'. The purpose of this Act is to promote a sound development of the labour market by redressing undue discrimination against fixed-term and part-time workers and strengthening the protection of their working conditions.[320]

273. This Act applies to all businesses or workplaces employing not fewer than five workers. However, this Act does not apply to a business or workplace which employs only relatives living together or to a worker who is hired for domestic work.[321] With respect to state and local government agencies, this Act shall apply to them regardless of the number of workers they ordinarily employ.[322]

C. Fixed-term Employees

1. Employment of Fixed-term Employees

274. As previously mentioned, an employer may hire a fixed-term employee for a period not exceeding two years (or in the case of repeated fixed-term labour contracts, the sum of such contracted periods shall not exceed two years). However, an employer may hire a fixed-term employee for a period in excess of two years where:

– the period needed to complete a project or particular task is defined;

319. For instance, regular workers, including blue-collar workers, are customarily paid daily or monthly, while part-timers are paid on an hourly basis, with the latter rate being much less than the former. While regular workers generally receive bonuses and retirement allowances, part-timers get no or very few such benefits. They are also treated differently with regard to the use of welfare and recreation facilities owned by the company (Takashi Araki, *op. cit.*, p. 37).

320. FPWPA, Article 1.

321. With respect to businesses or workplaces employing four workers or less, some of the provisions of this Act may apply to them as prescribed by presidential decree.

322. FPWPA, Article 3.

- the fixed-term employee is needed to fill a vacancy arising from a worker's temporary suspension from duty or dispatch until the worker returns to work;
- the period needed for a worker to complete schoolwork or vocational training is defined;
- the fixed-term labour contract is made with the aged as defined in Article 2 sub-paragraph 1 of the AEPA;
- the job requires professional knowledge and skills or the job is offered as part of the government's welfare or unemployment measures as prescribed by presidential decree;
- there is a rational reason equivalent to those described in sub-paragraphs 1 through 5 and prescribed by presidential decree.

275. Notwithstanding the fact that those grounds enumerated in the above provisos do not exist or cease to exist, if an employer hires a fixed-term employee for more than two years, the fixed-term employee shall be considered as a worker who has made a labour contract with no fixed term.[323]

2. Converting from a Fixed-term Contract to a Contract with No Such Limit

276. If an employer intends to make a labour contract without a fixed term, he/she shall make efforts to preferentially hire fixed-term employees who are engaged in the same or similar kinds of jobs in the business or workplace concerned.[324]

D. Part-time Employees

1. Definition and Working Conditions for Part-time Workers

277. The term part-time worker means an employee whose contractual working hours per week are shorter than those of a full-time worker engaged in the same kind of job in the same workplace (Article 2, subparagraph 8).

Working conditions for part-time workers shall be determined on the basis of the relative ratio of their working hours computed in comparison with those of full-time workers engaged in the same kind of job in the same workplace. The criteria or other matters to be considered for the determination of working conditions shall be prescribed by the Presidential Decree. With respect to workers whose contractual working hours is an average of less than 15 hours per week over a four-week period (the employment period, in case they are employed for less than four weeks), Articles 55 (holidays) and 60 (annual paid leave) shall not apply (Article 18).

323. FPWPA, Article 4.
324. FPWPA, Article 5.

2. Restrictions on the Overtime Work of Part-time Employees

278. 'Contractual working hours' refers to the working hours on which workers and employers have made an agreement within the limit of prescribed working hours under the LSA (Article 50 or Article 69) or the ISHA (Article 46).[325] If an employer intends to have a part-time employee work in excess of their contractual working hours, he or she shall obtain the consent of the employee in question. In this case, the overtime hours shall not exceed 12 hours a week. Any part-time employee can refuse to do overtime work if the employer orders the overtime work without obtaining their consent.[326]

3. Converting from a Part-time Contract to a Regular Working Contract, etc.

279. If an employer intends to hire a regular worker, he or she must make efforts to preferentially hire part-time employees who are engaged in the same or similar kinds of jobs in the business or workplace concerned. If a worker applies to work part-time on account of household duties, study or other reasons, the employer shall make efforts to convert the worker into a part-time employee.[327]

E. Prohibition and Redress of Discriminatory Treatment

1. Wage Differences between Regular Workers and Part-timers

280. The term 'discriminatory treatment' refers to unfavourable treatment in terms of wages and other working conditions given without any justifiable reason.[328] Part-timers are usually hired under fixed-term contracts and their employment is less secure than that of regular workers. Since most part-timers are women, sex discrimination further complicates the problems related to part-time workers.[329]

281. The inherent question about part-time work is this: if a worker is paid a lower wage for being a part-timer, despite the fact that the worker's job content is no different from that of a regular worker, is this illegal unequal treatment?

282. Article 6 of the LSA[330] prohibits an employer's discriminatory treatment with respect to working conditions on account of his or her nationality, creed or 'social status'. According to the generally accepted view, social status refers to a

325. LSA, Article 2, no. 7.
326. FPWPA, Article 6.
327. FPWPA, Article 7.
328. Article 2 no. 3.
329. However, the issues surrounding fixed-term contracts and discrimination against women are understood to be separate and are dealt with in accordance with the relevant legal theories.
330. No employer shall discriminate against workers on the basis of gender, nor give discriminatory treatment in relation to working conditions on the basis of nationality, religion or social status (Article 6).

social classification from which one cannot escape of one's own volition. Thus, class differentiation on the basis of being a part-time worker, a status created by mutual assent of the parties, does not fall within this category. Under the current law, moreover, there is no general provision establishing the principle of equal pay for equal work.[331] It is theoretically possible to argue that the discriminatory treatment of part-timers is against public order and morality (Civil Code Article 103) and should be deemed illegal.[332]

2. Prohibition of Discriminatory Treatment

283. An employer must not give discriminatory treatment to fixed-term employees on the grounds of their employment status compared with other workers engaged in the same or similar jobs under a labour contract without a fixed term in the business or workplace concerned. In addition, an employer must not discriminate against part-time workers on the grounds of their employment status compared with that of full-time workers who are engaged in the same or similar kinds of jobs in the business or workplace concerned.[333]

3. Application for Redress against Discriminatory Treatment

284. If a fixed-term or part-time employee receives discriminatory treatment, he or she can apply for redress to the Labour Relations Commission under the LRCAA. However, this shall not apply if six months or more have passed since the day when the discriminatory treatment occurred (or since the last day of the treatment in the case of continuous discriminatory treatment).

285. If a fixed-term or part-time employee makes an application for redress, he or she must clearly state the specific details of such discriminatory treatment.

---

331. Takashi Araki, *op. cit.*, pp. 37–38.
332. In Korea, however, as far as wages are concerned, there is no required correlation of wages to work performed. The basic principle for wages has been the seniority-based wage scheme coupled with the notion that wages should be sufficient to support the livelihood of a worker and his or her family. In other words, wages are perceived as compensation for a worker's entrusting his or her labour to the employer rather than as a direct compensation for some specific work performed. It follows that there is a notable difference between a complete entrustment of one's labour to the employer, in the case of a regular worker, who is expected to comply with overtime orders and transfer orders, and a part-time worker, who is not expected to follow such orders when or if they are issued. Thus, notwithstanding the fact that part-timers and regular workers may be performing the same work, when their respective work is compared at a certain point in time, a court may regard the wage disparity as being justified by the extent to which the worker surrenders his right to control the disposal of his labour. From an economic perspective, the wage of a regular worker is determined by the internal labour market, whereas the wage of a part-timer, who is not incorporated into the internal labour market and tends to move between companies, is determined by the external labour market. Given the difference in labour markets to which regular and part-time workers belong, it might be difficult to convince the court that the current wage scheme is categorically against public order and morals (Takashi Araki, *op. cit.*, p. 38).
333. FPWPA, Article 8.

286. Necessary considerations concerning procedures for, and methods of, the redress application shall be determined by the National Labour Relations Commission under the LRCAA. With regard to disputes relating to such discriminatory treatment, the burden of proof shall be placed on employers.[334]

4. Procedures for Redress, etc.

287. Upon receiving an application for redress, the Labour Relations Commission shall conduct the necessary investigation and an inquiry into the relevant parties without delay.[335]

288. The Labour Relations Commission can commence mediation procedures at the request of both or either of the parties concerned or by virtue of its authority during an inquiry. If the parties concerned file for arbitration under an agreement to follow an arbitration decision taken by the Labour Relations Commission, the commission may conduct such an arbitration.[336]

289. The Labour Relations Commission, if it judges that the treatment in question is discriminatory after the completion of their investigation and inquiry, shall issue a redress order to the employer. If it judges that the treatment in questions is not discriminatory, it shall make a decision to dismiss the application for redress.[337]

290. The judgment, redress order or dismissal decision must be made in writing and their reasons must be clearly specified and then be sent to the parties concerned. If a redress order is issued, its specific contents and compliance deadline shall be specified in writing. The contents of mediation or arbitration or of a redress order may include suspending discriminatory activities, improving working conditions, such as wages, and making adequate monetary compensation.[338]

291. If a party is dissatisfied with a redress order or dismissal decision by the Regional Labour Relations Commission, the party may apply for review to the National Labour Relations Commission within 10 days of receiving the notice of the redress order or dismissal decision.[339] If a party is dissatisfied with a review decision made by the National Labour Relations Commission, that party may bring an administrative lawsuit against the decision within 15 days of receiving notice of the review decision.

334. FPWPA, Article 9.
335. FPWPA, Article 10.
336. FPWPA, Article 11.
337. FPWPA, Article 12.
338. FPWPA, Article 13.
339. FPWPA, Article 14.

292. If a request for review is not made within the period prescribed and an administrative lawsuit is not brought within the period prescribed, the redress order, dismissal decision or review decision shall be confirmed as final.

293. The Minister of Employment and Labour can require employers to submit a status report on compliance with a confirmed redress order.[340] If an employer fails to comply with a confirmed redress order, the worker who applied for the redress may report the failure to the Minister of Employment and Labour.[341]

F. The Prohibition of Unfavourable Treatment

294. An employer shall not dismiss or give other unfavourable treatment to a fixed-term or part-time employee on the grounds that he or she has performed any of the following acts:[342]

- refusing to undertake overtime work when ordered to do so by the employer;
- applying for redress for discriminatory treatment, attending or making a statement at the Labour Relations Commission or applying for a review or bringing an administrative lawsuit;
- reporting a failure to comply with a redress order;
- giving notification to the Inspection Agency.

G. Written Statements of Working Conditions

295. When an employer makes a labour contract with a fixed-term or part-time employee, he/she must clearly state in writing all the matters described in the following sub-paragraphs, provided that sub-paragraph 6 shall apply only to part-time workers:[343]

1. matters concerning the contract period;
2. matters concerning working hours and rest hours;
3. matters concerning the components, calculation and payment methods of wages;
4. matters concerning holidays and leave;
5. matters concerning the place of work and the job to be done; and
6. work days and the working hours of each work day.

340. FPWPA, Article 15.
341. FPWPA, Article 15.
342. FPWPA, Article 16.
343. FPWPA, Article 17

H. Efforts of the State, etc., for Employment Promotion

296. The state and local governments shall make efforts to preferentially take necessary measures, such as providing employment information, vocational guidance, job placement services, vocational skills development services, etc., to promote the employment of fixed-term and part-time employees.[344]

VII. DWPA

A. Introduction

297. Non-regular workers include those external to the company. They can be divided into contract workers, dispatch workers, etc. The contract work arrangement is one where a worker works in the client's company, not under the supervision of the client company but of the contracting company who is his contractual employer. Supervision and direction of such workers by the client company constitutes an illegal labour-supply project. In fact, it is difficult to differentiate between an illegal labour-supply business and a legitimate contract work arrangement.[345] This led to the legalization of worker dispatching businesses. Worker dispatching was prohibited until the enactment of the 1998 DWPA. After several revisions, the current DWPA was promulgated in 2008. The number of dispatched workers has been steadily increasing and this increase is unquestionably providing employers with external or quantitative flexibility. However, the employment of non-regular workers serves as a complement to the core system. It should be emphasized that the key features of Korean employment relations, which have enabled employers to adapt to changing social and economic circumstances, still lie in the internal and qualitative flexibility of the employment relationship with regular workers.

298. 'Worker dispatch' means a system in which one employer, while maintaining employment relations with a worker it has hired, has the worker work for a second employer under the direction and order of the second employer in accordance with a worker dispatch contract.[346] The term 'worker dispatch undertaking' means conducting worker dispatching as a business. Other frequently used terms are 'sending employer', which refers to a person who carries out a worker dispatch undertaking, 'using employer', which refers to a person who uses a dispatched worker

344. Article 20.
345. For example, general requirements for legitimacy:

1. the contractor takes all financial and legal responsibility for the completion of the work;
2. the contractor itself directs and orders the workers who perform the work;
3. the contractor becomes the employer with respect to all obligations owed to its workers;
4. machinery, equipment, appliances or necessary materials are provided by the contractor or the work performed is not simply physical labor but is planning or work which requires professional technology or experience (Takashi Araki, *op. cit.*, p. 40).

346. Article 2, no. 1.

under a worker dispatch contract and 'dispatched worker', which refers to a person who is employed by a sending employer and subject to worker dispatch.

B. The Purpose of This Act

299. Worker dispatches are regulated by the law with the intention of securing the proper operation of worker dispatching undertakings and improved working conditions for dispatched workers. Therefore, the purpose of this Act is to enhance the flexibility of supply and demand of manpower by managing worker dispatch undertakings properly and setting up criteria such as the standards of working conditions for dispatched workers, thereby contributing to the employment security and welfare promotion of dispatched workers.[347]

C. The Worker Dispatching Relationship

300. Because worker dispatching relations involve a complicated triangular relationship, special regulations are required to protect dispatched workers. Dispatch workers maintain their employment relationship only with the dispatching agency and not with the client company. Therefore, as a general rule, the dispatching agency is responsible for compliance with the relevant protective labour laws, including the LSA. However, because the client company actually directs and controls the dispatched workers, the Act on the Protection, etc., of Dispatched Workers provides that the client company should be responsible for certain matters such as the guarantee of the worker's freedom to exercise his or her civil rights, regulations relating to working hours, and regulations for women and minors regarding hazardous work and mine work. The dispatching agency and the client company share responsibility for some other matters such as equal treatment, the prohibition of compulsory labour, the prohibition of apprenticeship abuse, and health and safety regulations.

347. Article 1.

Figure 1

Worker Dispatching Relationship

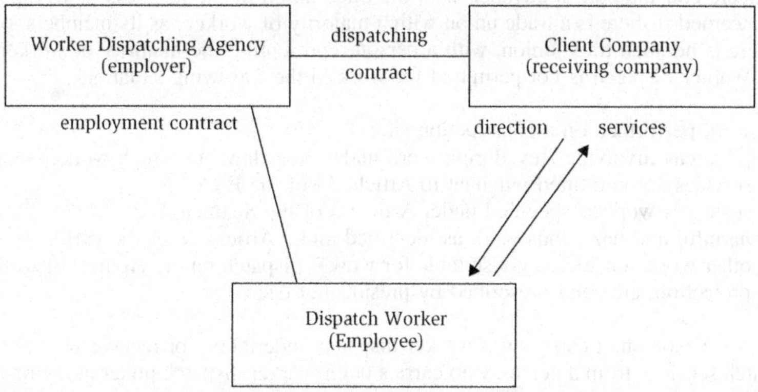

D. The Obligations of the Government

301. In order to protect dispatched workers and make it easier for workers to find jobs and for employers to secure manpower, the law requires the government to make efforts to ensure that workers be can be directly employed by employers, by coming up with and implementing various measures specified in the following methods:[348]

– the gathering and provision of employment information;
– research on jobs;
– vocational guidance;
– the establishment and operation of employment security organizations.

E. The Proper Management of Worker Dispatch Undertakings

1. Jobs Permissible for Worker Dispatch

302. Jobs permissible for worker dispatch are as follows.

Jobs permitted for worker dispatch shall be those considered suitable for that purpose given their nature and the required professional knowledge, skill or experience, and prescribed by presidential decree, but excluding those directly related to production in the manufacturing industry.

348. Article 3.

However, if there is a vacancy due to childbirth, illness, injury, etc., or there is a need to temporarily or intermittently secure manpower, worker dispatch may be permitted. If an employer intends to use a dispatched worker, he or she should have a sincere consultation in advance with the trade union of the business or workplace concerned if there is a trade union with a majority of workers as its members, or if there is no such trade union, with a person representing the majority of workers.

Worker dispatch is not permitted for work in the following situations:

- work performed on a construction site;
- job areas involving stevedoring work under other law, for which worker-supply services are permitted pursuant to Article 33 of the ESA;[349]
- seamen's work as specified under Article 3 of the Seamen Act;
- harmful and hazardous work as identified under Article 28 of the ISHA;
- other work considered not suitable for worker dispatch on the grounds of worker protection, etc., and prescribed by presidential decree.

No person shall carry out a worker dispatch undertaking or receive worker dispatch services from a person who carries out a worker dispatch undertaking in violation of these provisions.[350]

2. Length of Dispatch Period

303.

1. The length of a dispatch period shall not exceed one year, except for when the case falls under Article 5(2).
2. Notwithstanding the provision of paragraph (1), if there is an agreement between the sending employer, the using employer and the dispatched worker, the period may be extended. In this case, the extended period, if extended once, shall not exceed one year, and the total dispatch period, including the extended period, shall not exceed two years.
3. With regard to elderly dispatched workers under the AEPA, the dispatch period may be extended for more than two years.
4. The period of worker dispatch under Article 5(2) is as follows:
    1. a period required to resolve the cause in cases where there are such clear and objective causes as childbirth, illness or injury; and
    2. a period of less than three months in cases where there is a need to secure manpower on a temporary and intermittent basis: provided that if the cause is not resolved and there is an agreement among the dispatch employer, the

349. E.g. sub-paragraph 1 of Article 3 of the Harbour Transport Business Act, Article 9(1)1 of the Railroad Transport Business Act, Article 40 of the Act on Distribution and Price Stabilization of Agricultural and Fishery Products, and Article 2(1)1 of the Facilitation of Goods Distribution Act.
350. Article 5.

using employer and the dispatched worker, the period may be extended one time, not exceeding three months.[351]

3. Obligations for Direct Employment

304. If a using employer falls under any of the following categories, he or she shall directly employ the dispatched worker concerned:

1. if the using employer continues to use the dispatched worker in excess of two years in violation of Article 5(2);
2. if the using employer uses the dispatched worker in violation of Article 5(3);
3. if the using employer continues to use the dispatched worker in excess of two years in violation of Article 6(2) or (4);
4. if the using employer continues to be offered service by the dispatched worker in excess of two years in violation of Article 7(3).

However, the provisions of paragraph (1) shall not apply, if the dispatched worker clearly expresses an objection, or there is a justifiable reason as prescribed by presidential decree.

If a using employer directly employs a dispatched worker, working conditions for the dispatched worker shall be as follows:

– if among workers employed by the using employer, there is a worker performing the same or similar kind of work that the dispatched worker performs, working conditions prescribed in the employment rules applicable to the directly employed worker shall apply to the dispatched worker; and
– if among workers employed by the using employer, there is no worker performing the same or similar kind of work that the dispatched worker performs, the level of working conditions for the dispatched worker shall not be lower than the level of the existing ones for the dispatched worker.

If a using employer intends to directly employ a worker for a job for which a dispatched worker is already being used, he or she shall make efforts to preferentially employ the dispatched worker.[352]

4. Permission for Worker Dispatch Undertakings

305. A person who intends to carry out a worker dispatch undertaking must obtain permission from the Minister of Employment and Labour pursuant to the Ordinance of the Ministry of Employment and Labour. This requirement shall also apply when any change is made to major matters prescribed by the Ordinance of the Ministry of Employment and Labour, among those who have already gained permission.[353]

351. Article 6.
352. Article 6-2.
353. Article 7.

5. Criteria for Permission

306. If permission for worker dispatch undertakings is requested, the Minister of Employment and Labour may give that permission as long as the following requirements are met:

- the requesting party shall have assets and facilities, etc. that would enable him/her to carry out the worker dispatch undertaking properly; and
- the worker dispatch undertaking concerned shall not target a specific small number of using employers.

Detailed criteria for permission shall be prescribed by presidential decree.[354]

6. The Term of the Validity of Permission

307. The term of validity of permission for worker dispatch undertakings is three years. Any person who intends to continue to carry out a worker dispatch undertaking after the termination of the term of validity of permission must obtain permission for renewal pursuant to the Ordinance of the Ministry of Employment and Labour. The term of the validity of permission for such a renewal shall be three years, counted from the day after the previous term of validity of permission expired.[355]

7. Restrictions on Worker Dispatch

308. A sending employer shall not dispatch a worker to a firm where industrial action is underway to perform the work stopped due to such industrial action.

309. In addition, no person, after dismissing a worker for managerial reasons under the LSA,[356] shall use a dispatched worker for that work before the end of the certain period (two years) as prescribed by presidential decree.[357] For two years after dismissing a worker for a managerial reason under the LSA, a dispatched worker shall not be hired for the purpose of performing the concerned job: provided that if a trade union with a majority of workers (or a person who represents a majority of workers if such a union does not exist) that exists within the concerned business or workplace consents, then the period may be shortened to six months.[358]

354. Article 9.
355. Article 10.
356. LSA, Article 24.
357. Article 16.
358. Enforcement Decree of DWPA, Article 4.

F. Worker Dispatch Contracts

310. The contents of contracts, etc. shall be as follows:

The term 'worker dispatch contract' means an agreement prescribing worker dispatch between a sending employer and a using employer. The parties to a worker dispatch contract shall conclude the contract in writing detailing the following matters:[359]

1. the number of dispatched workers;
2. a description of the activities in which a dispatched worker will be engaged;
3. the reasons for dispatching the worker;
4. the name of the workplace, location and other working places in which a dispatched worker will be placed;
5. information on a person who will directly direct and command a dispatched worker during the dispatch period;
6. matters related to the dispatch period and the starting date for dispatch service;
7. matters related to the start and finish time of work, and recess hours;
8. matters related to holidays and leave;
9. matters related to extended, night and holiday work;
10. matters related to safety and health;
11. matters related to the price of worker dispatch;
12. other matters as prescribed by the Ordinance of the Ministry of Employment and Labour.

311. Methods resulting from the prohibition, correction, etc., of discriminatory treatments shall be as follows:

1. 'Discriminatory treatment' means giving unfavourable treatment in terms of wages and other working conditions etc. without justifiable reasons.
2. A sending employer and a using employer shall not treat a dispatched worker in a discriminatory manner in comparison with a worker who performs the same work in the business of the using employer. If a dispatched worker is discriminated against, he or she may apply for redress to the labour relations commission.
3. The FPWPA shall apply *mutatis mutandis* to applications for redress and other redress procedures.[360]

G. Prohibition of Contract Rescission, etc.

312. A using employer shall not rescind a worker dispatch contract on the grounds of the gender, religion or social status of the dispatched worker or their

359. Article 20.
360. Article 21.

legitimate involvement in the activities of a trade union. A sending employer may suspend worker dispatch or rescind a worker dispatch contract if, with regard to dispatch work, the using employer violates this Act or orders issued under this Act, the LSA or orders under the LSA, the ISHA or orders under the ISHA.[361]

H. Measures to be Sought by the Sending Employer

1. Welfare Enhancement for Dispatched Workers

313. A sending employer shall make efforts to enhance the welfare of dispatched workers by seeking measures necessary to secure employment, and education and training opportunities suitable for their desires and abilities, improvements in their working conditions, and securing their employment stability.[362]

2. Duty of Notice for Dispatched Workers

314. If a sending employer intends to employ a worker as a dispatched worker, he/she shall inform the worker in advance of the intent in writing. If a sending employer intends to choose a person to be dispatched from among workers who are hired by the employer not as dispatched workers, he or she shall notify the worker concerned of the intent in advance in writing, and obtain his or her consent.[363]

3. Prohibition of Employment Restriction for Dispatched Workers

315. A sending employer shall not, without a justifiable reason, conclude a contract with a dispatched worker or a person who desires to be hired as a dispatched worker, which contains such contents prohibiting the worker from being hired by a using employer after termination of employment relationships with the sending employer concerned. A sending employer shall not, without a justifiable reason, conclude a worker dispatch contract which contains contents prohibiting a using employer from hiring the dispatched worker after termination of employment relationships with the dispatched worker concerned.[364]

4. Notification of Placement Conditions

316. If a sending employer intends to dispatch a worker, he or she shall, in advance, notify in writing the worker concerned of matters described in the contents of contracts and other matters prescribed by the Ordinance of the Ministry of

361. Article 22.
362. Article 23.
363. Article 24.
364. Article 50.

Employment and Labour. A dispatched worker can ask the sending employer to provide detailed information on the price of worker dispatch. If a sending employer is asked to be provided detailed information, he or she shall provide it without delay.[365]

I. Measures to be Sought by a Using Employer

317. The using employer shall seek necessary measures not to violate the structure of a worker dispatch contract.[366]

J. Security on Proper Dispatch Work

318. If a dispatched worker files a grievance while undertaking dispatch work, the using employer shall notify the contents of the grievance to the sending employer, and handle such a grievance promptly and properly. Besides handling grievances, a using employer shall seek necessary measures to ensure the proper carrying out of dispatch work.[367]

VIII. Special Cases Relating to the Application of the Acts, etc.

A. Special Cases Relating to the Application of the LSA

319. With regard to the work of a dispatched worker during a dispatch period, the sending employer and the using employer shall be deemed to be an employer under the LSA and the same Act shall apply to them accordingly (with a few exceptions).

320. If a sending employer fails to pay wages to a dispatched worker due to causes attributable to the using employer as prescribed by presidential decree, the using employer shall be jointly liable for that failure along with the sending employer. In this case, the sending employer and the using employer share liability.

321. If a using employer grants paid holidays or paid leave under the LSA, the wages during such holidays or leave shall be paid by the sending employer.

322. If a sending employer and a using employer conclude a worker dispatch contract which contains contents violating the LSA, and violate the same Act by

365. Article 26.
366. Article 30.
367. Article 31.

having a dispatched worker work in accordance with the contract, they shall be subject to relevant penal provisions on the assumption that all parties to the contract should be deemed to be an employer under Article 15 of the same Act.[368]

B. Special Cases Relating to the Application of the ISHA

323. With regard to the work of a dispatched worker during a dispatch period, the using employer shall be deemed to be an employer under the ISHA in applying the same Act.

1. Enforcement of the Regulations

324. Acts violating the regulations of the DWPA are criminally sanctioned but are not necessarily regarded as null and void.

2. Regulations Concerning the Conclusion of Labour Contracts

a. Methods of concluding a labour contract

325. An individual contract may only be concluded with the consent of both parties. Since the Act does not require any specific form (be that in written form, an oral agreement, custom and practice,[369] etc.) for the conclusion of a labour contract, this consent may be deemed to be given tacitly. Also, both parties must agree only on all important matters (such as the nature of the job, the extent of remuneration, etc.) and, thereafter, the details may be left to works rules written out by the employer.

b. The statement or violation of agreed working conditions

326. For an employment contract to be concluded, the employer must clearly state the wages to be paid, contractual working hours, holiday entitlement as stipulated under Article 55, annual paid leave under Article 60 and other working conditions prescribed by the presidential decree. An employer shall issue a worker with a written statement specifying the components of, and methods of calculation and payment of, the wages and other matters described in Article 17 subparagraphs 2 through 4. Provided that if the matters above are altered due to the reasons prescribed by the Presidential Decree, such as changes in collective agreements or employment rules, etc., the statement shall be issued to the worker at his/her request. [370]

---

368. Article 34.
369. In general practice, both parties agree only on important matters (such as the type of job, remuneration, etc.) and the details are left to works rules written out by the employer.
370. Article 17 paragraph 2.

327. The purpose of this provision is to prohibit the employer from enticing workers with what appear to be good working conditions, which s/he has no intention of observing. The phrase 'other working conditions' as laid down in this article is interpreted as meaning such things as the location and condition of the workplace, the kind of work, matters which should be clarified by rules of employment,[371] and matters about dormitory regulations (if there is dormitory provision).

328. If any of the actual working conditions are found to be inconsistent with the conditions as agreed, the worker is entitled to claim damages resulting from the breach of the agreement or may terminate the labour contract forthwith. Any worker who intends to claim for damages, may do so with the Labour relations commission. If a labour contract has been terminated, an employer must pay travel expenses to a worker who changes his residence for the purpose of securing a new job.[372]

3. The Prohibition of the Predetermination of Non-observance

329. The employer shall not enter into a contract in which a penalty for or indemnity against possible damages incurred from breach of such a labour contract is predetermined.[373]

330. Because of inequality in their power, a penalty or compensation is usually decided by the employer and is unfairly disadvantageous to the worker. Therefore, unlike the Civil Code, labour law prohibits their prearrangement in order to protect the worker from unfair restraint.

4. The Prohibition of Offsetting Wages against Advances

331. An employer shall not offset wages against an advance or other credits given in advance on the condition of a worker's labour.[374] When an employer has forced labour service in return for an advance, this infringes Article 7 of the LSA which bans forced labour.[375] An action violating this provision is null and void and the employer concerned deserves the punishment as prescribed in Article 114 of the LSA.

371. Article 93.
372. Article 19 paragraph 1.
373. Article 21.
374. *Ibid.*
375. However, a loan itself is not prohibited unless it is made on the condition that the worker should offer labour service instead (Chi Sun Kim, *op. cit.*, p. 39).

5. The Prohibition of Compulsory Saving Policies

332. An employer shall not enter into a contract with a worker, in addition to a labour contract, which stipulates compulsory savings or the management of those savings.[376] Involuntary saving may be abused as a means of forced labour. Moreover, there is a possibility that deposited money may be misappropriated for business expenses. Because voluntary saving is not prohibited, when an employer is entrusted by a worker to manage his savings, the employer must observe the matters as following:

- The type and period of savings, as well as the financial institutions to manage the savings, shall be determined by the concerned worker and the savings account shall be in the name of the worker.
- Upon the request of the concerned worker to see any related materials such as a savings certificate, or to have them returned, the employer shall immediately comply with the request.

6. The Legal Effects of Labour Contracts that Run Contrary to the LSA

333. According to the principles of civil law, contracts which run contrary to imperative legal norms, public order, or morality are null and void in their whole. However, in the field of labour law, a labour contract which establishes working conditions which are inferior to the standards provided for in this Act shall be null and void only to that extent, and such conditions as are invalidated shall be replaced by those conditions as stipulated by the law.[377]

334. According to Article 33 of the TULRAA and Article 97 of the LSA, the same is true of contracts which run contrary to either collective agreements or to works rules.[378]

7. The Rights and Duties of the Respective Parties

335. In Korea, the rights and duties of employer and employee are not so much specified in individual labour contracts as formulated by rules established by collective agreements, works rules and numerous labour legislation.

376. Article 22.
377. Article 15.
378. Chi Sun Kim, *op. cit.*, p. 39.

336. Judging from the intent of both the provisions of the Constitution[379] and the LSA,[380] employers are considered to be under an obligation to provide their workers with decent working conditions. This obligation requires that employers not only observe the various labour protection law provisions concerning safety and health in relation to working conditions, but also to actively pursue standards above and beyond the minimum as laid down by legislation.

8. Other Duties of the Employer

337. As a result of the ever-increasing flow of labour legislation, the employer is obliged to carry out a number of other duties. For instance, an employer shall be responsible for the good management of workers' safety and health, ensure equal treatment of workers in the workplace, etc.

9. The Employee's Duties

338. The worker has an obligation to work under the instruction and direction of the employer. This includes the worker's duty to obey the provisions of works rules and the orders of superiors. In Korea, especially in the case of regular employees, it is not unusual to transfer employees from one job to another, or from one workplace to another. This raises an obvious question: does the duty to work include an obligation to work in any place or role designated by the employer? In some cases it is argued that the employer has abused their right of transfer by ordering a change of job or workplace which was not really necessary for the employer but which caused serious inconvenience to the employee. The courts balance the necessity of the transfer on the one hand, and what difficulties have been caused to the employee on the other. The courts will declare the order to transfer null and void if they find that the transfer has caused serious difficulties for the employee or that there was a possibility of finding a substitute or that the transfer itself was not really necessary. In addition, the dismissal of an employee because of disobedience of such an order will also be declared null and void, and the employee will be entitled to return to his or her former job or workplace.[381]

379. The Constitution provides that 'standards of working conditions shall be determined by law in such a way as to guarantee a life worthy of a human being' (Article 32, paragraph 3 of the Constitution).
380. The LSA provides that the working conditions provided herein shall prescribe the minimum standards and the parties to employment relations, therefore, shall not reduce the working conditions under the pretext of compliance with this Act: Article 3).
381. Chi Sun, Kim, *op. cit.*, p. 42.

339. The worker shall abide by such duties as the 'duty to keep company secrets',[382] the 'duty to uphold the company's honour',[383] faithfulness or sincerity, devotion,[384] etc.

382. The work rules of most companies provide that retired employees should not to reveal company secrets acquired during their employment. Further, some of them even provide that retired employees may not work for or engage in business with companies which are in direct competition with their previous employer. These provisions raise several legal problems, for the nature and extent of this obligation is not clear. As it is inevitable that employees will acquire some knowledge and techniques during their employment, such a restriction is considered illegal, because it curtails the employee's freedom of choice of work without just cause. Therefore, it is believed that an employee is free to use such knowledge and techniques as they have gained to find another job, as long as these are of a universal and general nature within the particular trade or industry. However, if the knowledge and techniques are peculiar to the company, and are the specific property of the company, they should be protected as business secrets. Even in such cases, however, the restriction should not go too far. In determining the scope with regard to the period of time, the geographical area and the trade or business to which competition is prohibited (Chi Sun Kim, *op. cit.*, p.42).

383. However, judicial precedents have been inclined to limit this broad obligation of loyalty and to restrict the employee's obligation mainly to matters concerning his or her job and within working hours. Some typical cases of this kind are those in which employees have been dismissed because of a minor crime, such as indecency, obscenity or drunkenness. The Courts usually look first at the status of the employee and the nature of the job; and if s/he is not a very high ranking employee, the Courts often deny the employer's argument that the employee has injured the company's honour, declaring that the employee's status is not high enough to endanger it. However, when the crime is one which involves money, the Courts will take the matter seriously if the employee concerned is doing a job which gives him or her easy access to the company's money (Chi Sun Kim, *op. cit.*, pp. 42-43).

384. The employee should work with the dedication expected of a normal employee – or what is generally expected of an average worker, not of the best one.

Chapter 3. Remuneration

§1. The Meaning of Wages

I. The Concept of Wages

340. The LSA defines wages as 'the wages, salary, or any other payment (all money and goods)[385] to the worker from the employer as remuneration for labour, regardless of the name by which such payment may be called'.[386] This definition in the LSA, also applies to the MWA (Article 2), the WCGA (Article 2), and the WRBSA (Article 2).

341. The first requirement (i.e. the key concept in distinguishing wages from other payments) is that they are paid 'as a remuneration for labour given'.

342. Within administrative practice, in classifying a payment as being remuneration for labour, three types of payment have been excluded from this category, they are:

1. the voluntary conferral of a benefit (for example congratulatory or condolence payments to celebrate a wedding or express sympathy upon the illness or death of a close relative and similar gestures);[387]
2. welfare payments (i.e. payment of benefits or expenditures for the workers' welfare);
3. payments for an enterprise's equipment and operational expenses (i.e. cost of that enterprise's equipment and work-related expenses needed for achieving the enterprise's business, etc.).

When the time and amount or method of calculation of these payments is prescribed in an employment contract, work rules or collective agreement, such bonuses or retirement allowances are regarded as wages.[388]

343. The second requirement for a wage is that it be a 'payment to the worker from the employer'.[389]

385. The Act prohibits the employer from paying wages other than in cash, but this may be allowed if otherwise provided for by special provisions of laws or ordinance, and collective agreement (Article 43 paragraph 1).
386. Article 2 paragraph 1.
387. Even those types of payments will be regarded as remuneration for labour and treated as wages, if they have been clearly required in advance by a collective agreement, or the like (Kazuo Sugeno, *op. cit.*, p. 218).
388. Takashi Araki, *op. cit.*, p. 76.
389. When a guest personally delivers a tip to an employee in an inn or eating house, because this is paid by the guest, it generally does not constitute wages. By contrast, service charges paid by guests in inns (i.e. hotels) and restaurants, which are mechanically divided between the workers who were on duty that day, can be labelled as payments from the employer.

344. The third requirement is that it be 'any payment regardless of the name'.

II. The Meaning of the Average Wage

345. Although wages are in principle paid for work done by the worker, they are now quite often paid for periods during which no work is done at all. Average wages apply in the cases of:

- retirement allowances;
- average wages stipulated by work rules or collective agreements, etc., to calculate annual paid leave, and in cases where the pay is under a paid allowance, not under ordinary wages as set out in the LSA;
- in accident compensation, etc., the notion of the average wage is a very important one, because it is the standard for calculating remuneration.

346. The LSA defines the average wage as 'The amount calculated by dividing the total amount of wages paid to the relevant worker during three calendar months (or the period of employment if it is less than three months) preceding the date on which the event necessitating such a calculation occurred by the total number of calendar days during those three calendar months'.[390]

347. In cases where the period concerning the calculation of average wages includes a period falling under any of the following situations, the period and wages paid for that period shall be deducted respectively from the base period for the calculation of average wages and, as a result, the total amount of average wages:

- any probationary period;
- any period of shutdown due to reasons attributable to an employer;
- any period of maternity leave;
- any period of suspension of work for medical treatment due to occupational injury or disease;
- any period of child-care leave under Article 19 of the EEWRA;
- any period of strike under sub-paragraph 6 of Article 2 of the TULRAA;
- any period of suspension of service or of non-work owing to the performance of duties under the Military Service Act, the Establishment of Homeland Reserve Forces Act, or the Framework Act on Civil Defence; provided that this shall not apply in the case that wages are paid during that period;
- any period of suspension of work with the approval of an employer due to non-occupational injuries, disease or other reasons.

348. Wages or allowances paid on an extraordinary basis and wages paid in forms other than that of currency shall not be included in the total amount of wages.[391]

390. Article 2.
391. Enforcement Ordinance of the LSA, Article 2.

349. The amount of average wages for daily workers shall be the one set by the Minister of Employment and Labour according to the relevant industry and occupation.[392] If it is impossible to calculate average wages, the sum deemed to be the average wage shall be that determined by the Minister of Employment and Labour.[393]

350. If the amount calculated pursuant to the Act[394] is lower than the ordinary wages of the worker concerned, the ordinary wage shall be deemed the average wage.[395]

III. The Meaning of Ordinary Wages

351. 'Ordinary wages' means those wages – whether they are paid hourly, daily, weekly, monthly, or on a contract basis – which have been determined to be paid periodically or in a lump sum to a worker for his or her prescribed work or the whole period of work.[396]

352. When calculating ordinary wages, the hourly wage rate is applied on the basis of the following principles:

1. if wages are determined on an hourly basis; the amount of the hourly wage;
2. if wages are determined on a daily basis, the amount is calculated by dividing the daily wage by the number of contractual working hours per day;
3. if wages are determined on a weekly basis, the amount is calculated by dividing the weekly wages by the number of hours (calculated by adding the contractual working hours per week, as prescribed in the Act, to paid hours beyond those contractual working hours) based on which weekly ordinary wages are calculated;
4. if wages are determined on a monthly basis, the amount is calculated by dividing the monthly wages by the number of hours (one-twelfth of the number of hours calculated by multiplying the number of hours based on which weekly ordinary wages are calculated, by the average number of weeks in the year) based on which monthly ordinary wages are calculated;
5. if wages are determined on the basis of a set period other than those of a day, week, or month, the amount calculated is done with reference to sub-paragraphs (2) through (4);
6. if wages are determined under a subcontracted wage system, the amount is calculated by dividing the total sum of wages under that subcontracted wage system during the period for which the wage calculation is relevant by the total

392. *Ibid.*, Article 3.
393. *Ibid.*, Article 4.
394. Article 2 paragraph 2. sub-paragraph 6 of LSA.
395. Article 2 paragraph 2.
396. Enforcement Ordinance of LSA, Article 6.

number of working hours during that period (referring to the period until the closing date of wages, if there is any closing date for the payment of wages); and

7. if ordinary wages are calculated at daily rates, the ordinary wage shall be calculated by multiplying the number of contractual working hours per day by the wage rate per hour.[397]

353. Consideration of ordinary wages shall apply in cases of:

1. dismissal allowances in lieu of an advance notice of dismissal;
2. wages added for overtime, night or off-day work;
3. ordinary wages as stipulated in the work rules or collective agreements, etc, to calculate the worker's annual paid leave;
4. in situations of paid allowances, such as overtime, the average wage must be higher than the ordinary wage.[398]

§2. Contractual Working Hours

354. The term 'contractual working hours' refers to those working hours upon which workers and their employers have made an agreement within the limit of legal working hours.[399] In cases where legal standard hours are regulated to be the same as contractual working hours, the calculation is as follows.

355. Where the legal standard hours are considered to mean 40 hours weekly, excluding rest hours: where standard hours are calculated for monthly purposes ordinary wages they shall equal 40 hours plus 8 hours, which in turn is multiplied by 365 days then divided by seven (days), further divided by 12 (months) resulting in a final figure of 209 hours (technically 208.57143 and then rounded off).

§3. Wage Systems

I. Wage Systems and Patterns in Korea

356. The main characteristic of the Korean wage system is that the basic wage includes various types of allowances, including family allowances, regional allowances, allowances for high attendance rate, etc. Usually, wages are roughly divided between those which are determined and paid on a monthly basis[400] and those others paid on a special bases (known as extraordinary wages). The former is further

397. *Ibid.*, Article 4 paragraph 3.
398. According to the LSA payment shall usually be deemed to be the ordinary payment rather than the average payment.
399. Article 2 paragraph 1 sub-paragraph. 7.
400. The pay period units are divided between daily, weekly and monthly systems. Most enterprises have adopted the monthly system.

subdivided between scheduled wages, which are made up of a basic wage plus various allowances, and non-scheduled wages for non-scheduled work (e.g. overtime allowances, allowances for work on rest days, and night-work allowances). Wages which are paid on a special basis are may be considered to be bonuses and retirement allowances.[401]

II. Characteristics and Recent Changes of Wage Systems in Korea

357. In other countries, wages are generally determined by the content of the job and the quantity and quality of the work performed. In Korea, however, the decisive factors in the determination of wages have been not the productivity of a worker's labour or the evaluation of the work they have performed. Rather these decisions relate to what might be termed the worker's attributes, namely length of service, age and educational background.[402] Therefore, basic wages increase annually and incrementally on the basis of length of service rather periodically on the basis of merit. Under this wage system, younger workers have usually been underpaid in relation to their productivity, while senior workers have generally been overpaid by the same criterion. In other words, in the Korean, seniority-based, wage system, the younger workers commit to their their company in the full knowledge that they will be underpaid but with the understanding that in the fulness of time they will be overpaid as they reach more senior levels.[403]

358. However, against the background of an ageing workforce and the intensification of international competition in enterprise, Korean companies have, in recent years, modified those wage systems, which previously placed great weight on the workers' length of service (specifically their years of continuous employment). In determining wage amounts they have increasingly moved to according great importance to the quality and productivity of the work provided. There has been a common policy shift toward, among other things, the consolidation of age-based wages into job-ability wages and to job-based wages, and the establishment of bonuses on the basis of assessments of merit as determined by work performance. The most striking phenomenon in such trends has been the changes in annual salary systems as this apply mainly to managerial workers.[404] In Korea, individualized, performance-based wage management is gradually replacing the more traditional collective system based on an employees length of service; this trend is becoming increasingly evident.

401. Kazuo Sugeno, *op. cit.*, p. 222.
402. The strong relationship between wages and education has contributed much to supplying a so-called high-quality labour force. The point at issue is a matter of degree. In Korea, starting wages are decided according to the employee's level of education rather than his or her ability.
403. Takashi Araki, *op. cit.*, pp. 70–71.
404. Kazuo Sugeno, *op. cit.*, p. 227.

§4. Labour Law Principles Concerning Wages in Korea

359. First of all it is important to set out the legal foundations of labour management negotiations which determine how wages can be decided on an equal footing (e.g. the guarantees of the right to combine, to bargain collectively, to engage in collective action, etc.). Secondly, as it is imperative to prevent a bottomless decline of wage rates within the labour market, standards for setting minimum wages are created and given effect (the MWA). Thirdly, policies guaranteeing the payment of wages by enterprises in normal times and in the event of bankruptcy are enacted. Fourthly, wages are secured during periods of inability to work (good examples might be compensation for days off while undergoing medical treatment for work-related injuries or illness, or sickness allowances for medical treatment unrelated to work). Finally, wage-related discrimination on specified and particular grounds is prohibited.[405]

I. Regulations Regarding the Payment of Wages

360. With regard to the means of the payment of wages, the LSA is quite clear and stipulates the following prescriptions: wages must be paid in cash, in full, directly to the workers, and in regular payments at least once a month.[406]

A. *Payment in Cash*

361. Wages must be paid in cash. Payment in kind is prohibited. Exceptions are allowed in cases otherwise stipulated by special provisions of laws or decrees or a collective agreement. In addition, 'cash' refers to money considered legal tender in Korea; as a result it does not include foreign currency.

B. *Direct Payment to the Worker*

362. To prohibit intermediate exploitation by any third party or the appropriation of minors' wages by their parents, wages must be paid directly to the worker. Payments to a worker's guardian or other legal representative or to his or her voluntarily appointed agent are both violations of this principle. The payment of wages to an envoy where someone is unwell or incapable of collecting their wages, having a partner or a similar close associate is lawful. None of this violates the principle that the right to receive a salary directly may not be traded or sold.

405. *Ibid., op. cit.*, p. 220.
406. Article 43.

C. Payment in Full

363. Wages must be paid in full. However, wages may be paid with partial deductions, if stipulated by law, ordinance or a collective agreement (a written agreement specifying such deductions). Under the current law, withholding income-tax, the deduction of social security premiums, the deduction of union dues and fees under check-off the system are all permitted to be removed from an employee's wages. An offset is considered a type of deduction that is banned by the principle of full payment.

D. Regular Payment at least Once a Month

364. Wages must be paid at least once a month on a specified date, except for extraordinary wages, allowances and the like as specified by presidential decree.[407]

365. If a company introduces an annual salary system, the designated monthly salary must be paid on the due date, as agreed. However, special allowances, or bonuses are not subject to this regulation. This principle aims to reduce potential instability in workers' lives due to there being excessively lengthy periods between payment.

E. The Statute of Limitations

366. The statutory limitation on exercising a claim for wages under the provisions of LSA is three years.[408] In the case of retirement pay, if the right to receive retirement pay under WRBSA has not been exercised for three years, it shall be annulled by extinctive prescription,[409] that is to say that the right to claim wages is annulled after this period automatically.

F. Emergency Payment

367. When a worker requests wage payment in order to meet expenses incurred as a result of occurrences such as childbirth, disease, accidents or something else specified by presidential decree, the employer shall pay all such wages for the work already performed even prior to the payday.[410]

407. Article 43 paragraph 2
408. Article 49.
409. Article 10 of the WRBSA.
410. Article 45.

§5. Regulations on the Amounts of Wages

I. An Introduction to the Minimum Wage System

368. Minimum wages are regulated under the MWA. Under the present Act, the country establishes minimum wage amounts and compels employers to observe them in accordance with the law. In theory rates of pay should be established voluntarily by employers and workers depending on the situation. However, because of the nature of the relationship between the two, as well as other social and economic factors, the government sets a minimum level of remuneration sufficient for basic survival.[411]

II. The Purpose and Scope of the MWA

369. The purpose of the MWA is to stabilize workers' lives and improve the quality of the labour force by guaranteeing them a minimum level of wages and thereby contributing to the sound development of the national economy.[412]

370. The MWA shall apply to all businesses or workplaces employing workers: provided that this Act shall not apply to any business using only relatives living together, and to those hired for household work. Furthermore the Act shall not apply to seamen who are subject to the Seamen Act or to ship owners employing such seamen.[413]

III. Criteria for Determining and Classifying the Minimum Wage

371. A minimum wage shall be set after taking into account the cost of living of workers, the wages of similar workers, labour productivity and the ratio of workers' compensation to the national income. As a result the level may be set differently for different types of business. This determination is made by the Minister of Employment and Labour following the consideration of the Minimum Wage Council.[414]

IV. Minimum Wage Rates

372. A minimum wage rate (referring to the amount determined as a minimum wage) shall be determined on a daily, weekly or monthly basis. In any of the cases, the minimum wage shall also be interpreted to an hourly rate.

411. Kazuo Sugeno, *op. cit.*, p. 242.
412. MWA, Article 1.
413. Article 3.
414. Article 4.

373. For workers who covered under any of the following paragraphs, the minimum wage rate may be set in an amounts different from the minimum wage rate prescribed.[415]

374. For a person who is in an apprentice period and for whom less than three months have passed since the beginning of his or her apprenticeship period; the rate may be reduced by 10 per cent.

V. Exceptions to the Application of a Minimum Wage

375. Where an employer has obtained the permission of the Minister of Employment and Labour, minimum wage policies will not apply to the following categories of workers:

- a person who has remarkably low abilities to work due to mental or physical impairment;
- other people as deemed inappropriate for the application of the the minimum wage.

VI. Methods for the Determination of Minimum Wages

376. The Minimum Wage Council shall be established within the Ministry of Employment and Labour to deliberate on the level of the minimum wage and other important matters related thereto.[416]

377. The Minister of Employment and Labour shall determine the minimum wage by 5 August of every year. By this date, the Minister shall have requested deliberation by the Minimum Wage Council, and make a determination of the minimum wage according to the proposal offered by the Council after its deliberations.[417]

378. Once the Minister of Employment and Labour has determined the minimum wage, he/she shall announce it publicly and without delay. In principle, the minimum wage, once announced publicly, shall come into effect on 1 January of the following year.[418]

379. An employer, to whom the minimum wage applies, shall inform his or her workers of the minimum wage concerned by displaying such a rate in a place where it can be easily seen by the workers, or by other appropriate means.[419]

415. Article 5.
416. Article 12.
417. Article 8.
418. Article 10.
419. Article 11.

VII. The Effects of a Minimum Wage

380. An employer must pay all workers who are covered under the stipulations of the minimum wage an amount not less than the rate prescribed by the minister. In addition, an employer shall not lower any previous wage level on the grounds of the minimum wage as set under this Act.

381. In any labour contract between an employer and a worker, which is subject to the provisions of minimum wage regulations, which provides for a wage that is less than the minimum wage rate, such provisions pertaining to payment shall be null and void and those invalidated provisions shall be regarded as stipulating that the same wage as the rate set under the MWA shall be paid.[420]

382. A person who pays wages lower than the minimum wage rate or who lowers the previously paid rates of wages on the grounds of the minimum wage rate in violation of MWA shall be punished by imprisonment for up to three years or a fine not exceeding 20 million won. In such a case, both the imprisonment and the fine may be imposed simultaneously.[421]

§6. The Guarantee of the Payment of Wages

I. Subcontracted Workers

383. For those workers who are employed on a subcontracted or equivalent system, an employer shall guarantee a certain amount of remuneration in proportion to their actual working hours.[422] This 'minimum fixed wage' (a certain amount of payment) is interpreted as guaranteeing a certain income to workers who are paid either piece-rates or by their results, but the minimum amount is not concretely specified in the Act. According to the intention of the Act, the amount of the fixed wage should follow the basic wage rate established by the labour contract or by works rules; and it should not be markedly lower than the mean wage for that particular industry.[423]

A. *Payment of Wages in Subcontracted Businesses*

384. If a project is carried out based upon several tiers of contracts and a subcontractor has failed to pay wages to its workers because of a fault attributable to its direct upper-tier contractor, the direct upper-tier contractor shall be jointly responsible along with the subcontractor concerned.

420. Article 6.
421. Article 28.
422. Article 47.
423. Chi Sun Kim, *op. cit.*, p. 50.

385. The scope of the fault attributable to the direct upper-tier contractor shall be determined by presidential decree.[424]

B. Joint Responsibility for Paying Wages in the Construction Industry

386. If a project in the construction industry is carried out through two or more tiers of contracts under subparagraph 11 of Article 2 of the Framework Act on the Construction Industry (hereinafter referred to as construction contracts) and its subcontractor who is not a constructor under subparagraph 7 of Article 2 of the same Act fails to pay wages (limited to wages incurred for the construction work concerned) to a worker it has employed, the immediate upper tier contractor shall take responsibility for paying wages to the worker employed by the subcontractor, jointly with the subcontractor(Article 44-2 paragraph 1).

387. If the immediate upper tier contractor under paragraph (1) is not a constructor under subparagraph 7 of Article 2 of the Framework Act on the Construction Industry, the lowest tier constructor among its upper tier contractors who are constructors under the same subparagraph shall be deemed the immediate upper tier contractor (Article 44-2 paragraph 2).[425]

C. Special Provisions Concerning Wages under a Construction Contract

388. If a construction contract falls within the purview of any of the following sub-paragraphs, a direct upper-tier contractor shall, at the request of a worker employed by its subcontractor, directly pay the worker an amount of wages (limited to the wages incurred for the construction work concerned) the subcontractor should have paid to the worker, up to the amount of the construction payment owed to the subcontractor (Article 44-3 paragraph 1):

1. where the direct upper-tier contractor and the subcontractor have agreed that the direct upper-tier contractor may pay wages directly to a worker employed by the subcontractor instead of the subcontractor and also agreed on the methods of and procedures for the payment;
2. if there is a payment order confirmed pursuant to Article 56, sub-paragraph 3, of the Civil Execution Act, an execution certificate pursuant to Article 56, sub-paragraph 4, which certifies that a worker employed by the subcontractor has the right to file a claim for wages against that subcontractor, a decision to recommend compliance made under Articles 5-7 of the Trials of Small Claims Act, and a certificate of other equivalent execution rights; or

424. Article 44.
425. Article 44-2.

3. if a subcontractor has informed the direct upper-tier contractor that it has unpaid wages owed to a worker and the direct upper-tier contractor has recognized that the subcontractor has apparent reasons not to be able to pay wages, such as bankruptcy.

389. If the contractor (hereinafter referred to as the prime contractor) of a person awarding a contract under subparagraph 10 of Article 2 of the Framework Act on the Construction Industry subcontracts the construction contract to two or more tiers of contractors, and a worker employed by a subcontractor (including subcontractors to the subcontractor; hereinafter the same shall apply in this paragraph.) has a title of deed under paragraph (1) 2 to such subcontractor, the worker may request the prime contractor to directly pay an amount of money equivalent to wages (limited to wages incurred for the construction work concerned) that the subcontractor is liable to pay. The prime contractor shall comply with such request to the extent of the amount of money for which the worker is entitled to exercise the subrogation right of a creditor against the prime contractor under Article 404 of the Civil Act (Article 44-3 paragraph 2).

390. If an immediate upper tier contractor or a prime contractor has paid an amount of money equivalent to wages to a worker employed by a subcontractor pursuant to paragraphs (1) and (2), it shall be deemed that the obligation to pay the subcontract price to the subcontractor has expired to such extent (Article 44-3 paragraph 3).[426]

II. Allowances during Business Suspension

391. If business is suspended for reasons attributable to an employer, the employer shall pay their workers allowances equivalent to 70 per cent or more of the average wages during that time. If this amount exceeds the ordinary wages, then the ordinary wages may be paid as allowances during the suspended period.

392. However, an employer who is unable to continue business for unavoidable reasons may, upon approval of the Labour Relations Commission, pay allowances during the suspension of business at an amount lower than the standards stipulated.[427]

426. Article 44-3.
427. Article 46.

III. Protection of Wage Claims

A. *Preferential Reimbursement for Claims of Wages*

393. When employers fall into either a management crisis or bankruptcy, leaving delayed wages unpaid, it is desirable for wage claims to be given priority and their payment secured because workers depend upon their wages for their livelihood.

394. In these cases, civil law gives priority to wage claims over other claims. However, if those other claims on the enterprise were also secured by bonds, mortgages or similar arrangements, then the LSA provides that:

> Wages, accident compensations and other claims arising from labor relations shall be paid in preference to taxes, public levies or other claims, except for the claims secured by pledges, mortgages or the liens under the Act on the Use of Movables, Receivables, etc., as Security on the total assets of the employer; however, this shall not apply to taxes or public levies which take precedence over pledges, mortgages or the liens under the Act on the Use of Movables, Receivables, etc., as Security (Article 38 paragraph 1). Notwithstanding the provision of paragraph (1), the claims which fall under the following subparagraphs shall be paid in preference to any obligations, taxes, public levies and other claims secured by pledges, mortgages or the liens under the Act on the Use of Movables, Receivables, etc., as Security on the total assets of an employer(Article 38 Paragraph 2).

B. *Late Payment Interest on Unpaid Wages*

395. With regard to the system of retirement benefits paid by employers to retiring workers, conditions prescribed by the Employee Retirement Benefit Security Act shall apply (Article34). If a worker dies or retires, an employer shall pay the wages, compensations, and other money or valuables within 14 days after the cause for such payment has occurred; however, the period, under special circumstances, may be extended by the mutual agreement between the parties concerned (Article36). If an employer fails to pay all or part of the wages and the benefits (referring to only lump-sum benefits) referred to in subparagraph 5 of Article 2 of the Employee Retirement Benefit Security Act which he/she is liable to pay pursuant to Article 36, within 14 days from the day when the cause for payment occurs, he/she shall pay late payment interest for the number of days from the following day to the day of payment at the interest rate prescribed by the presidential decree but not exceeding an annual rate of 40/100 in consideration of economic conditions, including the late payment interest rate applied by banks under the Banking Act (Article 37 paragraph 1). If an employer delays wage payment due to a natural disaster, an armed conflict or any other reason prescribed by the Presidential Decree, the provisions of paragraph (1) shall not apply to the period during which such reasons continue to exist (Article 37 paragraph 2).

§7. The Guarantee of the Payment of Wage Claims under the WCGA

396. The Asian economic crisis in 1997 led to a number of corporate bankruptcies. This led to a realization of the insufficiency of the above mentioned protections for wage claims, and in turn acted as a catalyst for the enactment of the WCGA of 1998.

I. The Purposes of the WCGA

397. The WCGA sets forth its purpose as contributing to the stabilization of workers' livelihood by coming up with measures to guarantee the payment of overdue wages, etc., to workers who have retired, having wages, etc. unpaid because the company cannot continue its business, or its business is unstable due to economic fluctuation, changes in industrial structure, etc.

II. Payment of Overdue Wages, etc.

398. Under this law, the government pays the unpaid wages to the worker in the place of the employer, if there are reasons, as prescribed by presidential decree, such as bankruptcy. In other words, notwithstanding the provision of the Civil Act[428] concerning payment by a third person, the Minister of Employment and Labour shall, on behalf of an employer, pay unpaid wages, or other payments due, to a retired worker at the request of that worker, if there are reasons, as prescribed by presidential decree, such as bankruptcy.

399. The scope of wages, or other payments (subrogated payment or the substitution of the payment of wages) paid by the Minister of Employment and Labour on behalf of an employer is as follows: provided that a ceiling may be put on the amount, in consideration of the worker's age, etc., at the time of retirement under the conditions prescribed by presidential decree and the subrogated payment may not be made in the case that the amount is small:

1. wages covered under the LSA;[429] and retirement pay for the final three years in accordance with the WRBSA;[430]
2. allowances for the suspension of business (limited to the final three months) in accordance with the LSA.[431]

400. The criteria for workers and employers who are subject to subrogated payments shall be prescribed by presidential decree.[432]

---

428. Article 469 of the Civil Act.
429. Article 38 paragraph 2 subparagraph 1.
430. Article 11 paragraph 2.
431. Article 46.
432. Article 7.

III. The Subrogation of the Right to Claim Unpaid Wages, etc.

401. If the Minister of Employment and Labour has made subrogated payment to a worker, the right of the worker to claim unpaid wages, etc., against his or her employer shall be transferred to the Minister of Employment and Labour. The right to preferential payment of wage claims under the LSA[433] and the right to preferential payment of retirement pay under the WRBSA[434] shall continue to exist with regard to the right having been transferred.[435]

IV. The Wage Claim Guarantee Fund

402. The Minister of Employment and Labour shall establish the Wage Claim Guarantee Fund to finance such subrogated payment as may be necessary.[436] The fund shall be created through the following financial means:[437]

- payments made by employers;
- charges paid by employers;
- loans;
- revenues from the operation of the fund;
- other revenues.

§8. The Employee Stock Ownership System

I. Purpose of the Employee Stock Ownership System

403. The purpose of the employee stock ownership system is to improve workers' economic and social status and enhance cooperation between labour and management by enabling workers to acquire and hold stocks (hereinafter referred to as the 'company's own stocks') of a company where an employee stock ownership association is set up through the employee stock ownership association.[438]

II. The Establishment, Membership and Operation of an Employee Stock Ownership Association

404. The term 'employee stock ownership association' refers to an entity which is organized by the workers of a corporation in accordance with the conditions prescribed in this Act in order to acquire and manage the stocks of the corporation concerned.

433. Article 38 paragraph 2.
434. Article 11 paragraph 2.
435. Article 8.
436. Article 17.
437. Article 18.
438. Article 27.

405. Workers may establish an employee stock ownership association as prescribed by presidential decree. In this situation, the workers shall consult with the company in advance.

406. With respect to the establishment and operation of an employee stock ownership association, the provisions of the Civil Act on corporate judicial persons shall be applied *mutatis mutandis*, unless otherwise provided for in this Act.[439]

407. In principle, all workers of a company with an employee stock ownership association can join the employee stock ownership association. In addition, a member of an employee stock ownership association may freely withdraw from the employee stock ownership association.[440]

408. An employee stock ownership association shall be operated in a democratic way by reflecting the opinions of all members of the association. An employee stock ownership association may have a meeting of delegates instead of a general meeting of the employee stock ownership association members according to the association's rules. Officers and delegates such as the representative of the employee stock ownership association shall be elected in a direct, secret and unsigned vote.[441]

409. The representative of an employee stock ownership association shall exercise voting rights ('voting rights') over the agenda of the general shareholders' meeting according to the opinions expressed by the members of the employee stock ownership association. The specific ways of exercising the voting rights shall be prescribed by presidential decree. However, if an employee stock ownership association member demands to be entrusted with their particular voting rights, the representative of the employee stock ownership association shall entrust that member with the voting right to shares owned in the employee stock ownership association by the member concerned.[442]

III. Preferential Allocation to Members of the Employee Stock Ownership Association

410. If a listed corporation (excluding corporations listed on the KOSDAQ market) or a corporation which intends to be listed on the securities market invites subscription for, or sells, its stocks, an employee stock ownership association member shall have the right to be preferentially allocated the stocks as prescribed in the Securities Transaction Act (Article 191-7).

411. When a corporation other than those prescribed above invites subscription for, or sells, its stocks or increases its capital with new stocks, it may preferentially

439. Article 28.
440. Article 29.
441. Article 30.
442. Article 31.

allocate the stocks to an employee stock ownership association member within the scope of the preferential allocation percentage prescribed in the Capital Market Consolidation Act,[443] notwithstanding the provision of the Commercial Act (Article 418).[444]

IV. Preferential Allocation and Restrictions on the Granting of Employee Stock Options

412. A company in which an employee stock ownership association has been established may grant its employee stock association members the right ('employee stock options') to subscribe to new stocks or buy its own stocks held by the company concerned within the limits of 20/100 of the total number of issued stocks for a price ('exercise price') set in advance within a certain period ('offering period'), after resolution at a general meeting of shareholders under the conditions prescribed by the articles of incorporation. However if the employee stock options are granted within the limits of 10/100 of the total number of issued stocks, it shall be granted after resolution at the board of directors under the conditions prescribed by the articles of incorporation.[445]

413. A company in which an employee stock ownership association has been established shall not preferentially allocate its stocks or grant employee stock options in such a way as to make the sum of preferentially allocated stocks, stocks that can be acquired in the case of exercising the employee stock options and stocks already held by the employee stock ownership association and its members exceed 20/100 of the sum of new stocks (including new stocks to be issued as a result of granting employee stock options) and those stocks already issued.[446]

V. Borrowing, and Acquisition of Company's Own Stocks by Employee Stock Ownership Association

414. An employee stock ownership association may take out a loan from the company, the shareholders and financial institutions as prescribed by presidential decree to acquire the company's own stocks. The company and the shareholders may make an agreement with the employee stock ownership association to contribute money or valuable goods for the repayment of the loan.

443. Capital Market Consolidation Act, Article 191-7 paragraph 1.
444. Article 32.
445. Article 32-2.
446. Article 32-3.

415. An employee stock ownership association may offer, as collateral, the company's own stocks acquired using a loan to the lender of the loan or the loan guarantor thereof. In this case, it shall be required that as for the company's stocks corresponding to the amount of repaid loan, the security right shall be terminated upon its repayment.[447]

416. An employee stock ownership association may acquire the company's own stocks through the contribution of the company's own stocks by the company, the shareholders, etc., and through the purchase, etc., of them using the employee stock ownership association fund created pursuant to this Act (Article 35). An employee stock ownership association shall allocate the company's own stocks acquired to the employee stock ownership association members concerned.[448]

VI. Deposit Period of Company's Own Stocks and Restrictions on Transactions by the Employee Stock Ownership Association

417. An employee stock ownership association member shall deposit the company's own stocks allocated to him or her as a trustee[449] for a period as prescribed by presidential decree within the ranges described in any of the following sub-paragraphs.[450]

However, an employee stock ownership association member may, if there occur reasons as prescribed by presidential decree, such as the dissolution of the employee stock ownership association or the death of its member, withdraw the company's own stocks through the employee stock ownership association even in the middle of the deposit period prescribed in this Act.[451]

418. An employee stock ownership association shall deposit the company's own stocks held by itself or allocated to its members through it in a trustee as prescribed by presidential decree. An employee stock ownership association or its members shall not transfer or offer as a security the company's own stocks deposited. However, this shall not apply in cases as prescribed by presidential decree.[452]

447. Article 32-4.
448. Article 33.
449. As prescribed in Article 37 paragraph 1.
450.
1. Stocks acquired through the contribution of the company's own stocks by the company, the shareholders, etc., pursuant to Article 33(1) and stocks acquired using financial resources prescribed in Article 35(1)1: eight years;
2. Stocks acquired using financial resources prescribed in Article 35(1)2: one year; and,
3. Stocks acquired using financial resources prescribed in Article 35(1)3 through 5: a period corresponding to the ones prescribed in sub-paragraphs 1 and 2.

451. Article 34.
452. Article 37.

VII. The Establishment of Employee Stock Ownership Association Funds and Support for Employee Stock Ownership Associations

419. An employee stock ownership association may create an employee stock ownership association fund using the following financial resources:

- money or other valuable goods contributed by the company, the shareholders, etc.;
- money contributed by employee stock ownership association members;
- loans;
- dividends on stocks held by the employee stock ownership association but not allocated to its members;
- other revenues.

420. In principle, the employee stock ownership association fund shall be used to acquire the company's own stocks, repay the loans and pay interests thereon.[453]

421. A company and its shareholders may contribute the company's own stocks or money or other valuable goods to the employee stock ownership association where workers of the company have joined, or provide support such as making loans or guaranteeing loans to finance the purchase of the company's own stocks by the employee stock ownership association or a member who is a worker of the company. In this case, the employee stock ownership association shall operate the company's own stocks acquired through said contributions and support, to ensure that the stocks are allocated to its members who are workers of the company. A company and its employee stock ownership association may set up an employee stock ownership administrative committee with equal numbers of members representing the company and the employee stock ownership association, respectively, as prescribed by presidential decree in order to discuss the contents, conditions, etc., of support for the employee stock ownership association.[454]

VIII. Dissolution of an Employee Stock Ownership Association

422. An employee stock ownership association shall be dissolved if there occur reasons falling under any of the following sub-paragraphs. In this case, the liquidator shall report this, along with clearly stated reasons for the dissolution, to the Minister of Employment and Labour as prescribed by presidential decree:

1. the bankruptcy of the company concerned;
2. the dissolution of the company concerned as a result of the discontinuation of business;
3. the dissolution of the company concerned as a result of the merger, split-up, or merger of the business;

453. Article 35.
454. Article 36.

4. if workers of an affiliated company join the employee stock ownership association of the controlling company pursuant to Article 29;
5. if the employee stock ownership association has no officer, has not held any assets such as the company's own stocks, employee stock ownership association funds, etc., for the past three fiscal years, and are as prescribed by the Ordinance of the Ministry of Employment and Labour.

423. If an employee stock ownership association is dissolved pursuant to paragraph (1), the property of the employee stock ownership association shall revert to the members of the employee stock ownership association as prescribed by the rules. However, if an employee stock ownership association has liabilities, the property which is left after the liabilities are cleared shall revert to members of the employee stock ownership association.[455]

IX. Support for the Activation of the Employee Stock Ownership System and Workers' Takeover of Companies

424. The state may provide necessary supports for the acquisition and holding of the company's own stocks by employee stock ownership association members, the support for the employee stock ownership association by a company, etc., and the guarantee, etc., of the conversion of the company's own stocks into cash by an unlisted corporation for the purpose of activating the employee stock ownership system.[456] Where workers take over their company through an employee stock ownership association due to the company's bankruptcy, etc., the state may provide the necessary support, such as providing the money needed to acquire the stocks.[457]

455. Article 39.
456. Article 40.
457. Article 42.

Chapter 4. Working Time

§1. Principles Concerning Working Hours and Rest Days

I. Principles Relating to Working Hours

425. Korea has traditionally been well known for its long working hours.[458] To reduce those long working hours, in an effort to cope with changes in the industrial structure, and to lead towards a life worthy of a human being,[459] the provisions concerning working hours and annual leave in the LSA have been continually revised. The 2003 revision introduced a 40-hour working week and an 8-hour working day system. The aim of this was to establish a five-day working week as a standard. Working hours as regulated by the LSA are those hours, excluding rest periods, that a worker is actually 'caused to work' (i.e. actual working hours). 'Actual working hours' refers not only to the work that is actually performed on a job the term also includes time spent in waiting between jobs (i.e. stand-by time).

426. The most basic legal regulation concerning working hours is simply the principle of legal working hours, which establishes the maximum number of working hours in either a week or a day. Employers may not cause their workers to work more than a 40-hour week, excluding recess hours. This is referred to as the the 40-hour workweek system. In addition, employers are not permitted to have a worker work more than eight hours a day, again excluding recess hours.[460]

427. This system of legal working hours has such functions as:

- creating a limitation upon the prescribed working hours in any set of work rules or contractual agreement (in most cases working hours are decided by agreement or are stated within the works rules);
- serving to limit the number of hours actually worked;
- the obligation on the employer to pay premium wages in the event of those stipulated hours being exceeded;
- the application of penalties, in instances of violation.

II. General Rules Concerning Legal Working Hours

428. The maximum number of working hours for adult workers (this is considered to be male workers, female workers, female workers within one year after giving birth and pregnant workers) is eight hours per day leading to a maximum of

458. There are several reasons for this, for example: (1) the five-day working week system did not permeate throughout SMEs; (2) overtime was incorporated into Korean employment relations as a means to absorb business fluctuations without resorting to economically driven dismissals; (3) a low utilization of annual paid leave, etc.
459. That is to say workers ought to sufficient time for the restoration of their physical and mental strength and the enjoyment of a cultural and social life.
460. Article 50.

40-hours per week, excluding recess hours.[461] Here, The term 'one week' refers to seven consecutive days including holidays.[462]

429. With respect to an employee who is engaged in hazardous or dangerous work, as prescribed by presidential decree, the employer shall not have him or her work in excess of aix hours per day, which should result in a 34-hour week.[463]

430. Working hours for a person aged between 15 and 18 shall not exceed seven hours per day and 35 hours per week. However, the working hours may be extended up to an hour per day, or 5 hours per week, by an agreement between the parties concerned.[464]

III. Contractual Working Hours

431. The term 'contractual working hours' in the context of the LSA means working hours on which workers and employers have made an agreement within the limit of those working hours as prescribed in Article 50 or Article 69 of LSA, or Article 46 of the Occupational Safety and Health Act.

§2. Principles Concerning Rest Periods

432. The LSA provides that an employer must provide recess periods of more than 30 minutes for every four hours worked and of more than one hour for every eight working hours during any given working period. Such a recess period may be used by workers at their own discretion without interference from the employer.[465] As long as the work is not affected, an employee may also leave the workplace. Stand-by time – during which a worker is required to stay on call – is interpreted as working time.

I. Principles of Weekly Rest

433. An employer shall allow a worker, on average, one or more 'paid holiday' per week.[466] Although the law requires one rest day per week, as a result of the regulation stipulating a 40-hour work week and an 8-hour working day anticipates the probability of a five-day working week, the majority of Korean workers have two rest days per week. National holidays are not regarded as mandatory rest days under

461. *Ibid.*
462. Article 2.
463. Occupational Safety and Health Act, Article 46.
464. Article 69.
465. Article 54.
466. Article 55.

the LSA. Therefore employers have no duty to provide a day off on national holidays. Generally speaking, the mandatory day of rest is considered to be Sunday, but it can be shifted by collective agreement or by works rules.

II. Special Provisions Relating to Working and Recess Hours

434. With regard to businesses to whom at least one of the following subparagraphs apply, employers may extend work hours beyond twelve hours or change recess hours which are respectively set by Article 53 paragraph (1) and Article 54. The following subparagraphs come from the divisions and sections of the Standard Classifications of Industry declared by the Minister of Statistics according to Article 22 paragraph (1) of the Statistics Act. [467] 1. Land transport and pipeline transport: Provided, That route passage transport businesses as determined in Article 3 paragraph (1) subparagraph 1 of the Passenger Transport Service Act are excluded. 2. Maritime transport 3. Air transport 4. Other transport-related businesses 5. Healthcare

III. Exceptions to Applications

435. The provisions relating to working hours, recesses and holidays are not applied to workers engaged in the following occupations:[468]

1. the cultivation of arable land, reclamation work, seeding and planting, gathering and picking-up or other agricultural and forestry work;
2. the breeding of livestock, the catching of marine animals and plants, the cultivation of marine products or similar cattle-breeding, sericulture-related or fisheries businesses;
3. surveillance or intermittent work, for which the employer has obtained the approval of the Minister of Employment and Labour;
4. any other work as prescribed by presidential decree.

§3. Regulations Relating to Overtime, Rest Day Work and Night Work

I. Definition and Restriction on 'Overtime Work (Extended Work)'

436. The term 'overtime work' (also known as extended work) means work performed in excess of the daily or weekly maximum number of hours as set out in the relevant regulation. 'Rest-day work' means work performed on rest days which are required by the legal standards for a weekly rest system. Night work is defined by the LSA as work done between 10 p.m. and 6 a.m. Considering the purposes of

467. Article 59.
468. Article 63.

work undertaken within these working hours, the LSA prescribes several restrictive provisions. Overtime work and so forth is only permissible with the agreement of both parties and in cases of emergency.

437. If the parties concerned have reached an agreement, the working hours stipulated in Article 50 may be extended by up to 12 hours per week (i.e. a worker's working week may be extended to 52 hours a week at maximum on the basis of mutual consent).[469]

438. If the parties concerned reach an agreement, the working hours stipulated as in Article 51 (the flexible working hour system) may be extended by up to 12 hours per week, and the working hours under Article 52 (the selective working hour system) may be extended by up to 12 hours per week averaged over an adjustment period, pursuant to sub-paragraph 2 of Article 52 (the selective working hour system/adjustment period).[470]

439. Under special circumstances, an employer may extend working hours as provided for in paragraphs (1) and (2) with the approval of the Minister of Employment and Labour and the consent of their workers; however, the employer shall immediately obtain the approval of the Minister of Employment and Labour *ex post facto*, if a situation is so urgent that time is not available to obtain such approval.[471] If the Minister of Employment and Labour finds that the extension of working hours is not appropriate, he or she may order the employer to grant recess hours or days-off equivalent to the extended working hours worked at later time(Article 53 paragraph 4).

440. The working hours of a person aged between 15 and 18 shall not exceed 7 hours per day or 35 hours per week. However, these working hours may be extended by up to an hour per day, or five hours per week, with the mutual consent of the parties concerned.[472]

II. Premium (Increased Rate) Payment for Overtime Work, Night Work and Holiday Work

441. An employer shall pay an additional 50 per cent, or more, of the ordinary wages for extended work, night work (work provided between 10 pm and 6 am) or for holiday work.[473] Holiday work beyond eight hours: 100 per cent of the ordinary wage. The primary purpose of this provision is, of course, to restrain overtime work. An employer may, in lieu of paying additional wages, grant the leave to a worker to

469. Article 53 paragraph 1.
470. Article 53 paragraph 2.
471. Article 53 paragraph 3.
472. Article 69.
473. Article 56.

compensation for the extended, night or holiday work, pursuant to a written agreement with the workers' representative (system of using leave as compensation).[474]

§4. VACATIONS

I. An Outline of Annual Paid Leave

442. In order to contribute to healthy and culturally fulfilled life, the LSA's annual-paid-leave system guarantees workers a certain number of days of paid leave each year over and above their regular rest days. In Korea, the utilization of annual leave to which a worker is entitled is low. Since the low utilization of annual leave was one of the reasons for Korea's long annual working hours, the current LSA establishes provisions (promoting the use of annual paid leave[475] and the substitution of paid leave)[476] to promote active use of annual leave.

II. Legal Regulations Regarding Annual Paid Leave

443. An employer must grant 15 days' paid leave to a worker who has recorded not less than 80 per cent of attendance during one calender year.

444. To acquire a right to annual leave, a worker must be employed continuously for one year, and must have reported for work for at least 80 per cent of the total number of days required. When these two conditions are met, the worker is entitled to 15 days of leave as of the first day after the completion of those 12 months' service. If he or she fails to report for work for more than 80 per cent of the time in the next year, he will have no right to annual leave at all in the following year. However, if the worker fulfils the reporting rate required in the subsequent year, he or she will be entitled annual leave in the following year.

445. An employer shall grant one day's paid leave per month to a worker whose consecutive service period is shorter than one year, if the worker has offered their work without an absence throughout a month.

446. If an employer grants a worker paid leave in the first year of his/her service, the number of leave days shall be 15 including the leave prescribed in paragraph 5(2)2.

447. After the first year of service, an employer shall grant one day's paid leave for each two years of consecutive service in addition to the leave set out in paragraph 5(2)1 to a worker who has worked consecutively for three years or more. In

474. Article 57.
475. Article 61.
476. An employer may have workers take paid leave on a particular working day in lieu of their annual paid leave, if the employer and the workers' representative agree in writing (Article 62).

this case, the total number of leave days, including the additional leave, shall not exceed 25. As a result, the number of leave days increases in proportion to the number of years of continuous service up to a maximum of 25 days.

448. An employer shall grant paid leave upon the request of a worker, and shall pay ordinary wages or average wages as prescribed in the relevant employment rules or other regulations during the period of leave. However, the leave period concerned may be changed, in cases where granting the period of leave requested by the worker might cause a serious impediment to the operation of the business.

449. The law gives the worker a right to designate the period of leave. If granting the leave at the period designated creates a 'serious impediment to the operation of the enterprise', the employer can change those designated dates. The enterprise in which the 'serious impediment to the operation of the enterprise' is understood to be the operational unit or section to which the worker belongs. Further, the test for interference is whether the worker in question is essential to such an operation and whether a substitute can be found without difficulty. Case law requires the employer to exercise reasonable efforts in finding a substitute and to endeavour to meet the worker's request to take the leave at the designated time.[477] Since the law does nor regulate the purpose for which a worker can use annual leave, it is understood that the individual can use the annual leave as he or she wishes (the principle of the free use of the annual leave)

450. In the application of paragraphs 443 through 446, a period falling under any of the following sub-paragraphs shall be considered a period of attendance:

1. a period during which a worker is unable to work due to occupational injuries or illnesses;
2. a period during which a pregnant woman does not work while on maternity leave;
3. a period during which a worker take a childcare leave.

451. The leave referred to in paragraphs 383 through 386 shall be forfeited if not used within one year. However, this shall not apply in cases where the worker concerned has been prevented from using the leave due to any cause attributable to the employer.[478]

III. Promoting the Use of Annual Paid Leave

452. To promote the utilization of annual leave, the law provides as follows.

453. If a worker's leave has been forfeited by non-usage despite the fact that the employer has taken measures described in any of the following sub-paragraphs to

477. Takashi Araki, *op. cit.*, p. 101.
478. Article 60.

promote the use of paid leave, the employer shall have no obligation to compensate the worker for the unused leave, and shall not be deemed to have caused such a non-usage as being attributable to the employer's actions.

454. Within the first 10 days of the six months before unused leave is to be forfeited, an employer shall notify each worker of the number of his or her unused leave days and urge them in writing to decide when they would like to use the leave and encourage them to inform the employer of the their requested leave period.

455. If a worker, despite this urging, has failed to decide when he or she wishes to use either the whole or a part of their unused leave and to inform their employer of the leave period upon which they have decided within 10 days after they were urged, an employer shall decide when the worker uses the unused leave and notify the worker of the decided leave period in writing no later than two months before the unused leave is to be forfeited.[479]

IV. Substitution of Paid Leave

456. An employer may have workers take paid leave on a particular working day in lieu of the annual paid leave, if the employer and the workers' representative agree in writing.[480]

§5. Flexible Working Systems

I. An Outline of Flexible Working Systems

457. The LSA introduces several forms of flexible work systems as they relate to working hours. There are two schemes for averaging out working hours over a certain period. First there is the flexible working hour scheme covering a period of not more than two weeks, next there is the flexible working hour scheme for a period of not more than three months. Finally there is the so-called flexitime system, the selective working hour system based on an adjustment period not more than one month.

458. The selective working hour system resembles the flexible working hour scheme in that exceeding the daily or weekly maximum of working hours is not regarded as overtime under the law as long as the average weekly hours during the period in consideration are within the weekly maximum. The flexible working hour scheme, however, allows the maximum number of hours only to be exceeded on days as specified in the work rules, whereas the selective working hour scheme does not require such a specification of daily working hours and concerns only total hours worked within a settled period.

479. Article 61.
480. Article 62.

459. The introduction of these flexible working hour schemes were made for the following reasons:

- to cope with the changes in industrial structures and types of work, such as the increase in the size of service industries and white-collar jobs;
- to reduce the number of working hours, by means of a flexible distribution of those hours.

II. Legal Regulations Relating to Flexible Working Hour Systems

460. The flexible working hour scheme (also known as the hour-averaging scheme) relates to periods of work-related time of not more than two weeks.

461. In accordance with work rules (or in accordance with rules or regulations equivalent thereto), an employer may have a worker work for a specific week in excess of the designated 40 hours, or on an specific day in excess of the stipulated 8 hours, on the condition that the average working hours per week within a certain unit period – of not more than two weeks – do not exceed 40 hours, with the proviso that the employee's working hours in any particular week shall not exceed 48 hours.[481]

III. The Flexible Working Hours Scheme within a Period of Not More Than Three Months

462. Where an employer reaches an agreement in writing with a representative of their workers on the following issues, the employer is allowed to have a worker work for a specific week in excess of 40 hours, or for a specific day in excess of 8 hours. However, this is predicated on the basis that the average working hours per week, within a certain unit of time – not more than three months – do not exceed the 40 hour maximum. Additionally, the working hours for a specific week or for a specific day should not exceed 52 hours and 12 hours respectively:

- the scope of workers subject to this paragraph;
- the period of time concerned (such a period may not exceed three months);
- the details of the relevant working days within a unit period and, likewise, the working hours for each working day; and
- such other matters as prescribed by presidential decree.[482]

463. However, the provisions are not applied to workers aged between 15 and 18, nor do they pertain to pregnant female workers. In addition, if an employer

481. Article 51 paragraph 1.
482. Article 51 paragraph 2.

needs to have a worker works in accordance with these provisions, the employer must prepare measures to ensure that the existing rate of payment is not reduced.[483]

IV. The Selective Working Hour System (Flexitime System)

464. The 'selective working hour scheme' is one in which workers can choose the start and end of their daily working hours as they wish as long as they work the designated number of hours over the course of a designated period of time.

465. Where an employer has reached a written agreement on each of the following items with a workers' representative regarding a worker who is entrusted with the decision as to when to begin and finish work in accordance with their rules of employment (including such rules as may by equivalent to rules of employment), the employer may have workers work in excess of 40 hours per week, or 8 hours per day, on the condition that their average working hours per week, computed on the basis of an adjustment period of not more than one month, do not exceed 40 hours. Such an agreement must cover the following criteria:

- the scope of the workers who shall be subject to this paragraph (excluding workers between the ages of 15 and of 18);
- an adjustment period (a finite period of not more than one month);
- an agreed number of total working hours within the adjustment period;
- the starting and finishing times of those working hours, if a mandatory work period is in force;
- such starting and finishing times for working hours as are allowed to be selected by workers;
- other matters as determined by presidential decree.[484]

§6. The Calculation of Working Time

I. The Concept of Working Time

466. The LSA does not define working time. Many scholars define working time, subject to the regulation of the LSA, as 'time during which a worker is under the direction of his or her employer'. In the calculation of working hours, the LSA provides two exceptions (special provisions for the calculation of working hours), namely work performed outside the workplace and discretionary work.

483. Article 51 paragraph 3–4.
484. Article 52.

II. Special Provisions for the Calculation of Working Hours

A. *Work Outside the Workplace*

467. The number of hours worked outside the workplace or related establishments is difficult for employers to determine. Therefore, the LSA provides that,

If it is difficult to compute working hours because a worker carries out his duty in whole or in part outside the workplace for business travel or for other reasons, it shall be deemed that the worker concerned has worked the contractual working hours. However, in cases where the completion of work requires a worker to work in excess of their contractual working hours, the worker is deemed to have worked for hours ordinarily required to complete the work concerned.[485] However, if an employer and the representative of their workers have agreed, in writing, on the work concerned, the working hours set by that agreement shall be deemed to be the working hours necessary for the performance of the work concerned.[486]

B. *The Discretionary Work Scheme (Relating to Professional and White-collar Modes of Work)*

468. It is believed to be reasonable to apply standard working hours regulations to workers engaged in creative and discretionary activities, because such workers are free from direction from their employer with regard to the manner of their performance and because the nature of their work requires that the work performed should be evaluated on the basis of results rather than by the amount of time spent conducting it.

469. Therefore, the LSA provides that 'in the case of works designated by presidential decree as those works which need, in the light of their characteristics, the worker's discretion with regard to the ways to perform the activities concerned, the worker shall be deemed to have worked such working hours as are determined by a written agreement between the employer and the workers' representative. Such written agreements shall contain each of the items described as follows':

- the provisions as to the work to be provided;
- the provisions in which the employer would not give directions to the worker regarding how to perform, and how to allocate working hours; and
- the provisions in which the computation of working hours shall be determined by the written agreement concerned.[487]

485. Article 58 paragraph 1.
486. Article 58 paragraph 2.
487. Article 58 paragraph 3.

Chapter 5. Safety and Health

§1. The Purpose and Structure of Workers' Accident Compensation

I. Purpose

470. The purpose of this Act is

a. to compensate workers rapidly and fairly for any work-related accidents endured in carrying activities within the purview of industrial accident compensation insurance;
b. to establish and operate insurance facilities to promote the rehabilitation of victims of accidents and ensure their return to being productive members of society;
c. to contribute to the protection of workers by preventing accidents and carrying out other projects that promote workers' welfare.

To achieve these objectives, insurance benefits are granted, and furthermore labour welfare is undertaken.

II. The Development and Structure of the Workers' Accident Compensation System

471. The detailed provisions of the ISHA protect workers' health and safety, but despite the actions of both employers and government, however vigorous, work-related accidents remain inevitable. The system of accident compensation was developed to deal with accidents at work or occupationally related diseases. The development of modern industry means that such occurrences happen with greater frequency.

472. According to the principles of civil law, an employer is liable for damages only when s/he has directly caused the accident or been responsible for the disease, whether on purpose or as a result of negligence (Civil Code, Article 750). However, it is very hard to verify or prove intent or negligence and even if it is somehow verified, it is often too late to relieve the injured worker as a civil suit usually lasts for a long time. In many countries principles of liability based on the premise of fault were gradually curtailed, and eventually abandoned to be replaced by a new system. In Korea, the LSA admits a causal relationship between industry and accidents and, as a result, saddles the employer with the responsibility for compensation, regardless of purpose or negligence, if the accident occurred in the workplace.

473. The liability for employment injuries under the LSA has several distinguishing characteristics compared to civil liability for damages. First, liability under the LSA is a strict liability (that is to say a liability without proof of fault) if the injury is work-related. Secondly, the LSA fixes the amount of compensation based on a calculation of a worker's average wage. Thirdly, the payment of such compensation is sanctioned by criminal provisions and subject to administrative supervision. Such strict liability, however, does not offer sufficient protection when the employer concerned cannot afford to pay. Therefore, a mandatory insurance system covering workers' compensation was developed. This is set out in the IACIA. The Act started as a liability insurance mechanism to ensure that employers can financially meet their duty to compensate workers for injuries suffered as a result of their employment. After numerous revisions, the IACIA has introduced additional protective measures and has expanded its coverage; as a result of this expansion, all enterprises are covered by the provisions of the Act. Additionally, the extent of the insurance payments was improved, and, as a result, became far superior to the compensation provided under the LSA. As a result, the LSA has come to play a limited role (that is to say that it relates to the first three days or fewer of medical care benefits and wage replacement benefits) while the IACIA has become the principal law governing compensation for workers' accidents in place of the LSA, and more important than the regulations contained within the LSA for providing injury compensation to workers.

474. One of the unique characteristics of Korea's workers' compensation and insurance system is that, in spite of the existence of a mandatory compensation system, damages that have not been fully compensated by the LSA's workers' compensation payments or IACIA insurance benefits can be claimed in court based on traditional civil liability.

§2. The Workers' Accident Compensation System under the LSA

475. The LSA provides that if workers suffer any injuries, illness or death, resulting from their employment, the employer is required to furnish the following forms of compensation.

I. Medical Treatment Compensation

476. An employer should provide the necessary medical treatment at his or her own expense or bear the corresponding expenses for any worker who suffers an occupational injury or from a work-related disease. The interpretation of what is meant by terms such as 'occupational disease' and 'medical treatment' as well as the timing of the resulting compensation for medical treatment are prescribed by presidential decree.

II. Compensation for the Suspension of Work

477. An employer must provide a worker undergoing medical treatment an allowance during their suspension of work at a level equivalent to 60 per cent of their average wages during that period of medical treatment. The purpose of this provision is to maintain the employee's minimum standard of living. If a person who is to be provided with such compensation has received part of his or her wages during the period for which the compensation is provided, the employer must provide compensation at the same rate but having subtracted the amount of ordinary wages already paid. The timing of the compensation is prescribed by presidential decree.

III. Compensation for Disability

478. If a worker continues to be disabled after the completion of such treatment as is deemed appropriate for his or her occupational injuries or diseases, the employer shall provide disability compensation at an amount equivalent to the worker's average wages multiplied by the number of days previous to the accident set according to grade of disability as shown in Table 1.

Table 1 Disability grade and accident compensation (in a day's average wages)

Grade	*Accident compensation*	*Grade*	*Accident compensation*
Grade 1	1,340	Grade 8	450
Grade 2	1,190	Grade 9	350
Grade 3	1,050	Grade 10	270
Grade 4	920	Grade 11	200
Grade 5	790	Grade 12	140
Grade 6	670	Grade 13	90
Grade 7	560	Grade 14	50

479. For a person who already has a physical disability and has that disability aggravated by an occupational injury or disease, the amount of compensation for disability shall be the amount calculated by subtracting the number of compensation days for the previous disability grade from the number of compensation days for the aggravated disability grade and then multiplying the resulting number by the average wages at the time when the cause for the claim occurred.

IV. Exceptions to the Provisions for Compensation for the Suspension of Work or for Disability

480. If a worker suffers an occupational injury or contracts a work-related disease as a result of gross negligence on his or her own part, and the employer obtains the acknowledgment of the Labour Relations Commission of that negligence, the employer shall not be liable to provide compensation for either the suspension of work nor compensation for disability.

V. Compensation for Survivors

481. If a worker dies on duty, the employer shall provide survivors' compensation equivalent to 1,000 days of the worker's average wages to his or her surviving family and shall do so without delay following the death. The scope of surviving family members, their order of priority for the receipt of survivors' compensation and their order of priority in terms of receiving survivors' compensation in any case where a person eligible to receive survivors' compensation dies shall be prescribed by presidential decree.

VI. Funeral Expenses

482. If a worker dies on duty, the employer shall provide funeral expenses equivalent to 90 days of the average wages without delay after the worker's death. Usually this means that the fatality must occur in the workplace and be clearly related to work.

VII. Lump-sum Compensation

483. If a worker receiving compensation has not completely recovered from the said occupational injury or disease even after two years since the medical care began, the employer may be exonerated from any further obligation of compensation under this Act by providing a lump-sum payment equivalent to 1,340 days of the average wage of the worker. Yet she or he is not necessarily free from tort as stipulated in the Civil Code.

If an employer proves his ability to pay compensation, and has obtained the consent of a recipient, he may pay the compensation pursuant to Articles 80, 82 or 84 in instalments over a period of one year.

VIII. Claims for Compensation

484. A claim for compensation shall not be revoked or changed in other ways due to retirement and must not be either transferred or confiscated.

IX. The Relationship of Compensation to Other Damage Claims

485. When an accident has happened, a worker may claim compensation in three ways, which are prescribed, in the LSA, the Civil Code and the IACIA. Because each of them is not always identical in its legal nature and the required necessary conditions, an employee has the right to choose between them. However, if a person to receive compensation has received money or other valuables corresponding to accident compensation as stipulated in this Act by way of the Civil Code, or other laws or decrees for the same reason, the employer shall be exonerated from the obligation of compensation to the extent of the value received, for there is no need to pay double compensation.

X. Reappraisal and Arbitration by the Minister of Employment and Labour

486. If a person has an objection to the determination of occupational injury, disease or death, methods of medical care, determination of compensation or any other matters regarding compensation, that person concerned may request the Minister of Employment and Labour to reappraise or arbitrate the case. If such a request is filed, the Minister of Employment and Labour must reappraise or arbitrate the case within one month. The Minister of Employment and Labour may reappraise or arbitrate a dispute on his or her authority, if necessary. The Minister of Employment and Labour may have a doctor diagnose or examine the worker concerned, if it is deemed necessary for reappraisal or arbitration. The purposes of the statute of limitation, the request for reappraisal or arbitration and the commencement of reappraisal or arbitration shall be regarded as the institution of a judicial proceeding.

XI. Reappraisal and Arbitration of Labour Relations Commission

487. If reappraisal or arbitration has not been made by the Minister of Employment and Labour within one month, or if a person is dissatisfied with the result of reappraisal or arbitration, a request may be filed with the Labour Relations Commission for reappraisal or arbitration. If a request is filed, the Labour Relations Commission shall reappraise or arbitrate the case within one month.

XII. Exception to Subcontracted Work and Keeping of Documents

488. The party who bears the responsibility for compensation is, needless to say, the employer. When she or he has workmen's accident compensation insurance, the compensation is made by the insurance company. However, when a business is operated based upon several tiers of subcontracts, the primary contractor shall be regarded as the employer for the purposes of accident compensation. The purpose of this provision is to ensure the payment of compensation, because subcontractors are generally smaller than the primary contractor with regard to their means of payment.

If a subcontractor is delegated to pay compensation by a written agreement with the primary contractor, the subcontractor shall also be regarded as the employer; however, the primary contractor shall not have more than one subcontractor bear overlapping compensation for the same business. The primary contractor who has been requested to provide compensation may ask the applicant to demand compensation first from the subcontractor who has agreed to the responsibility for such compensation. However, this shall not apply if the subcontractor concerned is missing or is declared bankrupt.

489. An employer shall not discard important documents concerning accident compensation unless accident compensation is finished or before the right to claim accident compensation is extinguished by the prescribed limit of three years.

The statute of limitation to exercise a claim for accident compensation in accordance with this Act shall be three years.

§3. IACIA

490. The IACIA is a compulsory state-run social insurance system. Therefore, industrial accident compensation insurance activities shall be managed by the Minister of Employment and Labour. In order to carry out efficiently activities aimed at achieving the purposes prescribed in this Act, under the auspices of the Minister of Employment and Labour, the Korean Workers' Compensation and Welfare Service was established.

The government collects insurance premiums from employers and provides insurance benefits directly to injured workers or their survivors. When the injured workers or their survivors receive insurance benefits, employers are exempted from liability for those workers compensation under the LSA.

I. The Scope of Application

491. This Act applies to all businesses or workplaces employing workers: provided that this Act shall not apply to businesses determined in the presidential decree in consideration of their hazard rate, size, location, etc.

The LSA and IACIA apply to all individuals, irrespective of nationality or legal status, working on Korean soil according to the principle of territorial application. Illegal migrant workers can legally claim insurance benefits against the government programme.

II. Insurance Premiums

492. The premiums and other charges to be collected to finance the expenses required for insurance activities under this Act shall be subject to the conditions prescribed by the Act on the Collection, etc., of Premiums for Employment Insurance and Industrial Accident Compensation Insurance (otherwise known as the Insurance Premium Collection Act). According to the Insurance Premium Collection Act, an employer's premium is determined by multiplying the total amount of wages paid to workers by the industrial accident compensation insurance premium rate.

493. The industrial accident compensation insurance premium rate is fixed for each occupation between 0.6 per cent and 22.5 per cent considering the frequency of work-related accidents in their particular industry. In other words, these rates shall be prescribed according to the type of business as set out in the Ordinance of the Ministry of Employment and Labour, on the basis of the ratio of the total industrial accident compensation insurance benefits to the total wages for the past three years as of 30 June each year, after taking into account the amount needed for industrial accident compensation insurance benefits, such as annuities under the IACIA, the costs of preventing industrial accidents and improving welfare for accident victims, and so forth.

III. The Conditions Required to Define an Injury as Employment Related

494. Insurance benefits are only payable when a worker's injury, disease, physical disability or death 'results from employment'. The term 'work-related accident' (employment injury) within the IACIA means any injuries, diseases, disabilities or death of a worker, which is caused by his or her duties resulting from employment.

However, the interpretation of this term has always been controversial. Generally speaking, the injury must occur in the course of employment or it must be caused by employment duties. 'In the course of employment' means that 'the worker is under the employer's control and management'. In addition the term 'caused by employment duties' means that 'the accident has a causal relation with acts incidental to duty, working conditions or the working environment'. 'Caused by duties' (resulting from employment) has been stated formally as meaning that, under principles of experience, it is recognized that the hazard inherent in the worker being under an employer's control under a labour contract, including the execution of his or her duties is realized. Thus it is held, in 'caused by duties', 'duties' has almost the broad meaning of 'in the course of employment'.

495. The criteria for recognition of work-related accidents in the IACIA, based on the latest medical knowledge about work-related accidents, are established as follows.

If a worker sustains an injury, a disability or disease or dies for any of the causes described in the following regards, that injury, disease, disability or death shall be considered to be a work-related accident. This shall not apply if there is no causal relationship between the work and the accident.

A. *Work-related Accidents*

496. A work-related accident is:

a. an accident which happens while the worker is performing work or an act in accordance with his/her employment contract;
b. an accident which happens due to a defect in, or the careless management of, facilities, etc., provided by the employer while the worker is using those facilities, etc.;
c. an accident which happens while the worker is commuting to and from work;

d. an accident that happens while the worker is participating in or preparing an event organized by the employer or an event following the directions of the employer;
e. an accident which happens during recess hours due to an act that can be seen as being under the control of the employer;
f. other accidents which happen in relation to work.

B. Work-related Diseases

497. A work-related Disease is:

a. a disease which occurs due to the handling of, or exposure to, harmful or hazardous elements while the worker is performing his or her duties;
b. a disease which occurs as a result of a work–related injury;
c. other diseases which occur in relation to work.

498. An injury, disease, disability or death of a worker, which arises from, or is caused by, his or her intentional, self-harming or criminal act shall not be considered as a work-related accident: provided that if the injury, disease, disability or death occured due to an act committed when the worker's level of cognitive ability, etc., was obviously low and the cause is prescribed by presidential decree, it shall be considered as a work-related accident.

Though this provision is based on the principle of equity, it is too severe for workers. At least, 'gross negligence (intentional acts)' on the part of employee should be interpreted strictly and narrowly.

The specific criteria for the recognition of work-related accidents shall be prescribed by presidential decree.

IV. Contents of Insurance Benefits

A. Medical Care Benefits

499. Medical care benefits shall be paid to a worker if the worker sustains an injury or disease as a result of work-related causes. Medical care benefits require the worker to receive medical care at an industrial accident insurance-related medical institution: provided that in inevitable cases medical care expenses may be paid in lieu of providing medical care. If the injury or disease can be cured after three days or less of medical care, the medical care benefits need not be paid. The scope of the medical care benefits is as follows:

– medical examinations and tests;
– the provision of medicines or medical supplies, artificial limbs and other prosthetic devices;
– treatments, operations and other procedures;

- rehabilitation treatment;
- hospitalization;
- nursing and payment to carers;
- transfers;
- other matters as prescribed by the Ordinance of the Ministry of Employment and Labour.

500. A person who intends to receive medical care benefits shall make an application for medical care benefits to the corporation; this application should include documents indicating his or her workplace, the background of the accident, and medical opinions about the accident.

A person who applies for medical care benefits may receive such benefits under of the National Health Insurance Act or do so under the Medical Benefits Act.

501. If a worker receiving medical care due to a work-related accident falls under any of the following categories, he or she may apply for medical care benefits for an additional injury or disease:

- where medical care is needed as an injury or a disease, which has arisen from the work-related accident, is additionally found;
- where medical care is needed to deal with an ailment that has occurred as a result of the initial injury or disease, which in turn arose from the work-related accident.

If a person who has previously received medical care benefits relapses into their former work-related injury or disease and is once again subject to medical care after their initial recovery or, if due to the deterioration of the injury or disease, there is a medical opinion that he or she needs active medical care to treat it, he or she may receive medical care again.

502. Nursing benefits shall be paid to those who received medical care benefits pursuant to Article 40 and, due to constant or frequent nursing needs after medical care, receives actual nursing services.

B. Wage Replacement Benefits

503. Wage replacement benefits shall be paid to any worker who is injured or contracts a disease due to work-related activities for that period during which the worker concerned is unable to work due to the need to receive medical care, and the amount to be paid shall be calculated on a daily basis at an amount equivalent to 70/100 of the average wages: provided that if the period of not being able to work is three days or less, then they shall not be paid.

504. If a worker who is undergoing either medical care or additional medical care but returns to employment for a certain period or works part–time, he or she may be paid 90 per cent of the amount due as calculated by subtracting those wages paid for either days or hours employed from the average wage corresponding to the number of days or hours for which he or she is employed.

For a person who receives additional medical care, an amount equivalent to 70 percent of the average wage, calculated on the basis of the wage at the time of the receipt of additional medical care, shall be the daily wage replacement benefits.

C. Disability Benefits

505. Disability benefits shall be paid to any worker who has a continuing disability after receiving medical care due to injuries or diseases sustained in work–related situations.

Disability benefits shall be paid in the form of a disability compensation annuity or as a lump sum disability compensation payment with regard to the grade of disability, and the criteria for such grades of disablement are prescribed by presidential decree. The choice between an annuity or a lump sum shall be made by the person entitled to receive such payments. However a worker who disability falls within those grades, as prescribed by presidential decree which are characterized as a complete loss of work ability, shall be paid a disability compensation annuity. In addition a worker who was not a Korean national when the incident leading to the claim occurred and resides in a foreign country shall receive a lump sum disability compensation.

506. Any person whose grade of disability alters, following the point at which they were deemed to be cured, may request an adjustment of that grade, or the relevant corporation may do so on its own authority, in any instance where the situation has improved or worsened.

D. Survivors' Benefits

507. Survivors' benefits shall be paid to the surviving family members of any worker who has died as a result of work-related activities. Survivors' benefits shall be paid in the form of a survivors' compensation annuity or as a lump sum.

Those who are qualified to receive survivors' compensation annuities shall be the worker's spouse (including a person in a *de facto* marital relationship) and those falling under any of the following sub-paragraphs among their surviving family members (excluding surviving family members who are not Korean nationals or were living in a foreign country at the time of his or her death) whose livelihood was dependent on the income of the worker concerned at the time of his or her death. In this case, the criteria for judging which surviving family members livelihood was so supported shall be prescribed by presidential decree:

- the spouse (including a person in a *de facto* marital relationship), parents and grandparents aged 60 or older;
- children and grandchildren aged less than 25;
- brothers and sisters aged less than 18, or aged 60 or older, etc.

E. Injury or Disease Compensation Annuity

508. If a worker who has received medical care benefits, continues to be in a state that meets all of the requirements described in the following sub-paragraphs, following two years since the start of medical care, he or she shall be paid an injury or disease compensation annuity instead of a wage replacement benefit:

- the injury or disease remains uncured;
- the degree of invalidity caused by the wound or disease meets the standards for invalidity grades as prescribed by presidential decree.

F. Funeral Expenses

509. Funeral expenses shall be paid if a worker has died due to one or more work-related accidents, and an amount equivalent to 120 days of the worker's average wages shall be paid to the surviving family member who performs the funeral service providing if there is no surviving family member who performs the funeral service or a person other than surviving family members has performed the funeral service for inevitable reasons, the amount actually spent within the limits of an amount equivalent to 120 days of the average wages shall be paid to the person who has performed the funeral service.

G. Vocational Rehabilitation Benefits

510. The types of vocational rehabilitation benefit are as follows:

- vocational training allowances and the costs of providing vocational training for those who need such training to be reemployed and have been recipients of disability benefits;
- the return-to-work subsidy, work adaption training costs, rehabilitation exercise costs – which are paid if an employer retains, or carries out work adaptation training or a rehabilitation exercise programme – for recipients of disability benefits who have returned to the same workplace where the work–related accident happened.

H. Lump-sum Payment of Insurance Benefits

511. If a worker who is not a Korean national applies for the lump-sum for the payment of insurance benefits with the intention of departing from Korea while receiving medical care due to an injury or disease resulting from a work-related accident before it is cured, the insurance benefits which are expected to be claimed following the application day may be paid in a lump sum.

The amount which may be paid in a lump sum is the sum of each amount as follows:

- medical care benefits from the day when an application is made for a lump-sum payment to the day when the injury or disease resulting from the work-related accident is expected to be cured;
- wage replacement benefits or injury or disease compensation annuities from the day when an application is made for the said lump-sum payment to the day before the worker is expected to find employment;
- disability benefits corresponding to the grade of the disability expected to remain after the injury or disease resulting from the work-related accident is cured.

I. Special Disability Benefits and Special Survivors' Benefits

512. If a worker has sustained any disability falling under the grades of disability prescribed by presidential decree due to a work-related accident caused by the intention or due to the negligence of the insurance subscriber, if the entitled person claims special disability benefits in lieu of a claim for damages as prescribed by the Civil Act, special disability benefits, as prescribed by presidential decree, may be paid in addition to the disability benefits. This shall only apply in cases where the worker and the insurance subscriber reach an agreement on special disability benefits.

If an entitled person receives special disability benefits, he or she shall not bring the claim for damages under the Civil Act or other Acts – and subordinate statutes – against the insurance subscriber for the same cause.

If a worker has died due to a work–related accident caused by the intention or negligence of the insurance subscriber, if the entitled person claims special survivors' benefits in lieu of a claim for damages as prescribed by the Civil Act, the special survivors' benefits prescribed by presidential decree may be paid in addition to the survivors' benefits referred to in Article 62, provided that this shall apply only in cases where the worker and the insurance subscriber have reached an agreement with regard to Special Survivors' Benefits.

If an entitled person receives Special Survivors' Benefits, he or she shall not bring the claim for damages under the Civil Act or other Acts – and subordinate statutes – against the insurance subscriber for the same cause.

V. The Relationship to Other Forms of Compensation or Indemnity

513. If an entitled person was paid or may be paid insurance benefits pursuant to this Act, the insurance subscriber shall be exempted from the liability for accident compensation as prescribed by the LSA for the same cause.

Furthermore, if an entitled person has received insurance benefits pursuant to this Act for the same cause, the insurance subscriber shall be exempted from the liability for indemnity as prescribed by the Civil Act and other Acts and subordinate statutes, to the extent of that amount. In this case, a person who receives a disability or survivors' compensation annuity shall be considered to have received a lump sum disability or survivors' compensation.

If an entitled person has received under the Civil Act or other Acts and subordinate statutes, money or valuable goods equivalent to the insurance benefits as prescribed by this Act, for the same cause, the corporation shall not pay the insurance benefits as prescribed by this Act to the extent of the amount calculated by converting the money and valuable goods received according to the method as prescribed by the relevant presidential decree.

If a worker who receives medical care benefits receives an injury/disease compensation annuity after three years have passed since the start of the medical care, the employer concerned shall be considered to have paid the lump sum of compensation as prescribed by the LSA on the day that three years have elapsed since the initial payment.

VI. Claims for Damages Against a Third Person

514. If the corporation concerned has paid insurance benefits for an accident caused by a third person's act, it may subrogate the right of the person who has received the benefits to file a damages claim against that third person within the limits of the benefit amount.

VII. Protection of Right to Benefits

515. The right of a worker to receive insurance benefits shall not be extinguished by his or her retirement. The right to receive insurance benefits shall not be transferred, seized or offered as collateral.

VIII. Request for Examination and Re-examination

A. *Request for Examination*

516. A person who is dissatisfied with decisions, etc., by the corporation, falling under any of the following matters, may make a request for examination to the corporation:

- decisions on the insurance benefits;
- decisions on the medical expenses;
- decisions on the medicine expenses;
- measures, etc., to change a medical treatment plan;
- decisions on the lump-sum payment of insurance benefits;
- decisions on the collection of undue gains;
- decisions on the subrogation of the right to receive benefits.

B. Request for Re-examination

517. A person, who is dissatisfied with a decision on a request for examination, may make a request for reexamination to the Industrial Accident Compensation Insurance Reexamination Committee within the Ministry of Employment and Labour as prescribed in Article 107.

IX. Prescription

518. If the right to receive insurance benefits under this Act has not been exercised for three years, it shall become extinct by prescription.

§4. The Purpose and Reasons for the ISHA and Related Legislation

519. A worker's life, body and health are, obviously, very important to him or her. How to prevent these from being harmed in the course of employment is the major concern of this law.

520. According to labour law, the employer is under an obligation to guarantee employees' safety, while the workers should take corresponding precautions. As seen already, in Korean labour law, there are many safety and health-related laws (ISHA, LSA, IACIA, the Act on the Prevention of Pneumoconiosis and Protection, etc., of Pneumoconiosis Workers, and so forth) and related provisions to secure safety and health in the workplace itself, and thereby prevent workers' accidents.

521. The ISHA of 1990 can be considered the immediate and primary Act as it sets minimum standards for safety and health. Under the terms of the LSA, the safety and health of workers shall be subject to those conditions as prescribed by the ISHA.[488]

522. The purpose of the ISHA is to maintain and promote the safety and health of workers by preventing industrial accidents and diseases through establishing standards relating to industrial safety and health, clarifying where the responsibility lies for maintaining them, and by creating a comfortable work environment. (Article 1).[489] To implement workplace safety and health, it also imposes a duty, backed up by penal sanctions, upon persons involved in the manufacture and circulation of dangerous machinery and harmful materials, and upon general contractors and their clients with regard to hazardous construction practices.

523. The ISHA defines 'worker' as it is defined under the LSA, and defines an enterprise as 'one who carries on an enterprise and employs workers'. This law is,

488. LSA, Article 76.
489. ISHA, Article 1.

therefore, not directed at the 'employer', but rather regulates the 'entrepreneur' (ultimately corresponding to the 'owner of an enterprise' (paragraph 2 LSA).[490]

I. Basic Provisions

A. The Scope of Application

524. This ISHA shall apply to all businesses or workplaces, excepting that this Act may not apply wholly or partially to businesses as prescribed by presidential decree which will take into consideration the degree of hazard and danger innate within the business, the nature and scale of the business, the location of business, etc.

525. This Act and any order issued under this Act shall apply to the state, local governments, and government-invested institutions.[491]

B. Duties of the Government, the Employer and the Worker

526. In order to accomplish the goals of the ISHA, the government must faithfully fulfil the following responsibilities:[492]

- matters concerning the establishment, execution, coordination and control of the occupational safety and health policy;
- matters concerning support and guidance relating to accident and disease prevention within workplaces where accidents and diseases occur frequently;
- matters concerning the assessment of safety and the subsequent improvement of harmful and dangerous machinery, tools or equipment as well as protective devices and personal protective equipment, etc.;
- matters concerning the preparation of specific criteria for safety and health measures and those providing guidance relating to the control of hazardous or dangerous machinery, tools, equipment and materials, etc.;
- matters concerning support for the establishment of autonomous safety and health management system by workplaces;
- matters concerning the promotion of public relations, education, and accident-reduction campaigns to raise public awareness about safety and health;
- matters concerning research into and the subsequent development of technology as well as the the installation and operation of facilities for the enhancement of safety and health;
- matters concerning the maintenance and management of investigations and statistics relating to industrial accidents and diseases;

490. Kazuo Sugeno, *op. cit.*, p. 339.
491. Article 3.
492. Article 4.

- matters concerning the support, guidance and control of organizations related to safety and health;
- other matters concerning measures for the prevention of dangers and health problems for workers.

527. The government must consider policies to carry out effectively the above matters, and if it is deemed necessary, may provide the Korea Occupational Safety and Health Agency and other related organizations and institutes with administrative and financial support.[493]

528. An employer must observe the standards for the prevention of industrial accidents and diseases as prescribed by this Act and any order issued under this Act, provide workers with information on safety and health in the workplace, prevent workers developing health problems as a result of physical fatigue or mental stress, safeguard their lives, maintain and promote the safety and health of workers by creating a proper working environment through the improvement of working conditions, and comply with the industrial accident and disease prevention policy executed by the state. Any person who designs, manufactures or imports machinery, tools and other equipment, who manufactures or imports raw materials, or who designs or builds any construction, shall observe the standards as prescribed by this Act and orders issued under this Act in carrying out such design, manufacture, import or construction, and strive to prevent the occurrence of industrial accidents and diseases caused by the use of these objects.[494]

529. All workers shall observe the standards for the prevention of industrial accidents and diseases as prescribed by this Act and orders issued under this Act, and they are further subject to measures taken for the prevention of industrial accidents and diseases by the employer or other related organizations.[495]

C. *Safety and Health Management Systems*

1. Safety and Health Managers

530. An employer must assign a safety and health manager to be in charge of safety and health management.[496]

a. Supervisors

531. In addition, an employer shall have the supervisor of any workplace take the responsibility for carrying out measures concerning safety and health as prescribed by presidential decree, such as safety and health inspections. For work – as

493. Article 4.
494. Article 5.
495. Article 6.
496. Article 13.

prescribed by presidential decree – which is deemed particularly dangerous, the designated individual shall perform measures concerning safety and health – again prescribed by presidential decree – such as special education for assigned personnel. The term 'supervisor' refers to the head of a division within any given management structure, who directly manages and supervises business and employees related to production or who takes charge of such a position; hereinafter the same definition shall apply.[497]

b. Safety managers

532. An employer shall designate a safety manager for the workplace to assist the employer or the safety and health manager in technical matters concerning safety, and to instruct and give advice to the supervisor or person responsible for safety on such matters.[498]

c. Health managers

533. An employer shall assign a health manager for the workplace to assist the employer or the safety and health manager in technical matters concerning health, and to instruct and give advice to the supervisor or person responsible for health on such matters.[499]

d. Industrial physicians

534. An employer shall assign an occupational physician to the workplace for the purpose of guiding the health management of workers and the other duties of the health manager, except in cases where the designated health manager is themselves a doctor.[500]

e. General safety and health managers

535. Any employer, a part of whose business is carried out under a contract at the same place, and which is prescribed by presidential decree, shall designate the safety and health manager for the business as the general safety and health manager for the purpose of the general control over the prevention of industrial accidents and diseases that may take place when workers employed by the employer and those employed by his or her contractor (including any subcontractors) work together at the same place. In the case of an employer whose business is not required to assign a safety and health manager, they shall designate the person who exercises general control over the business at the workplace as a general safety and health manager.[501]

497. Article 14.
498. Article 15.
499. Article 16.
500. Article 17.
501. Article 18.

2. Industrial Safety and Health Committees

536. In order to deliberate over or to resolve important matters concerning occupational safety and health, an employer shall establish and operate an occupational safety and health committee composed of an equal number of workers and employers.[502]

537. In order to maintain safety and health in workplace, an employer shall prepare safety and health management regulations in relation to the following matters, post or keep them in workplace, and notify all members of their workforce:[503]

- matters concerning the safety and health management organization and its functions;
- matters concerning safety and health education;
- matters concerning safety management within the workplace;
- matters concerning health management within the workplace;
- matters concerning accident investigations and the formulation of accident prevention plans.
- other matters concerning safety and health.

538. The safety and health management regulations shall not be contrary to any collective agreement or work rules which are applicable to the workplace concerned. In the case that any part of the safety and health management regulations are contrary to such agreements or rules, it shall be subject to the standards as set out within the agreement or rules.

§5. Observance, etc., of Safety and Health Management Regulations

539. An employer and workers shall observe safety and health management regulations. Except as provided fort by this Act, the provisions of the LSA concerning employment regulations shall be applicable to safety and health management regulations, unless they are contrary to the nature thereof.[504]

I. Measures for Preventing Hazards and Danger

A. Safety Measures and Health Measures

540. An employer shall take all measures necessary for the prevention of hazards in operating their business. An employer shall take measures necessary for the

502. Article 19.
503. Article 20.
504. Article 22.

prevention of hazards caused by improper working methods in excavating, quarrying, lumber-jacking, transporting, operating, dismantling, the handing of heavy objects, and other work.

541. An employer shall take measures necessary for the prevention of hazards in places where workers might fall down, where sand or structures, etc. might collapse, where material objects might fall or come flying off, or any other hazard that may be anticipated, in the course of carrying out work, due to natural disasters or acts of God.[505]

542. An employer shall take the measures necessary for the prevention of the health problems caused the operation of their business.[506]

B. Suspension, etc., of Work

543. If there is an imminent danger that an industrial accident or disease may occur, or that a serious accident and disease has occurred, an employer shall take necessary measures for the preservation of safety and health, such as the immediate suspension of operations, the evacuation of workers from the workplace, and so on, and only then may work be resumed. If any worker suspends their work and takes shelter due to an urgent risk of industrial accident or disease, he or she shall report it without delay to their immediate superior officer, who shall take appropriate measures to address the situation. If there are reasonable grounds to believe that there exists any imminent danger of an industrial accident and disease, an employer shall not mistreat or dismiss the workers concerned, on the basis that they have suspended their work and taken shelter.[507]

C. Prohibition of Contract for Hazardous Work

544. Sectors of work deemed to be particularly hazardous or dangerous to workers' safety and health – as prescribed by presidential decree – may not be tendered out for contract (including a subcontract) without obtaining the approval of the Minister of Employment and Labour.[508]

D. Safety and Health Measures for Contracting Businesses

545. The owner of a business, part of whose work is done under a contract and which is designated by presidential decree, shall take the following measures with

505. Article 23.
506. Article 24.
507. Article 26.
508. Article 28.

the purpose of preventing industrial accidents and diseases which may occur when those employed by the owner and those employed by the contractor work together in the same place.[509]

E. *Safety and Health Education*

546. An employer shall periodically conduct safety and health education for the workers engaged at their place of business. In addition, when an employer initially employs a worker, or when the nature of their work changes significantly, the employer shall conduct education for the workers relating to the safety and health issues related to their work. When an employer employs workers for a particularly hazardous or dangerous job, he shall conduct special education on the safety and health issues related to the work they are undertaking.[510]

II. Safety Inspections

547. An employer who uses hazardous or dangerous machines, instruments or equipment ('hazardous or dangerous machines, etc'. shall request an inspection, administered by the Minister of Employment and Labour, on whether the safety performance of hazardous or dangerous machines, etc. meets the inspection standard ('safety inspection').

548. Hazardous or dangerous machines, etc. falling under any of the following categories shall not be used:

- hazardous or dangerous machines, etc. which have not received a safety inspection (excluding a case where a safety inspection is exempted pursuant to the proviso of paragraph (1)); and
- hazardous or dangerous machines, etc. which have failed to pass a safety inspection.[511]

III. Prohibition of Manufacturing, etc.

549. No person shall manufacture, import, transfer, offer or use the substances falling under any of the following categories and those determined by presidential decree:

- substances proven to cause occupational cancers and identified as especially hazardous to workers' health;

509. Article 29.
510. Article 31.
511. Article 36.

– substances likely to cause significant health problems to workers based on the results of risk assessment under Article 39 or Article 40.[512]

IV. Management, etc. of Hazardous Agents

550. The Minister of Employment and Labour shall classify and manage the use of chemicals, physical agents, etc. causing health problems to workers ('hazardous agents') according to the classification standards as determined by the Ordinance of the Ministry of Employment and Labour.

551. The Minister of Employment and Labour shall set occupational exposure limits for the hazardous agents and announce them in an official gazette, etc.[513]

V. Compliance with the Permission Standards for Hazardous Agents

552. As for hazardous agents as prescribed by presidential decree, which could cause serious health problems to workers, such as a carcinogen, an employer shall maintain the exposure density of the agents within the workplace below the level of the permission standards determined by the Ordinance of the Ministry of Employment and Labour.[514]

VI. Hazard and Risk Evaluation of a New Chemical

553. Any employer who desires to manufacture or import any chemical other than those prescribed by presidential decree ('new chemical'), shall submit to the Minister of Employment and Labour a hazard and risk evaluation report on the new chemical, to prevent any health problems for their workers which may be caused by the chemical, as prescribed by presidential decree.[515]

VII. Preparation and Maintenance, etc. of Material Safety Data Sheet

554. If an employer desires to manufacture, import, use, transport or store any chemical or preparations containing chemicals, he or she shall prepare in advance data specifying all the following matters ('material safety data sheet'), and post and maintain such information in a work area where it can be seen easily by workers handling substances concerned:

512. Article 37.
513. Article 39.
514. Article 39-2.
515. Article 40.

- the name, ingredients and composition of the chemical;
- handling precautions which ensure safety and health;
- health and ecological hazards identifications; and
- other matters as determined by the Ordinance of the Ministry of Employment and Labour.[516]

§6. HEALTH MANAGEMENT OF WORKERS

I. Monitoring of the Working Environment, etc.

555. An employer shall have the person holding the qualification determined by the Ordinance of the Ministry of Employment and Labour monitor and evaluate the working environment of places of business where work which is potentially hazardous to workers' health is carried out as determined by the Ordinance of the Ministry of Employment and Labour, and then record and keep the results and report them to the Minister of Employment and Labour. In such cases, if the workers' representative requests, he or she shall allow the workers' representative to observe the process of monitoring.[517] The Minister of Employment and Labour may, if it is deemed necessary to assess the accuracy and precision of the results of such monitoring, conduct a reliability assessment.[518]

II. Health Examinations

556. An employer shall conduct health examinations for workers at an institution designated by the Minister of Employment and Labour or an institution conducting a health examination in accordance with the National Health Insurance Act ('health examination institution') to protect and maintain workers' health. If there is a request from a workers' representative, the employer shall allow the workers' representative to attend the health examination.

557. Workers shall undergo health examinations requested by the employer. When the examination is complete and the results are known the employer shall notify the relevant workers of the result without delay and report it to the Minister of Employment and Labour.

558. If it is deemed necessary for the protection of the health of all workers, the Minister of Employment and Labour may order an employer to conduct a preemptive health examination of specific workers or to take other necessary measures.[519]

516. Article 41.
517. Article 42.
518. Article 42-2.
519. Article 43.

III. Disease Investigation

559. The Minister of Employment and Labour may, if deemed necessary for the diagnosis of occupational diseases and the identification of the causes of the diseases or, alternatively, the prevention of occupational diseases, conduct an investigation ('disease investigation') on any possible correlations between the workers' diseases and the hazardous elements of their workplace. In the case that a disease investigation is conducted, the employer or the worker concerned shall fully cooperate with the investigation.[520]

IV. Prohibition of, or Restrictions on, the Work of Sick Persons

560. With respect to a person who is affected by an infectious or mental disease, or a disease which might grow worse due to work and which is prescribed by the Ordinance of the Ministry of Employment and Labour, the employer shall prohibit or restrict the work according to the diagnosis of a doctor. When an employee whose work has been prohibited or restricted, regains his or her health, the employer shall, without delay, allow him or her to resume their work.[521]

V. Restriction on Employment by Qualification

561. For hazardous or dangerous work which is prescribed by the Ordinance of the Ministry of Employment and Labour, the employer shall not allow any person other than those who have the qualifications, licence, experience or skills required for that work, to perform it.[522]

§7. SUPERVISION AND ORDER

I. Submission, etc., of Hazard and Danger Prevention Plan

562. If an employer, operating a business of the category and scale as prescribed by the Ordinance of the Ministry of Employment and Labour, installs or moves any structure, machinery, instrument or equipment related to the business concerned, or alters major structural parts thereof, he shall prepare and submit to the Minister of Employment and Labour a plan for preventing any hazard or danger prescribed by this Act, or orders issued under this Act ('hazard and danger prevention plan') as prescribed by the Ordinance of the Ministry of Employment and Labour.[523]

520. Article 43-2.
521. Article 45.
522. Article 47.
523. Article 48.

II. Safety and Health Diagnoses

563. The Minister of Employment and Labour may order any such workplaces as are prescribed by Ordinance of the Ministry of Employment and Labour to undergo a safety and health diagnosis conducted by those who are designated by the Minister of Employment and Labour ('safety and health diagnosis institution'). An employer shall cooperate positively with these activities, and shall not refuse, interfere with or evade such activities without justifiable reason.[524]

III. Submission, etc. of a Process Safety Report

564. The designated employer within any workplace using hazardous or dangerous equipment – as prescribed by the presidential decree – shall prepare and submit a process safety report to the Minister of Employment and Labour and keep a copy of it in the workplace, with the aim of preventing any accident which could inflict immediate damage on workers either within the workplace or areas within its immediate vicinity, due to dangerous substances from such equipment leaking, catching fire, exploding, etc. ('the serious industrial accident') as prescribed by presidential decree.[525]

IV. Safety and Health Improvement Plans

565. If it is deemed necessary to take comprehensive improvement measures for the prevention of industrial accidents and diseases with respect to workplaces, facilities and related issues, the Minister of Employment and Labour may order an employer to formulate and execute a safety and health improvement plan with relation to those workplaces, facilities or other matters as prescribed by the Ordinance of the Ministry of Employment and Labour.

566. When the Minister of Employment and Labour issues such an order, he or she may, if it is deemed necessary, order the employer to undergo a safety and health diagnosis and to formulate and submit a safety and health improvement plan, as prescribed by the Ordinance of the Ministry of Employment and Labour.[526]

V. Supervisory Measures

567. A labour inspector may, when it is necessary to execute an action under this Act or any orders issued under this Act, as determined by the Ordinance of the Ministry of Employment and Labour, enter any workplace etc., to ask questions to the persons concerned, carry out an inspection of their books, documents and other

524. Article 49.
525. Article 49-2.
526. Article 50.

materials, check out the safety and health situation, and remove products, raw materials or apparatuses from the workplace to any extent necessary for the inspection without being charged. In such cases, the labour inspector shall notify the employer concerned, etc. of the results in writing.[527]

VI. Requests for the Suspension of Business

568. In cases concerning industrial accidents or diseases which under any of the following considerations, and the where causes are attributable to the employer, have occurred, the Minister of Employment and Labour may make a request for the suspension of related work or other sanctions as prescribed in the provisions of relevant Acts and subordinate statutes to the head of the administrative agency concerned, or he make a request to the head of a government-invested institution for the necessary restrictions regarding orders about work to be put in place by the concerned institution:

- when accidents prescribed by presidential decree occur, such as those resulting in deaths of a large number of workers or serious damage to a district neighbouring the working area;
- when work in contravention of the order costs a worker his or her life.[528]

VII. Reports to a Supervisory Body

569. If an act violating this Act, or an order issued under this Act, occurs at a workplace, any worker may report it to the Minister of Employment and Labour or a labour inspector. No employer shall dismiss or mistreat a worker for making such a report.[529]

527. Article 51.
528. Article 51-2.
529. Article 52.

Chapter 6. The Termination of Individual Labour Contracts

§1. Job Security and the Right to Work

I. Freedom in Matters of Hiring and Restrictions on Dismissal

570. As stated above, Korean law and courts permit employers to exercise broad discretion with regard to hiring. At the same time, once an employment relationship is formed with such broad discretion, the cancellation of those employment relations or dismissal is strictly limited by the law and by case law.

II. The Right to Work and Restrictions on Dismissal

571. The Constitution declares the right to work as a fundamental human right of all Korean people.[530] This raises the question of whether Article 32 of the Constitution can also be interpreted as a basis for restricting the employer's right to dismiss their workers. Opinions are divided. Some deny it on the grounds that the right to work governs only the relationship between the state and the people, not that between the employer and the worker. However, the majority opinion seems to confirm that it does have such an implication. It is true that the freedom to dismiss, together with the freedom to conclude contracts, is one of the fundamental legal principles of the capitalist system. However, if Article 32 of the Constitution were not applied to the relations between labour and capital, the provision would lose most of its significance. Thus, the decisions of the courts often proclaim that the employer must respect this provision as guaranteeing job security and not abuse their right to dismiss employees. The courts often require a proven just cause, even in instances where the dismissal takes place with notice. In such situations, whenever they find it to be illegal, the courts declare the dismissal null and void as it is in violation of the Constitution. As a result, a dismissed worker can continue with the employment contract (reinstatement) unless s/he prefers to claim damages instead. However, the wisdom of this legal principle may not be so satisfactory as one imagines, for reinstated workers often do not remain long in their old jobs because of the damage done to their personal relationship with management and their former colleagues.[531]

530. Article 32, paragraph 1 of the Constitution.
531. Chi Sun Kim, *op. cit.*, pp. 67 to 68.

III. Ending the Contract by Means Other than Dismissal

A. *The Expiry of a Labour Contract after a Fixed Period*

572. Every lawful labour contract with a fixed periods generally expire when that period come to an end. This principle of civil law cannot be sustained unconditionally in labour law. If labour relations were to cease only because of the expiration of the period, as fixed in the contract, and without a further, objective reason, this would contradict the basic purpose of restricting dismissal.

573. Successive contracts are illegal. However, this does not mean that they are null and void. They are only regarded as having no term of contract, and an employer should renew the contract as long as there is no inevitable social or economic reason to terminate it.[532] When a worker continues to work after the period fixed in the contract, without any objection from the employer, the contract is regarded as having been tacitly renewed (Civil Code, Article 662).

574. Where there is such a labour contract with a fixed period, however, the actual continuation of the labour relationship will cause the contract to be renewed by implication. After such a contract has been repeatedly renewed it will resemble a contract without a fixed period, and the legal principles governing a abusive dismissal will be applicable by analogy to a refusal to renew the contract.[533]

B. *Consensual Termination*

575. A consensual contract termination refers to an agreement between a worker and an employer to prospectively terminate a labour contract and is not subject to the dismissal rules of the LSA or the legal principles governing abusive dismissals. It is subject, however, to the Civil Code provisions dealing with legal acts (e.g., expression of intention) and a variety of other legal principles.[534]

C. *Resignations*

576. A resignation is a termination of the labour contract by the worker. If the contract is one without a fixed period, the worker may terminate it at any time (i.e. without any reason). Termination of the contract by the worker is no matter of concern in labour law. According to the provisions of the Civil Code, an employee may terminate a contract with one month's notice, or even without notice if there is an unavoidable reason. A termination to which both parties agree is not a dismissal, and therefore not regulated by the restrictions on dismissal in the LSA. However, because of the inequality between employer and worker, there is the possibility that

532. Chi Sun Kim, *op. cit.*, p. 68
533. Kazuo Sugeno, *op. cit.*, p. 460.
534. *Ibid.*

the agreement has, in fact, been forced on the worker by the employer to avoid the restrictions on dismissal. Thus, the courts should examine this possibility carefully; and if they deem it to be so, the rules relating to dismissal must be applied regardless of the form of any agreement.[535]

D. Mandatory Retirement Systems

577. A mandatory retirement system refers to a system under which a labour contract terminates when the worker reaches a certain age. A mandatory retirement system is universally adopted by Korean firms.

IV. Extinction of a Party

A. Death of a Party

578. Where the employer is an individual and dies, or where a worker dies, there is no alternative but to terminate the contract because their status under the labour contract is as exclusive individuals and cannot be inherited.[536]

B. Extinction of One's Status as a Juridical Person (Dissolution)

579. Where the employer is a juridical person, and its status as such is dissolved, its labour contracts will be terminated by no later than the liquidation of its estate (i.e. its extinction as a juridical person). Until then, its labour contracts can usually be canceled (i.e. by dismissal).[537] In the case of a corporate employer, the death of the representative or a change in the legal form of the corporate employer does not affect the contractual relationship. Only the dissolution of the legal personality will end the contract.

V. Reorganization of Enterprises and Labour Contracts

A. Merger of Companies and Labour Contracts

580. In the case of a merger of companies or a transfer of business, the matter in question is somewhat delicate. If there is a merger of companies, the majority view is that the contract concluded by the merged company passes to the new company or to the company which has taken over, for the business property of the former is inclusively handed over to the latter.

535. Chi Sun Kim, *op. cit.*, p. 69.
536. Kazuo Sugeno, *op. cit.*, p. 464.
537. *Ibid.*

B. The Transfer of Business and Labour Contracts

581. In the case of a transfer of business, the majority opinion contends that the business property is handed over individually; and therefore the labour relationship is not necessarily transferred to the transferee, apart from when she or he consents to continue the labour relationship by mutual agreement with the workers. In the field of labour law, the question is how to ensure that labour relations continue regardless of consent between the party transferring the business and the transferee, in order to protect the workers from collective unemployment. Recently, many scholars have affirmed the transference of labour relations without consent between the transferer and the transferee on the grounds that, in most cases, a simple alteration in the employer does not affect the substance of labour service. However, when labour relations are based upon a strong human relationship or when a new company cannot maintain the organization of the former, this theory leaves many problems awaiting solutions. On the other hand, when a change in name, form or ownership of the enterprise proves to be an intentional avoidance of the law, the courts will declare the continuance of the contract with the real successor as long as they can identify it.[538]

§2. Restrictions on Dismissal

I. Introduction

582. Dismissal means the termination of a labour contract unilaterally by the employer regardless of – or rather, against – the worker's will. Generally speaking, there are two reasons for dismissal. When an enterprise is in decline, the employer may need to reduce the number of workers by dismissing those who have become redundant (collective dismissal). In addition, when a worker violates a company's discipline policy or proves not to manifest the expected ability, an employer would rather dismiss him or her and hire a replacement (individual dismissal). In these respects, dismissal is very convenient and useful for the employer. However, at the same time, to the employee it means the loss of their job and a resulting threat to his or her livelihood. In addition, an increase in the unemployment rate is not only undesirable for the state economy but also causes serious social unrest. The Civil Code requires an unavoidable reason to terminate an employment contract without notice. With one month's notice, an employer is free to terminate it even without cause. Labour law modifies this civil law principle and lays down several restrictions on dismissal which will be explained in the following section.[539]

538. Chi Sun Kim, *op. cit.*, p. 68.
539. *Ibid.*, p. 69.

A. Characteristics of Legal Protection for Employment Security

583. As stated above, Korean law and courts permit employers to exercise broad discretion with regard to hiring. At the same time, once an employment relationship is formed using such broad discretion, the cancellation of those employment relations or dismissal is strictly limited by both statute and case law.

584. The most important characteristics of legal protection for employment security, or restraint on dismissals, is imposed by legislation (statutes). Like most European countries, there is a statute that generally requires just cause for dismissals in Korea. Statutes regulate employers' freedom to dismiss. Under the current statutes, several provisions restring dismissal exist:

- restrictions on dismissal, etc;[540]
- restrictions on the timing of dismissal;[541]
- restrictions on dismissal for managerial reasons[542] and preferential re-employment;[543]
- requirement for advance notice of dismissal[544] and exceptions to that requirement;[545]
- the requirement for a written notification of the reasons for dismissal;[546]
- the process for application for remedy in the case of unfair dismissal and related acts[547] – investigations, etc.,[548] remedy orders, etc.,[549] – and the Subsequent confirmation of said remedy orders, etc.,[550] and the effects of remedy orders, etc.[551]

B. Restrictions on Dismissal, etc., and Reasons for Dismissal – 'Just Cause'

1. Legislative Restrictions on Dismissals

585. There are legal provisions restricting the employers' freedom to dismiss their workers. The LSA provides that 'No employer shall dismiss, lay off, suspend, or transfer a worker, or reduce their wages, or take other punitive measures ("unfair dismissal, etc.") against a worker without justifiable reasons'.[552]

540. Article 23.
541. Article 23 paragraph 2.
542. Article 24
543. Article 25.
544. Article 26.
545. Article 35.
546. Article 27.
547. Article 28.
548. Article 29.
549. Article 30.
550. Article 31.
551. Article 32.
552. Article 23 paragraph 1.

586. Therefore, current written laws require employers to demonstrate the existence of just cause for dismissal, other similar actions.

587. Korean courts recognize the protection of workers from arbitrary dismissal, etc. Such a dismissal, or similar act, without just cause should be held to be void. An objectively unreasonable or socially unacceptable punitive decision is an abuse of the right to dismiss. Under this provisions, an employer must demonstrate the existence of just cause. If an employer has dismissed an employee without just cause, the dismissal is null and void legally, and a punitive provision (LSA, Article 110) applies thereto.

2. Reasons for Dismissal, etc. – 'Just Cause'

588. Although the LSA provides that the employer cannot dismiss an employee without just cause, it remains silent as to what 'just cause' means. 'Just cause' may be established in work rules or by collective agreements as an internal standard for dismissal. However, to obtain substantial justice, they should pass legal evaluation. Legal theories often categorize just cause in a manner that distinguishes between personal reasons, behavioural reasons and managerial reasons.

589. Personal reasons include such situations as a lack of vocational aptitude, the performance of a defective labour service, kinship with the owner of a rival company, malignant disease, etc. Behavioural reasons include breach of contract, poor relations with colleagues, violating the company's discipline policy, and other difficulties with management. Managerial reasons include management rationalization to reduce expenses, partial shutdown or reduction in operating hours caused by shortages of raw materials or a sales ban. If we classify these reasons into the circumstances of the employee and those of the employer, the first and second belong to the former, while the third belongs to the latter; and an individual dismissal usually results from the former, while collective dismissals result from the latter.[553]

590. Just cause should be judged on the grounds of generally accepted social ideas. If a collective agreement or a work rule stipulates a dismissal procedure (such as affording the opportunity of making a statement to the employee), a dismissal which has ignored it cannot be a just one – even if there is a just cause. A dismissal which does not indicate the reasons for dismissal clearly and concretely is also null and void. And as aforesaid, even in a contract for a definite period, a refusal to renew a labour contract should be identified as a dismissal without just cause when the renewal is normal practice in the company and when there is no necessary reason to refuse it. A similar problem may arise in case of any designated probationary period.[554]

553. Chi Sun Kim, *op. cit.*, p. 70.
554. *Ibid.*

591. Apart from the ambiguous concept of 'just cause', current labour law prohibits dismissal for the following specific reasons. In each case, dismissal contrary to these provisions is null and void:

1. an employer must not dismiss a worker on the grounds that she or he has joined or tried to join a trade union, has attempted to organize a union or has engaged in justifiable acts for the operation of a union (TULRAA, Article 81);
2. an employer shall not dismiss a worker on the grounds that she or he has joined in a legitimate collective action, has reported to, or given a testimony to, the labour committee that the employer has violated the provisions of this article, or has presented evidence of such violation to the administrative office (TULRAA, Article 81) - the details of (1)and (2) will be described below as unfair labour practice);
3. since Article 6 of the LSA lays down the principle of equal treatment, an employer cannot dismiss an employee for reasons of sex, marriage, nationality, religion or social status.

592. When the legal effect of an individual dismissal is challenged in court, the worker's claim should be either that it is based of his or her political or religious creed, union activity, sex, nationality or race; or that the dismissal is an abuse of the employer's right to dismiss. And the employer will submit some reasonable cause for the dismissal in order to refute the worker's argument. Theoretically speaking, the burden of proof is on the worker according to the normal rules of civil procedure. However, considering the difficulty of proving someone's intentions, the courts often switches the burden of proof to the employer if some circumstantial evidence is submitted. Taking into account the seriousness of the effect of dismissal on the worker, the courts interpret 'just cause' rather strictly. A worker's inefficiency, laziness or other minor misconduct does not constitute 'just cause' for dismissal.[555]

3. Restrictions of Dismissal for Managerial Reasons

593. Where an employer has dismissed workers in accordance with the requirements as set forth under the following criteria, the dismissal concerned shall be deemed to have been made for justifiable reasons:[556]

1. Dismissal of a worker by an employer for managerial reasons shall be based on urgent managerial needs. In such cases as the transfer, acquisition or merger of businesses, which are aimed to avoid financial difficulties, it shall be deemed that an urgent managerial need exists (Article 24 paragraph 1).

---

555. *Ibid.*
556. Article 24.

2. An employer shall make every effort to avoid the dismissal of workers and shall select workers to be dismissed by establishing rational and fair criteria for dismissal. In such cases, there shall be no discrimination on the basis of gender (Article 24 paragraph 2).
3. With regard to the possible methods for avoiding dismissal and the criteria for dismissal, an employer shall give notice 50 days prior to the date of the dismissal to a trade union which is formed by the consent of the majority of all workers in the business or workplace concerned (or to a person representing the majority of all workers if such a trade union does not exist, hereinafter referred to as a 'workers' representative') and have a consultation in good faith (Article 24 paragraph 3).
4. An employer intending to dismiss more than the number of workers prescribed by the presidential decree pursuant to paragraph (1), shall report the this to the Minister of Employment and Labor as prescribed by the presidential decree (Article 24 paragraph 4).
5. In cases where an employer has dismissed workers in accordance with the requirements as set forth in paragraphs (1) to (3), the dismissal concerned shall be deemed to have been made for the justifiable reasons under paragraph 1 of Article 23 (Article 24 paragraph 5).

594. An employer intending to dismiss more than the number of workers as prescribed by presidential decree, must report this to the Minister of Employment and Labour as prescribed by presidential decree.

595. In short, any dismissal for managerial reasons is an abuse of the right to dismiss unless it meets the following four requirements:

1. There must be urgent managerial necessity to resort to a reduction of the workforce.
2. The employer is obliged to take various measures to avoid dismissals, such as a reduction in overtime, a reduction in mid-term recruitment, an implementation of transfers or the farming out of employees, non-renewal of fixed term contracts, curtailment of regular hiring, a reduction in the salaries of executives and managers, a temporary stoppage of operation with reduced pay, and the solicitation of voluntary retirement.
3. The rational and fair criteria for dismissal must be established on an objective and reasonable basis.
4. Management is required to explain the necessity for the dismissal, its timing, scale and method to the labour union, or worker group if no union exists, and consult with them concerning methods for avoiding dismissal(s) and the criteria for dismissal(s) in good faith.

596. Traditionally, the validity of dismissal for managerial reasons has been determined on the bases of whether the above-mentioned four requirements are met or not. If one of the four requirements is not satisfied, although there may be much room for doubt, generally speaking the dismissal has been regarded as abuse of the right to dismiss.[557] And, in such a case, dismissal contrary to these provisions is considered null and void.

4. Preferential Re-employment

597. If an employer who dismissed a worker intends to employ a worker for the same job the dismissed worker was in charge of at the time of dismissal, within three years from the day when the worker was dismissed, he or she shall preferentially employ the worker dismissed pursuant to Article 24, if the worker wants that job. The government shall give priority to workers dismissed for managerial reasons by taking necessary measures including securing their livelihood, reemployment, and vocational training.[558]

5. Restrictions on the Timing of Dismissal

598. When a worker has been injured or due to duty, the employer is bound to provide the necessary medical care or reimburse the corresponding expenses, and should provide recuperation compensation equivalent to 60 per cent of average wages during that period. Besides, the LSA prohibits dismissal during certain periods. An employer cannot dismiss any worker during a period of temporary interruption of work for medical treatment of a work-related injury or disease and within 30 days thereafter, and any female worker during a period of temporary interruption of work before and after childbirth as provided herein and within 30 days thereafter.[559]

599. During the foregoing period, dismissal is not allowed even if there are so-called 'just causes'. However, an employer may dismiss a worker on payment of a lump sum of compensation in an amount equivalent to 1340 days' average wage[560] or when the enterprise must close due to natural calamity or other inevitable reason.[561]

6. The Requirement for Advance Notice of Dismissal

600. The LSA provides that when an employer wants to dismiss an employee, she or he must give the employee at least 30 days' notice before the dismissal (including dismissal for managerial reasons). If the notice is not given 30 days before the dismissal, ordinary wages for more than 30 days shall be paid to the

557. Takashi Araki, *op. cit.*, p. 26.
558. Article 25.
559. Article 23 paragraph 2.
560. LSA, Article 84.
561. LSA, Article 23 paragraph 2.

worker.[562] However, there are exceptions in cases, prescribed by the Ordinance of the Ministry of Employment and Labour, where it is impossible to continue business because of natural disasters, armed conflicts, or other unavoidable causes, or where a worker has caused considerable difficulties to business, or damage to related property, on purpose.[563]

601. According to a judicial precedent, an employer still cannot dismiss a worker without just cause even though giving them prior notice. The purpose of this provision in merely to afford the worker with the minimum time or money to provide a livelihood until he or she gets another job.[564] As the Act requires no special form of notice, it can be given orally or in writing.[565] If an employer dismisses a worker with just cause but without either giving prior notice or paying 30 days' normal wages, what is its legal effect? Opinions are divided, but the majority view denies the legal effect of such dismissal on the grounds that Article 26 of the LSA stipulates the immutable conditions of dismissal. Although there is no written requirement, an employer must give 30 days' notice, as well as just cause, to terminate the contract for a definite period, because a refusal to renew it is identified as a dismissal if renewal is the usual practice.[566]

7. Dismissal without Notice

602. An immediate dismissal without advance notice, or an advance notice allowance in lieu of advance notice, is allowed in exceptional circumstances: In the event that the continued operation of the enterprise has been made impossible by a natural disaster or other unavoidable causes, or where a worker has caused considerable difficulties to business, or damage to related properties, on purpose and in the event that the worker is dismissed for reasons for which the worker is responsible. Here an 'unavoidable cause' is interpreted as meaning a reason equivalent to a natural calamity: that is, an act of God. It must be caused by something outside the employer's control which happened so suddenly that there was no chance to avoid it under normal circumstances and thus no time to give notice.[567]

562. And the amount of wages paid in place of prior notice should be paid in cash, in full and at a time – before or at the time of notice – otherwise the dismissal is not effective.
563. Article 26.
564. Therefore, the employer should pay wages when the employer and worker can mutually ask for labour service and wages during the period of notice.
565. However, in order to avoid trouble, employers are recommended to give notice in writing along with the reason(s) for dismissal. In any case, the date of dismissal must be clearly shown. Notice with an indefinite term or conditions does not hold water.
566. Chi Sun Kim, *op. cit.*, p. 71.
567. For example, when a company has had all or most of its raw materials or plant lost in a fire and, therefore, cannot continue production in the near future, the employer may dismiss employees without notice.

603. The principle of advance notice of dismissal[568] does not applied to the following workers, for they should realize that these kind of labour relations are only temporary or short term:

- a worker who has been employed on a daily basis for less than three consecutive months;
- a worker who has been employed for a fixed period not exceeding two months;
- a worker who has been employed for seasonal work for a fixed period not exceeding six months;
- a worker in a probationary period.[569]

604. However, just cause is still required in the above cases.

8. The Requirement for Written Notification of the Reasons for Dismissal

605. If an employer intends to dismiss a worker, the employer shall notify that worker of the reasons for dismissal and the date of such a dismissal in writing. The dismissal of a worker shall take effect only after the written notification is given to the worker.[570]

§3. Remedies for Unfair Dismissal

I. Application for Remedy for Unfair Dismissal

606. If an employer dismisses a worker unfairly, the worker may apply for remedy to the labour relations commission. The application for remedy must be made within three months of the date on which the unfair dismissal, and related acts, took place.[571]

607. Upon receiving the application for remedy, the Labour Relations Commission shall conduct the necessary investigations and question relevant parties without delay.

608. When conducting an inquiry, the labour relations commission may, at the request of the parties concerned or by virtue of its own authority, have witnesses appear before the Commission and question them regarding necessary matters.

568. Article 26.
569. Article 35.
570. Article 27.
571. Article 28.

609. When conducting an inquiry, the labour relations commission shall give sufficient opportunities for the parties concerned to present evidence and to cross-examine the witnesses. Detailed procedures for the investigation and inquiry by the labour relations commission shall be determined by the National Labour Relations Commission under the LRCA.[572]

II. Remedy Orders, etc.

610. The Labour Relations Commission shall issue a remedy order to the employer, if the case is determined to constitute an unfair dismissal, etc. after the completion of the inquiry, and shall dismiss the application for remedy if the case is determined not to constitute an unfair dismissal, etc.

611. The judgment, remedy order and dismissal decision shall be notified to the employer and worker concerned in writing.

612. When issuing a remedy order (referring only to an order of remedy for dismissal), if the worker does not want reinstatement, the Labour Relations Commission may order the employer to pay to the worker an amount not less than the amount of wages he or she would have received if he or she had worked during the period since dismissal, in lieu of ordering his or her reinstatement.[573]

III. Confirmation of Remedy Orders, etc.

613. If an employer or a worker is aggrieved by a remedy order or dismissal decision rendered by a Regional Labour Relations Commission in accordance with the Labour Relations Commission Act, he/she may apply for a re-examination of the case to the National Labour Relations Commission within ten days of the date on which he/she received the notice of the remedy order or dismissal decision.

614. An employer or a worker may file a lawsuit in accordance with the Administrative Litigation Act against the decision made by the National Labour Relations Commission after the re examination within 15 days from the date on which he/she received the notice of the decision relating to the re-examination.

615. If no application for re-examination is made or no administrative lawsuit is filed within these periods, the remedy order, dismissal decision or decision on reexamination shall be finally confirmed.[574]

572. Article 29.
573. Article 30.
574. Article 31.

IV. Effect of Remedy Orders, etc.

616. The effect of a remedy order, dismissal decisions or decisions on reexamination rendered by the Labour Relations Commission shall not be suspended by an application for reexamination to the National Labour Relations Commission or by the initiation of an administrative lawsuit.[575]

V. Enforcement Levies

617. If an employer, after receiving the remedy order (including a decision on reexamination concerning a remedy order; hereinafter the same shall apply in this Act) from the Labour Relations Commission, fails to comply with that remedy order by the compliance deadline, an enforcement levy of an amount not exceeding 20 million won shall be imposed on the employer.

618. The Labour Relations Commission shall inform the employer in writing of its intention to impose and collect such an enforcement levy, at least 30 days before the imposition of the levy.

619. The imposition of an enforcement levy shall be done in writing which shall specify, among other things, the amount of the enforcement levy, the reasons for its imposition, the payment deadline, the recipient organization, how to raise an objection, and to what organization such an objection can be made.

620. Types of violations for which an enforcement levy may be imposed, the amounts of charges based on the degree of violation, procedures for a refund of the enforcement levy and other necessary matters shall be prescribed by presidential decree.

621. The Labour Relations Commission may impose and collect the enforcement levy repeatedly until the order is complied with, up to twice per year from the date on which the first remedy order was issued.

622. The Labour Relations Commission shall not newly impose an enforcement levy once a person who received a remedy order has complied with that order, but shall collect enforcement levies that have already been imposed before the compliance.

623. If a person upon whom an enforcement levy has been imposed fails to pay it by the payment deadline, the Labour Relations Commission may set a new deadline and urge payment and, if the person continues to fail to pay the levy, may collect payment in accordance with the process for recovery of unpaid national taxes.

---

575. Article 32.

624. If an employer, who has received a remedy order, fails to comply with the order by the compliance deadline, the worker may inform the labour relations commission of said non-compliance within 15 days of the compliance deadline.[576]

576. Article 32.

Part II. Collective Labour Relations

Chapter 1. Freedom of Association, Trade Unions and Employers' Associations

§1. Labour Unions

I. Introduction

A. The Purpose of the TULRAA

625. The purpose of this Act is to maintain and improve working conditions and to improve the economic and social status of workers by securing the workers' rights to association, right to collective bargaining and collective action pursuant to the Constitution, and to contribute to the maintenance of industrial peace and to the development of the national economy by preventing and resolving labour disputes through the fair adjustment of labour relations.[577] The maintenance and improvement of working conditions is the ultimate purpose of all labour law. While the LSA attains this purpose directly by prescribing minimum standards of working conditions, the TULRAA attains this purpose indirectly by making manifest the right to organize collectively, the right to bargain collectively and the right to act collectively. An organization which workers form obtains improved working conditions by bargaining with an employer, or using dispute tactics if negotiations with the employer fail.[578]

B. Definition of Worker and Employer

626. 'Worker' means a person who lives on wages, salary, or another equivalent form of income earned in pursuit of any type of job.[579] The scope of the definition of worker in the TULRAA is broader than that of the worker in the LSA in that the former includes the unemployed. 'Worker', according to the LSA means only a person who is employed, in other words the person now offering labour. A worker is a person who lives on wages (including salaries and any other income) and 'wages'

577. TULRAA, Article 1.
578. Chi Sun Kim, *op. cit.*, p. 75.
579. Article 2.

are the money and goods paid to the worker in compensation for labour service. A subordinate relationship exists between worker and employer.

627. 'Employer' means a business owner, a person responsible for the management of a business, or a person who acts on behalf of the owner of the enterprise with respect to matters concerning workers in the business.[580] The employer as the owner of the enterprises is one of the parties to the labour contract and demands the offer of labour service from a worker. This may be a natural person or a legal person. The employer is the person who is in charge of the operation of the enterprise, and represents the enterprise. Members of the executive body are those in charge of the operation of the enterprise. A person who executes the rights of the owner of the enterprise or of the members of the executive body to command or control on their behalf is regarded as an employer by this Act. We may enumerate the heads of department, and sections of the enterprise, for example the planning department, personnel department, business department, general affairs department, labour–management department, etc. Besides these persons of high rank, a person of low rank who is invested with the authority to deal with matters concerning workers is regarded as an employer by this Act. The persons mentioned above, even though they were originally workers, are prohibited from organizing or joining a trade union.[581]

628. The term used in this Act 'employers association' means an organization of employers which has an authority to adjust and control its constituent members with regard to labour relations.

629. The term 'labour disputes', as used in this Act, means any controversy or differences arising from a disagreement between the trade union and employer or employers' association (hereinafter referred to as 'parties to labour relations') concerning the determination of terms and conditions of employment such as wages, working hours, welfare, dismissal, other treatment issues, etc. In such cases, 'disagreement' refers to situations in which no agreement is likely to be reached by the parties even if they continued to attempt to make such an agreement.

630. The term 'industrial action', used in this Act, means actions or counteractions which obstruct the normal operation of a business, such as strikes, sabotage, lock-outs, or other activities through which the parties to labour relations intend to achieve their respective claims.

II. The Legal Framework Regulating Collective Labour Relations in Korea

631. Collective labour relations concern mainly the formation and operation of workers' organizations to represent workers in seeking various benefits within their labour relationships (including the relationships between the workers' organizations

580. Article 2.
581. Chi Sun Kim, *op. cit.*, p. 76.

and their members), and consultations and negotiations between those organizations and an employer or an organization representing employers.[582] Collective labour relations law is the legal field in which such collective labour relations are regulated. Collective Labour relations are primarily regulated by the Constitution, the TULRAA of 1997, and are additionally regulated under the Act on the Promotion of Worker Participation and Cooperation of 1997, the Act on the Establishment, Operation, etc., of Public Officials' Trade Unions of 2006, and Act on the Establishment, Operation, Etc., of Trade Unions for Teachers[583] of 1999, etc.

632. Korea's Constitution which was promulgated in 1948 guarantees fundamental rights for workers. Article 33 of the Constitution provides that (1) 'to enhance working conditions, workers shall have the right to independent association, collective bargaining and collective action.' (2) 'Only those public officials who are designated by Act, shall have the right to association, collective bargaining and collective action.' (3) 'The right to collective action of workers employed by important defence industries may be either restricted or denied under the conditions as prescribed by Act.'

633. Therefore, any legislative or administrative act that infringes on these rights without reasonable justification is unconstitutional and void. Workers are immune from any criminal or civil liability for proper union activities. This article is construed as protecting not only relations between the state and private citizens, that is, employer and workers. Consequently, workers have a cause of action against an employer who has infringed their union rights.[584]

634. Article 33 is further interpreted to entrust the National Assembly to enact statutes to effectuate basic union rights.

635. Accordingly, the TULRAA sets requirements for recognition as a qualified union, establishes the unfair labour practice system prohibiting employers' anti-union actions, gives collective bargaining agreements normative effects and establishes the labour relations commissions, administrative tripartite bodies which adjudicate unfair labour practice cases and help resolve labour disputes.

636. The Labour Relations Commission Act was enacted to facilitate the resolution of collective labour disputes. Under this Law, the Labour Relations Commissions are entrusted with the conciliation, mediation and arbitration of labour disputes. Although special regulations exist for public sector workers, the above mentioned laws provide a basic framework for industrial relations in the private sector.[585]

---

582. Kazuo Sugeno, *op. cit.*, p. 494.
583. The purpose of this Act is to stipulate matters concerning the organization of trade unions for teachers in conformity with the proviso of Article 5 of the TULRAA and to regulate the special provisions necessary for the TULRAA to be applied to teachers, notwithstanding Article 66(1) of the State Public Officials Act and Article 55 of the Private School Act.
584. Takashi Araki, *op. cit.*, p. 159.
585. *Ibid.*, p. 160.

§2. THE RIGHT TO ORGANIZE

I. The Right to Organize and the Freedom of Association

637. Article 21 of the Constitution provides that 'all citizens shall enjoy freedom of association and the licensing or censorship of association shall not be recognized'. Even in cases where the right of workers to organize is not expressly provided in law, workers are entitled to form and join workers' organizations as a result of their freedom of association.[586]

638. In Korea, the right to organize is recognized independently from that of the freedom of association. The freedom of association has different aspects in terms of its historical origin, legal character and legal effect. The right to organize is a fundamental economic right essentially different from the freedom of association. That is why the right to organize is guaranteed for workers in addition to the freedom of association.

II. The Right to Organize and Union Security

639. The right to organize is generally interpreted as meaning both the right of workers to form or join a trade union and, as a natural extension, the right of trade unions to continue their existence. These two rights are closely related to each other.

640. The problem is that whether the right to organize implies the right not to organize. Since the right to organize has also the character of the freedom of organization it may be reasonably said that the right to not organize may be interpreted as implied in the right to organize. But the right to organize has a legal character essentially different from freedom of association. And workers face the urgent need for a powerful organization of their own to fight for their interests against employers who have much higher social status and much greater economic power than individual workers. So most legal theorists are of the same opinion, namely that the right to not organize is not included in the right to organize. In other words, the Constitution guarantees the right to organize, but not the right to not organize. Accepting this view, there still remains the problem of to what extent workers are forced to organize. This problem has been closely related to so-called union security clauses.[587]

641. These clauses are inserted in a collective agreement to protect the continued existence of a trade union. Typical examples are as follows: closed shop clauses, union shop clauses, maintenance of membership clauses, preferential shop clauses and check-off clauses.

---

586. Chi Sun Kim, *op cit.*, pp. 77–78.
587. *Ibid.*, p. 79.

642. When a closed shop agreement is made, only members of a certain trade union are hired. When a union shop clause is included, non-union members may be hired, but they must join the trade union within a specified period.[588]

643. In Korea, it is common practice for an employer and union to include a union shop agreement which requires the employer to dismiss a worker who does not join that union. Thus the Constitution has not been interpreted to prohibit union shop agreements. However, if union shop agreements are construed so as to expel members of other unions that would infringe the other union's right to organize guaranteed under the system of plural unionism, where each union has the right to organize regardless of their size. Simultaneously, workers have the right to choose membership in a particular union as part of their right to organize under the Constitution. To reconcile these conflicting principles, the Supreme Court has held that a union shop agreement should be interpreted to require the employer to dismiss workers who refuse to join any union as a corollary to the fact that there is no guaranteed right not to organize, but that this rule does not apply to workers who choose to join another union.[589] The rationale for this rule is that the workers right to join the union of their choice stems from their constitutional right to organize. Accordingly, the employer is not required to dismiss a worker who does not join, or who is expelled from the union which is the party to the union shop agreement but does join another union. When a worker is expelled from the union and does not join another union, the employer then has no option but to dismiss the worker. Case law also dictates that when the expulsion from a union is regarded as null and avoid, the dismissal from the company is also nullified as lacking reasonable grounds for dismissal.[590]

§3. The Establishment of Unions under Korean Laws

I. The Definition of a Trade Union

644. The TULRAA gives as the definition of a trade union. 'The "trade union" means an organization of workers or a federation of organizations, which is formed in a voluntary and collective manner upon the workers' initiative for the purpose of maintaining and improving working conditions, or improving the economic and social status of workers.'[591]

588. *Ibid.*
589. The *Mitsui Soko Ko-un* case, Japan's Supreme Court (14 December 1989) 43 Minshu 2051 (Takashi Araki, *op cit.*, p. 163).
590. The *Nihon Shokuen* case, Japan's Supreme Court (25 April 1975) 29 Minshu 456 (Takashi Araki, *op cit.*, p. 163).
591. Article 2.

A. *Positive Essential Requirements for Establishing a Qualified Union under the TULRAA*

645. The TULRAA sets forth five requirements for a labour organizations to enjoy statutory rights and remedies.[592] The first four requirements are provide in Article 2 and the last contained in Article 11.

1. Membership (Workers or Predominantly So)

646. The organization must be 'predominantly formed by workers and organized by workers on their own initiative'. They are at core organizations of the workers, by the workers and for the workers. 'Workers' for the purposes of the TULRAA are defined in the Act as 'those who live by their wages, salaries or other remuneration assimilable thereto'.[593]

2. Independence (Autonomy, Exclusion of Managerial Workers from Membership and Non-receipt of Financial Assistance from the Employer)

647. The organization must be independent of the employer. The Act requires three specific types of independence. One is that organization must be 'autonomously' formed by the workers themselves. The organization must also not allow within its membership those who represent the employer's interest, such as board members, supervisory workers having direct authority to hire, fire, promote or transfer workers, and supervisory personnel who have access to confidential information relating to the employer's labour-relation plans and policies such that their official duties responsibilities would be in direct conflict their loyalties and responsibilities as a member of the union concerned.[594] The third issue is financial independence: the organization must not receive financial support from the employer, with the exception of certain enumerated matters; these exceptions include the employer's permitting workers to confer or negotiate with the employer during working time without loss of time or pay, the employer's contributing the welfare funds and the furnishing of minimal office space.[595]

3. Purpose

648. The main purpose of the organization must be 'to maintain and improve working conditions and to raise the economic status of workers'.[596] Therefore, an

592. TULRAA, Articles 2 and 7.
593. TULRAA, Article 2 sub-paragraph 4, proviso no. 1.
594. *Ibid.*, proviso nos. 1 and 4.
595. *Ibid.*, proviso no. 2.
596. *Ibid.*, proviso no. 3.

organization which has the limited objectives of 'mutual aid or conducting other welfare activities'[597] or which 'mainly aims at political or social movements' are not unions under that law'.[598]

4. Character as an Organization

649. An organization must be an 'organization or federation thereof'.[599] To be deemed an organization, there must be more than two members.

5. Trade Union Constitutions: Requirements

650. The organization must establish a trade union constitution which includes the items enumerated in Article 11 of the TULRAA Most of the enumerated items concern the democratic administration of the internal affairs of the Union, such as the equal treatment of union members and the use of secret ballots for the election for union officers or for strike decisions.[600]

651. Other than the foregoing prerequisites, there are no further requirements. The majority support of the workers is not required, neither is a minimum number, or registration with a government agency, in short, Korea has few requirements for organizing unions.[601]

---

597. *Ibid.*
598. *Ibid.*, proviso no. 5.
599. *Ibid.*, sub-paragraph 4.
600. Article 11 (Bylaws)

> In order to guarantee an autonomous and democratic operation of the organization, a trade union shall include the following matters in its bylaws.
>
> 1. the name of the trade union;
> 2. its purposes and activities;
> 3. the location of its main office or headquarters;
> 4. matters relevant to union members (matters regarding its constituent organizations in the case of a trade union in the form of an associated organization);
> 5. the name of the associated organization which it belongs to;
> 6. matters relating to a council of delegates if such council of delegates has been established;
> 7. matters concerning meetings;
> 8. matters concerning representatives or officials;
> 9. matters concerning accounting, including union dues and others;
> 10. matters concerning the modification of the union bylaws;
> 11. matters concerning dissolution;
> 12. matters concerning the disclosure of the result of a vote on industrial action, the keeping of and access to voters' roll and ballot papers;
> 13. matters concerning impeachment of representatives or officials for violation of the bylaws;
> 14. matters concerning the election of officials and delegates; and
> 15. matters concerning discipline and control.

601. Takashi Araki, *op. cit.*, p. 161.

B. Negative Essential Requirements

652. In cases where an organization falls into one of the following categories, the organization shall not be regarded as a trade union.[602]

653. In cases where an employer or other persons who always act in their employer's interests are allowed to join the organization.

654. Trade unions should not accept as members employers and those persons who always act for the benefit of employers. Those who are in charge of the operation of the enterprise or act on behalf of the owner of the enterprise with regard to matters concerning workers may not participate in the organization of trade unions and may not join any trade union.[603] This is to secure for trade unions autonomy and independence.

655. In cases where most of the expenditure is supported by the employer.

656. Trade unions should not receive assistance mainly from the employers in the disbursement of their expenses. This is to secure for trade unions financial independence. Without financial independence trade unions cannot but be dominated by employers. Not only substantial financial assistance but also partial financial assistance is prohibited as constituting interference in and control over trade unions, namely, as unfair labour practices. But the Act allows that 'an employer may allow the workers to take part in consultation or bargaining with the employer during the working hours, may provide subsidies for the welfare of the workers, or for the prevention and alleviation of financial difficulties and other such disasters, and may offer union office accommodation on a minimal scale for a trade union'.[604]

657. In cases where the activities of an organization are only aimed at mutual benefits, moral culture and other welfare undertakings.

658. Workers' organizations having only the purpose of providing mutual benefits and welfare services cannot be recognized as legal trade unions.

659. In cases where those who are not workers are allowed to join the organization. However, a dismissed person shall not be regarded as a person who is not a worker, until a review decision is made by the National Labour relations commission when he or she has made an application to the labour relations commission for remedies for unfair labour practices.

660. In cases where the aims of the organization are mainly directed at political movements.

602. Article 2, subparagraph 4.
603. Speaking generally, executives, managers, supervisors and others given responsibility and authority for management affairs of the enterprise cannot be members of a trade union.
604. Article 81, section 4.

661. Any organization which 'mainly aims at political or social movements are not unions under that law'.

662. As stated above, organizations of workers should not fall under any category of the negative requirement made in the proviso, Article 2, to be recognized as legal trade unions. These unqualified trade unions are deprived of part of the protection guaranteed by this Act.

C. Formal Requirements

1. Report on the Establishment of a Trade Union

663. A person who intends to establish a trade union shall prepare a report containing the matters described in the following sub-paragraphs, attached with the bylaws (Article 11) and submit it to the Minister of Employment and Labour. Alternatively, in the case that the trade union takes the form of an associated organization or is a unit trade union spanning not less than two areas out of the Special City, Metropolitan cities, Provinces and Special Self-Governing Provinces, to the Special City Mayor, relevant Metropolitan City Mayors and relevant Provincial Governors. In the case that the trade union is a unit trade union spanning not less than two areas out of Sis/Guns/ Gus (referring to autonomous Gus); and to relevant governors of special self-governing provinces and relevant heads of Sis/Guns/Gus (referring to heads of autonomous Gus) in the case of other trade unions:

1. the name of the trade union;
2. the location of their main office or headquarters;
3. the number of union members;
4. the name and address of union officials;
5. the name of any associated organization to which it belongs;
6. in the case of a trade union in the form of an associated organization, the name of its constituent organizations, the number of union members, the address of its main office or headquarters, and the name and address of its officials.

664. A trade union which is an associated organization means an industry-wide organization comprised of unit trade unions in the same industry and a federation comprised of industry-level organizations or nationwide industry-level unit trade unions.[605]

605. Article 10.

2. Trade Union Constitutions (Bylaws)

665. In order to guarantee the autonomous and democratic operation of the organization, a trade union shall include the following matters in its bylaws:[606]

1. the name of the trade union;
2. its purposes and activities;
3. the location of its main office or headquarters;
4. matters relevant to union members (matters regarding its constituent organizations in the case of a trade union in the form of an associated organization);
5. the name of the associated organization to which it belongs;
6. matters regarding a council of delegates if such a council of delegates has been established;
7. matters concerning meetings;
8. matters concerning representatives or officials;
9. matters concerning accounting, including union dues and others;
10. matters concerning the modification of the union bylaws;
11. matters concerning dissolution;
12. matters concerning the disclosure of the result of a vote on industrial action, the keeping of and access to the voters' roll and ballot papers;
13. matters concerning the impeachment of representatives or officials for violation of the bylaws;
14. matters concerning the election of officials and delegates;
15. matters concerning discipline and control.

3. Issuance of Certificate[607]

666. The Minister of Employment and Labour, the mayor of a special city, the mayor of a metropolitan city, the provincial governor, the governor of special self-governing province or the head of Si/Gun/Gu (hereinafter referred to as the 'administrative authorities') must issue a certificate within three days of receiving the report on the establishment, except for cases as prescribed in paragraphs (2) and (3).

667. In cases where a report or bylaws need to be supplemented because of any omission or other reasons, the administrative authorities shall order a supplement thereof by designating a submission period of up to 20 days in accordance with presidential decree. Upon receiving the supplemented report or bylaws, a certificate shall be issued within three days.

668. The administrative authorities must return a report filed in cases where a trade union which made the report falls under the purview of any of the following sub-paragraphs:

606. Article 11.
607. Article 12.

1. where a trade union falls within the categories of sub-paragraph 4 of Article 2 (negative requirements);[608]
2. where supplements are not submitted within the designated period in spite of the order to supplement a report in accordance with the provisions of paragraph (2).

669. With regard to the issuance of a certificate, a trade union shall be construed to have been established at the time when a report of the establishment of the trade union was submitted.

4. Notification of Modifications, etc.[609]

670. A trade union shall notify any modifications of the contents to the administrative authorities within 30 days from the date when changes occur in any of the following sub-paragraphs from among those which have been filed:

1. its name;
2. the location of its main office or headquarters;
3. the names of representatives;
4. the name of the associated organization to which it belongs.

671. A trade union shall give notice as to matters which fall within each of the following sub-paragraphs to the administrative authorities by 31 January of each year. However, this shall not apply to matters whose modification was notified in the previous year pursuant to paragraph (1):

1. in cases where the bylaws were modified in the previous year, then, the contents of the modifications to the bylaws;
2. in cases where union officials were replaced in the previous year, then, the names of the union officials replaced;
3. the number of union members as of 31 December of the previous year (the number of union members in each constituent organization in the case of a trade union in the form of an associated organization).

608. Sub-paragraph 4 of Article 2:

1. in cases where an employer or other persons who always act in their employer's interests are allowed to join the organization;
2. in cases where most of the expenditure is supported by the employer;
3. in cases where the activities of an organization are only aimed at mutual benefits, moral culture and other welfare-related undertakings;
4. in cases where those who are not workers are allowed to join the organization; provided that a dismissed person shall not be regarded as a person who is not a worker, until a review decision is made by the National Labour Relations Commission when he or she has made an application to the Labour Relations Commission for remedies for unfair labour practices;
5. in cases where the aims of the organization are mainly directed at political activities.

609. Article 13.

§4. GENERAL PROVISIONS REGARDING TRADE UNIONS

I. The Organization and Membership of Trade Unions

672. Workers are free to organize a trade union or to join one, except for public servants or teachers who are subject to other enactments.[610]

II. The Incorporation of a Trade Union[611]

673. A trade union shall be incorporated according to the bylaws of the trade union.

674. In the case of the incorporation of a trade union, the trade union shall be registered in accordance with presidential decree.

675. With respect to an incorporated trade union, except for such matters are prescribed by this Act, the provisions on incorporated associations in the Civil Code shall apply.

III. Requirements for the Protection of Trade Unions

676. The requirements for the protection of trade unions are as follows:[612]

1. trade unions which are not established by this Act shall not make an application for adjustment of labour disputes and for remedy for unfair labour practices to the Labour relations commission;
2. the provisions of paragraph (1) shall not be construed as excluding the protection of workers under sub-paragraphs (1), (2) and (5) of Article 81;
3. except specifically for the trade unions formed under this Act, the term 'trade union' shall not be used.

IV. Exemption from Taxation

677. No tax shall be imposed on a trade union except for its affiliated businesses.[613]

610. Article 5.
611. Article 6.
612. Article 7.
613. Article 8.

§5. TYPES OF TRADE UNION

678. Workers are free to organize a trade union or to join it, except for public servants or teachers who are subject to other enactments.[614] The TULRAA envisages not only enterprise unions but also industrial unions or other types of unions as seen in other countries.

679. To speak generally, trade unions are divided into craft unions, industrial unions and company unions according to whether they are organized on the craft level, on the industrial level or on the company or enterprise level. The craft union is made up of workers of the same occupation or the same industrial process. It is organized on a horizontal basis, cutting across industries and enterprises.[615] The industrial union is organized by industry, regardless of occupation, enterprise and region. The company or enterprise union is established within an individual enterprise, irrespective of their members' jobs, and collectively bargain with a single employer, and conclude collective agreements at the enterprise level. Enterprise unions normally confine their membership to regular workers although there are no legal obstacles which prevent enterprise unions from organizing part-time or temporary workers. This is due to the fact that the interests of regular workers and those of non-regular workers are usually different, and sometimes even conflict.

680. Enterprise unions within the same industry often join an industrial federation of unions, and the industrial federations are affiliated with national confederations. However, in Korea industry-level collective bargaining is very rare. In the case of a company union working conditions may be properly established between labour and management. But it may also be easily dominated by the employer. An enterprise union also has several difficulties, such as weak bargaining power, the lack of universal impact across an industry or the nation, and the lack of social and political influence on national labour policy.

681. Depending on whether their members are individual workers or trade unions, trade unions can be divided into federal unions and non-federal unions. In case of federal unions the member unions organize a federation of trade unions. When trade unions are organized at enterprise level, these enterprise unions often form a federation of unions. However, when trade unions are organized at an industry level, workers organize one trade union as a whole irrespective of the diversity of enterprises and occupations in an entire industry.[616]

---

614. Article 5.

615. The craft union has the following advantages:

1. a high degree of solidarity among its members;
2. collective bargaining is not complicated and working conditions are established uniformly;
3. it is not easily dominated by employers. For these reasons it also has the disadvantage of being exclusive and peremptory (Chi Sun Kim, *op. cit.*, p. 85).

616. Branches or chapters are usually established at the enterprise level and at the regional level. In principal these branches do not have the essential nature of individual unions. Sometimes they are

§6. ADMINISTRATION OF TRADE UNIONS

I. Documents to Be Kept, etc.

682. A trade union shall prepare each of the following documents within 30 days from the date of its establishment, and keep them at its headquarters or main offices. Documents stipulated in sub-paragraphs (4)and (5) shall be retained for three years:[617]

1. a register of union members (the name of its constituent organizations in the case of a trade union in the form of an associated organization);
2. the union's bylaws;
3. the names and addresses of the union's officials;
4. minutes of meetings;
5. financial records and documents.

II. General Meetings

683. A trade union shall hold one or more general meeting each year. The representative of a trade union shall preside over general meetings.[618]

684. Each of the following matters shall require a resolution adopted by the general meeting:[619]

1. the adoption and modification of bylaws;
2. the election or discharge of union officials;
3. collective bargaining arrangements;
4. budgets and final Accounts;
5. the establishment, operation, and disposition of funds;
6. the establishment of, admission to, or withdrawal from an associated organization;
7. merger, division, or dissolution;
8. structural changes; or
9. other important matters.

685. The general meeting shall adopt resolutions by the affirmative vote of a majority of the members present at a general meeting where a majority of all members are present. However, resolutions as to the introduction and modification of bylaws, discharge of union officials, and merger, division, dissolution and structural

regarded as individual trade unions when that essential authority is delegated to them by an industrial union. But their individuality is not as strong as that of member unions as part of a federation (Chi Sun Kim, *op. cit.*, p. 85).

617. Article 14.
618. Article 15.
619. Article 16.

change of a trade union shall be passed by the affirmative vote of at least two-thirds of members present at a general meeting where a majority of all members are present.

686. Union officials shall be elected from among the union members. The tenure of union officials shall be determined by the union bylaws, but shall not exceed three years.[620] In an election in which no candidate running for the position of a union official has obtained the consent of a majority of the union members present, a runoff election may be held and the candidate with the highest number votes may be elected in accordance with the bylaws. Resolutions as to the adoption and modification of union bylaws, or the election and discharge of union officials shall be made by a direct, secret, and unsigned ballot.

687. A trade union may, in accordance with its bylaws, establish a council of delegates in lieu of a general meeting. Delegates shall be elected in a direct, secret, and unsigned ballot by union members. The tenure of delegates shall be specified in the bylaws of the trade union but shall not exceed three years. Where a council of delegates has been established, the provisions on general meetings shall be applied *mutatis mutandis.*[621]

688. The representative of a trade union may, if he or she deems necessary, convene an extraordinary general meeting or council of delegates. The representative of a trade union shall convene, without delay, an extraordinary general meeting or a council of delegates in cases where more than a third of the union members or delegates bring the matters to be referred to meetings, and require him or her to call such a meeting (in the case of a trade union in the form of an associated organization, more than one-third of its constituent organizations). Where a representative of a trade union deliberately neglects or avoids the convening of the general meeting, and a request is made by one third or more of the union members to appoint a convener of the meeting, the administrative authorities shall ask the labour relations commission to adopt a resolution within 15 days, and upon adoption of such resolution by the labour relations commission, immediately appoint a person to convene the meeting. Where there is no person entitled to convene a general meeting or a council of delegates, if one third or more of the union members or delegates bring matters to be referred to the meeting, and submit a request to appoint a person to convene the meeting, the administrative authorities shall appoint a person within fifteen days of such a request.[622]

689. A general meeting or council of delegates shall give public notice of matters to be discussed at least seven days prior to the commencement date of such meeting or council, and shall convene such meeting or council pursuant to the methods prescribed by the bylaws. However, the notification period may be reduced in

620. Article 23.
621. Article 17.
622. Article 18.

accordance with the bylaws of a trade union in cases where a trade union is composed of workers in the same workplace.[623]

690. In cases where a trade union is to make a resolution on matters regarding a particular union member, that union member shall have no right to partake in the vote.[624]

III. Correction of Bylaws, Resolutions and Measures

691. The administrative authorities may, with the resolution of the labour relations commission, order the correction of union bylaws which are in conflict with the related labour laws.

692. The administrative authorities may, with the resolution of the Labour Relations Commission, order the correction of resolution or measures made by a trade union, which are determined to be in conflict with the related labour laws and union bylaws. An order for the correction of bylaws shall be made only by the application of the interested party.

693. In the case of orders for correction, a trade union shall implement such orders within 30 days, except that the period may be extended for a reasonable cause.[625]

IV. Full-time Officials of Trade Unions

694. If stipulated in a collective bargaining agreement or with the consent of an employer, a worker may perform duties only for a trade union, without providing work specified in his or her employment contract. Those who are engaged in duties only for trade unions ('full-time officials') shall not be remunerated in any way by their employers for the duration of their tenure.[626]

695. A worker may perform duties only for a trade union, without providing the services specified in his/her employment contract, if it is stipulated in the collective bargaining agreement or with the employer's consent(Article 24 paragraph (1). A person who is engaged in duties only for a trade union in accordance with paragraph (1) (hereinafter referred to as full-time official) shall not be remunerated in any way by the employer for the duration of his/her tenure (paragraph (2)). An employer shall not restrict legitimate union activities of a full-time union official (paragraph (3)).

623. Article 19.
624. Article 20.
625. Article 21.
626. Article 24.

696. Notwithstanding paragraph (2), a worker may take time off from work to carry out the functions prescribed by this Act or other applicable Acts, including consulting and bargaining with the employer, handling of grievance and occupational safety activities, and the functions of maintaining and managing the trade union for the sound development of industrial relations without any loss of wages as long as he/she does not exceed the maximum time-off limit (hereinafter referred to as the maximum time-off limit) set in consideration of the number of union members, in each business or workplace in accordance with Article 24-2, if it is stipulated in the collective agreement or consented by the employer (paragraph (4)). A trade union shall not demand the payment of wages in violation of paragraphs (2) and (4) and take industrial action to achieve such a goal (paragraph (5)).

V. Time-off System Deliberation Committee

697. In order to set the maximum time-off limit, the time-off system deliberation committee (hereinafter referred to as the committee in this article) shall be set up by the Ministry of Employment and Labour (Article 24-2 paragraph(1)).

The maximum time-off limit shall be announced by the Minister of Employment and Labour according to the results of deliberation and decision by the Committee, and may be decided anew every three years after a re-deliberation on whether it is adequate or not (paragraph(2)). The Committee shall be composed of five members recommended by labor circles, five members recommended by business circles, and five public interest members recommended by the government (paragraph(3)). The members of the Committee shall be appointed by the Minister of Employment and Labour. The members appointed on the recommendation of labour circles shall be appointed from among those recommended by nation-wide labour organizations and the members appointed on the recommendation of business circles shall be appointed from among those recommended by nation-wide employers' organizations (Enforcement Decree of the Trade Union and Labour Relations Adjustment Act Article 11-3). When the Time-off System Deliberation Committee sets the maximum time-off limit, it may set the limit in the form of the number of time-off hours and the number of people who can take time-off, after taking into consideration the number of all union members in the business or workplace and the scope of the functions concerned pursuant to Article 24 (4) of the Act((Enforcement Decree of the Trade Union and Labour Relations Adjustment Act Article 11-2).

698. The chairperson shall be elected by the Committee from among the public interest members (Article 24-2 paragraph(4)). Decisions of the Committee shall require the attendance of a majority of all members and the approval of a majority of the members present (paragraph(5)). Necessary matters concerning the qualifications and appointment of members, the operation of the Committee, etc., shall be prescribed by the presidential decree (paragraph(6)).

VI. Auditing of Accounts and Disclosure of Operations

699. The representative of a trade union shall have an auditor conduct, at least once every six months, an audit of all of the financial resources of a trade union, the purposes of those financial resources, the names of major contributors and its current financial and accounting status, and shall disclose the results of audit to all the union's members. The auditor of a trade union may, if necessary, conduct an audit of the trade union, and disclose the results of the audit.[627]

700. The representative of a trade union shall notify union members of the financial closing and the status of operation each fiscal year, and have them available for inspection when union members so request.[628]

701. A trade union shall report the results of their end of year accounts, and the status of operations upon a request from the Administrative Authorities.[629]

§7. Dissolution or Reorganization of Trade Unions

I. Dissolution

702. A trade union shall be dissolved if it falls within the purview of any of the following reasons:[630]

1. occurrence of causes for dissolution prescribed by its bylaws;
2. dissolution due to merger or division;
3. dissolution by a resolution adopted by a general meeting or council of delegates;
4. dissolution by the administrative authorities, with the resolution of the Labour Relations Commission, when the trade union in question has no officials and has not carried out any activity for more than one year.

703. If a trade union is dissolved on the reasons as stated above (1)to (3), the representative of the trade union shall report it to the administrative authorities within 15 days of the date of the dissolution.

704. When a union that has the status of a juridical person is dissolved, the TULRAA makes applicable to the reversion of the remaining assets and the procedures for settling its accounts the provisions of the Civil Code dealing with incorporated associations.[631] If a union does not have the status of a juridical person, its residual

627. Article 25.
628. Article 26.
629. Article 27.
630. Article 28.
631. Civil Code, Articles 77–80.

assets belong to its members in 'communal ownership' the decisions require the consent of all the members in order to discontinue this 'communal ownership'.

II. Organizational Changes

705. A modification of a union's structure during its existence is generally referred to as an organizational change. There are various kinds of organizational changes with different requirements and procedures: changes in the scope of its membership, reorganization (from 'unit union' to federation or from 'federation' to unit union or from a unit union to an enterprise-based local union), entry of a unit union into federation or secession of a unit union from a federation.

706. When an organizational change has been completed, the post-change union, which is recognized as being the same as the pre-change union, inherits its finances and labour agreements.

III. Schisms

707. A union schism is a social phenomenon under which a union is split into two or more separate unions as a result of internal opposition. Among the legal questions raised by this social phenomenon is the major one of how to treat the union's property (including its liabilities). The court's position (for instance, Japan) was that, as in the great majority of cases of social schism, the former union's collective agreements and property are inherited by the surviving union. On the other hand, if a schism is affirmed in very exceptional cases, the old union is not the same as either the remaining union or the new union, then such things as the old union's collective agreements and its right to use an office will be extinguished.[632]

708. There is also a question of how to deal with a schism that occurs in a unit union's subordinate organizations (i.e. schism within local unions that are part of unit unions). We can see that in the case of a union's local union, there will generally be no schism (i.e. a division of the union's property and its distribution to the seceding union and the remaining union). Where there has been an organizational change (secession from a union and the formation of an independent union) then, depending on whether it was validly decided, either the seceding or the remaining union will inherit the property.[633]

IV. Amalgamation

709. The TULRAA contains no provisions recognizing the amalgamation of unions, although legal commentators have acknowledged its possibility.

632. Kazuo Sugeno, *op. cit.*, p. 545.
633. *Ibid.*, p. 546

710. An amalgamation is the integration of two or more continuing unions into a single union. It is the same as a merger of corporations. When union A and union B amalgamate, they form union C, which is a newly-created amalgamation. At times, union A will absorb union B, and the union will continue as union A. This is an example of amalgamation by absorption.

711. As for the effects of an amalgamation, the principle is that such things as the property of both unions, the rights–duties relationships with each union member, and the obligations of each party to a collective bargaining agreement, which existed prior to the amalgamation, will be succeeded to the new union or the absorbing union following the amalgamation. According to common opinion, the debts of both unions will generally also be inherited.[634]

§8. Internal Union Affairs

I. Union Autonomy and the Principle of Union Democracy

712. Unions are voluntary associations independently formed by workers to protect their own interests. It is, therefore, both necessary and desirable to recognize the principle of autonomy, under which their management is determined by their constitutions and by majority decision and by the principle of autonomy. On the other hand, since the law provides labour unions with special benefits, a union to some extent bears the characteristic of a public organization. This special nature of a union requires judicial intervention to guarantee democratic internal administration.

713. Because of these two conflicting aspects, many problems relating to internal union administration must be decided by striking a fair balance between protecting union autonomy and ensuring democratic practices. These two principles sometime conflict in areas such as the regulations for admission, resignation or expulsion from unions, regulations on union dues and the validity of union discipline.[635]

II. Rights and Duties of Union Members

714. No member of a trade union shall be discriminated against on the basis of race, religion, sex, age, physical condition, employment type, political affiliation, or social status.[636] In addition, every union member has equal rights and duties to participate in all the affairs of the trade union. However, a trade union may restrict, under union bylaws, the rights of those members who do not pay union dues.[637]

634. *Ibid.*
635. Takashi Araki, *op. cit.*, p. 168.
636. Article 9.
637. Article 22.

715. As a private voluntary association, a union may decide the scope of its membership. Therefore, a union may limit its membership to regular workers of the company. However, discrimination based on race, religion, sex or creed is understood to be illegal in light of the principle of union democracy. Therefore, the provisions of trade union charters which restrict the right of workers to join it because of their sex, social status or political and religious creed are regarded as unconstitutional and as a natural consequence null and void. Further other discriminatory treatment on account of these reasons is null and void.

716. Since the freedom to resign from a union is one of the most basic aspects of a voluntary association, the courts have nullified restrictions on resignation. For instance, provisions requiring that resignation be approved in advance by the executive committees or a general meeting have been held null and void. A union shop agreement is the exception to a worker's right to resign freely from a union.

717. The TULRAA makes an exception to this. A trade union may, by virtue of its charter, impose restrictions on the rights of those union members who do not pay membership fees.[638] All union members have an equal right to vote. If a trade union is to make a decision in connection with specific members of the trade union, those members of the trade union at issue cannot vote.[639] But this does not mean that those members at issue are deprived of the right to express their opinions.

III. Control of a Trade Union over Its Members

718. The right to organize means both the right of workers to unionize or to join a trade union and the right of a trade union to continue its existence.

719. The rights of a trade union may conflict with the rights of its members.

720. The fundamental duties of union members to their union are to observe the union's general policy and constitution, to abide by union decisions and directives and to pay union dues.

721. A union's constitution usually provides that the union can discipline members who disrupt the union's solidarity; expulsion from a trade union, disqualification, suspension of qualification and other disciplinary penalties are examples of disciplinary measures. When a trade union takes necessary measures, the activities of its members may be restricted by them.

722. Speaking generally, as long as a trade union exercises its control over its members within the limit of legal provisions and the limit of its purpose to maintain

638. Proviso of Article 22.
639. Article 20.

and promote workers' working conditions and to promote workers' welfare, disciplinary measures taken against those who act in violation of the orders of the trade union are regarded as legal.

723. These measures should be taken with just cause and according to due process. Expulsion should be taken particularly seriously because it is most disadvantageous for members of a trade union. Above all, the opportunity for members to express their opinions and to safeguard their rights must be given to them in cases of expulsion.[640]

724. The courts have actively intervened in disciplinary measures imposed by unions when the measures infringe on the worker's fundamental human rights, such as freedom of speech or political creed. Even disciplinary actions against union members who have tried to divide a union have often been nullified by the courts. The courts often find that the disciplinary measure is too severe in light of the limited damage to union cohesiveness.[641]

§9. Check-off

725. A check-off system is an arrangement between an employer and a union under which the employer deducts union dues from wages and transfers them automatically to the union. Such arrangements raise legal questions about whether the employer's deduction of wages violates the principle of the full payment of wages as established in Article 43 of the LSA.[642] The Supreme Court held that a check-off violates the full payment of wages unless there exists an agreement between the employer and the majority representative of workers which allows this as an exception to the full payment principle provided in the LSA.[643] Another legal question arises when a workers asks an employer to stop automatic deductions for that specific worker. The Supreme Court has held that an employer must obey such requests because a check-off agreements is only an agreement between the employer and the union.[644] It has no normative effects on individual employment contracts.[645]

640. Chi Sun Kim, *op. cit.*, pp. 94–95.
641. Takashi Araki, *op. cit.*, p. 170.
642. In the past, it was assumed that such deductions were legal because it was an arrangement that was beneficial to labour (Takashi Araki, *op. cit.*, p. 169).
643. The *Saise-kai Chuo Byoin* case, Japan Supreme Court (11 December 1989) 43 Minshu 1786.
644. The *Esso* case, Supreme Court (25 March 1993) 650 Rohan 6; the *Nestle Japan, Kasumigaura Kojo* case, Japan Supreme Court (23 February 1999) 670 Rohan10.
645. Takashi Araki, *op. cit.*, p. 169.

§10. The Acts on the Establishment, Operation, etc., of Trade Unions for Teachers and Public Officials' Trade Unions

I. Introduction

726. In the case of public servants, only those public officials who are designated by Act, shall have the right to association, collective bargaining and collective action. And Article 5 of the TULRAA provides that 'workers are free to organize a trade union or to join it, except for public servants or teachers who are subject to other enactments'. Therefore, the employees in national and local public service are subject to special regulations, namely by the Act on the Establishment, Operation, etc., of Public Officials' Trade Unions (2006). Employees in the police services, the prison services, the fire defence services, etc., are prohibited not only from going on strike, but also from organizing labour unions. All public employees both in national and local civil services are prohibited from striking and any violation is punishable by criminal sanctions. The right to collective action of workers employed by important defence industries may be either restricted or denied under conditions as prescribed by Act.[646]

727. In addition, to stipulate matters concerning the organization of trade unions for teachers, the Act on the Establishment, Operation, etc., of Trade Unions for Teachers[647] was enacted in 1999.

II. Act on the Establishment, Operation, etc., of Trade Unions for Teachers

A. The Purpose of This Act

728. The purposes of this Act are:

1. to stipulate matters concerning the organization of trade unions for teachers in conformity with the proviso of Article 5 of the TULRAA and;
2. to regulate special provisions necessary for the TULRAA as they are applied to teachers.[648]

729. The term 'teacher' in this Act refers to a person prescribed in Article 19(1) of the Elementary and Secondary Education Act. However, any dismissed persons

646. Constitution, Article 33 paragraph 3.
647. The purpose of this Act is to stipulate matters concerning the organization of trade unions for teachers in conformity with the proviso of Article 5 of the TULRAA and to regulate special provisions necessary for the TULRAA to be applied to teachers, notwithstanding Article 66(1) of the State Public Officials Act and Article 55 of the Private Schools Act.
648. Article 1.

who have made an application to remedy unfair labour practices to the labour relations commission under the provision of Article 82 (1) of the TULRAA shall be regarded as teachers until a review decision is made by the National Labour Relations Commission.[649]

B. The Establishment of Trade Unions

730. Teachers may establish a trade union at the special city, metropolitan city, province or special self-governing province ('cities and provinces') level or at the national level. Anyone who wants to establish a trade union must submit an application to the Minister of Employment and Labour.[650]

C. The Status of Full-time Officials of Trade Unions

731. A teacher may be solely engaged in trade union affairs with the approval of the relevant government authority. A teacher who is solely engaged in a trade union (full-time official) with the approval of the the relevant government authority shall be regarded as complying with an order to take a leave of absence under the Public Educational Official[651] Act and of the Private Schools Act.[652] A full-time official shall not be entitled to wages during the period of service as a full-time official. A full-time official shall not be subject to any disadvantages in promotion or in other matters related to personal status on the grounds of his/her position as a full-time official during their period of service as a full-time official.[653]

III. The Act on the Establishment, Operation, etc., of Public Officials' Trade Unions

A. The Purpose of This Act

732. The purpose of this Act is to stipulate matters concerning the organization of trade unions for public officials in conformity with the proviso of Article 5 of the TULRAA, and to guarantee the public officials' rights of association and collective bargaining pursuant to the Constitution.[654]

649. Article 2.
650. Article 4.
651. Article 44.
652. Article 59.
653. Article 5.
654. Article 33 paragraph 2; Article 1.

B. The Establishment of Trade Unions

733. Public officials may establish a trade union at the National Assembly, the Court, the Constitutional Court, election commissions, the administration, the Special City, metropolitan city, provincial or special self-governing provincial ('cities and provinces') level or at the education office of the respective city and provincial level. Anyone who wants to establish a trade union shall submit an application to the Minister of Employment and Labour.[655]

C. The Status of Full-time Officials of Trade Unions

734. A public official may be solely engaged in trade union affairs with the consent of the relevant government authority. A public official who is solely engaged in a trade union (full-time official) with the consent of the relevant government authority, that authority shall be regarded as complying with an order to take leave of absence under the Government Officials Act and Local Public Servants Act. A full-time official shall not be entitled to wages during the period of service as a full-time official. A full-time official shall not be subject to any disadvantages in promotion or in other matters related to personal status on grounds of his or her position as a full-time official during the period of service as a full-time official.[656]

D. Scope of Public Officials Prohibited from Joining Trade Unions

735. The scope of public officials prohibited from joining a trade union is as follows:[657]

- public officials more senior than deputy director;
- public officials who exercise the right to direct and supervise other public officials or engage in generally managing other public officials' affairs;
- public officials, such as those performing jobs related to personnel and remuneration, who stand in the position of administrative agencies in relations to a trade union;
- public officials who engage in correction, investigation and other similar jobs;
- public officials whose main jobs, such as mediating and inspecting labour relations, are considered inappropriate to be performed by someone with the status of a union member.[658]

655. Article 5.
656. Article 7.
657. Article 6.
658. *Ibid.*

Chapter 2. Workers' Participation

§1. The Act on the Promotion of Workers' Participation and Cooperation

I. The Purpose of the Act on the Promotion of Worker Participation and Cooperation

736. Traditional labour relations have been interpreted as being based on antagonistic relations.[659] When workers and employer cannot reach agreement, workers go on strike and an employer uses the lock-out to accomplish his or her purpose. Accepting that labour relations are based on antagonistic relations, it cannot be said that labour relations have only an antagonistic character. Both labour and management have common interests[660] in constructive and cooperative relations. These cooperative relations could create great benefits for them. Therefore, we may say that labour relations have both an antagonistic character and a cooperative character, and that cooperative relationships are based on antagonistic relations.[661]

737. Cooperative labour relations have been established by developing the system of workers' participation in management. Through workers' participation in management,[662] common interests could be improved and mutual understanding and cooperation could be established. However, there is a problem in ascertaining to what extent workers should participate in management.[663] We admit that this problem in reality depends on economic and social circumstances. And it also depends on the actual state of labour–management relations.[664]

738. European countries typically have dual systems, with industry-level collective bargaining by unions, and company or plant level consultation by works councils. In Korea, the demarcation between joint consultation and collective bargaining is blurred.

659. This concept of antagonism is derived from the fact that while workers are vendors of their labour, an employer is a purchaser of labour. Their interests run counter to each other, both in making labour contracts and in fulfilling them. Therefore, struggle for their respective interests breaks out in all labour–management relations. The collective bargaining system provides peaceful it may be, this system is based on the concept of antagonism (Chi Sun Kim, *op. cit.*, p. 142).
660. Both employees and an employer profit by the expansion and the success of their enterprise.
661. In other words labour–management relations are essentially antagonistic but in addition they may also have a cooperative nature (Chi Sun Kim, *op. cit.*, p. 142).
662. Formerly management was exclusively the prerogative of the employer. However due to spontaneous cooperation from workers, matters concerning the enterprise management needed to be opened to workers.
663. For example, labour–management consultation about matters concerning management policy, production plans. manpower plans, workers' grievances and the improvement of the working environment, etc. Generally speaking, the more labour-management joint consultation there is, the more both sides will profit by it.
664. Chi Sun Kim, *op. cit.*, p. 143.

739. There are several reasons for this lack of a clear distinction between the two channels. First, both joint consultation and collective bargaining take place at the same plant or enterprise level. Second, the parties involved in joint consultation and collective bargaining are, in many cases, the same. Third, the subjects discussed in joint consultation and collective bargaining usually overlap.[665]

740. The vague distinction between labour–management councils and collective bargaining leads to an degree of informality. Usually, joint consultation occurs prior to collective bargaining, and the participants and subjects discussed are similar to those in collective bargaining.[666]

741. In Korea, there is a legal requirement to establish joint consultative bodies. A new Act called the Labour–Management Council Act was enacted as an independent law in 1980 for the furthering of common interests and for establishing cooperative relations between management and labour.[667] After numerous revisions, the current Act on the Promotion of Worker Participation and Cooperation was enacted. The Act provides that its purpose is to keep industrial peace and to contribute to the development of the national economy by promoting the common interests of labour and management through their participation and cooperation.[668]

742. It goes on to provide for the labour–management council, a consultative body which is established to promote the welfare of workers and to seek the sound development of businesses through the participation and cooperation of workers and employers.[669]

---

665. Takashi Araki, *op. cit.*, pp. 179–180.
666. *Ibid.*, p. 180.
667. In Korea labour-management consultation was introduced for the first time by the amended Trade Union Act (TUA, Article 6) in 1963. Labour-management consultation was not imposed by law but only encouraged by administrative guidance. The TUA itself did not make any distinction between labour–management joint consultation and collective bargaining. For this reason the system of labour–management consultation did not develop either in name or in reality. As the labour movement became stronger and strikes became more destructive and more violent in the process of industrial modernization, the Government thought that traditional antagonistic labour relations should be transformed into cooperative ones. To further economic development and to induce foreign capital required for industrial modernization the Government began to turn its attention to labour-management consultation. Thus Article 6 of the TUA was amended in 1973. The subject of labour-management consultation was newly introduced and the provision giving the capacity to undertake collective bargaining to the representative of the labour–management council was abolished. But this was not enough to establish systematic machinery for the furthering of common interests and for establishing cooperative relations between management and labour. In the 5th Republic a new Act called the 'Labour-Management Council Act' was enacted as an independent law in 1980 for the above purpose (Chi Sun Kim, *op. cit.*, p. 143).
668. Article 1.
669. Article 3, no. 1.

II. Basic Principles of the Labour–Management Council System

A. The Obligation for Good Faith and Public Notice and of the Implementation of Resolutions

743. Cooperative labour relations can be established not by legal compulsion but by mutual understanding and spontaneous contribution, in other words by a sincere attitude of good faith. This is particularly required of management. The employer must open matters concerning management as far as possible to their employees. The Act imposes on both sides the duty of good faith by providing that the employers and workers must consult with each other in good faith and on the basis of mutual trust.[670] This duty is an intrinsic one. To the same effect the Act also imposes on both sides the obligation of observance. The Act provides that the Council shall promptly notify workers of matters resolved by it[671] and both workers and the employer shall implement in good faith resolutions made by the Council.[672] When either the management side or the labour side has failed to implement a resolution made by a Council, without justifiable reason, a fine not exceeding 10 million won is to be imposed.[673]

B. The Principle of Mutual Independence between the Labour–Management Council and the Collective Bargaining Process

744. With relation to trade unions, the Act provides that collective bargaining or any other activities of a trade union shall not be affected by this Act.[674]

745. Therefore, these two systems, labour–management councils and collective bargaining, have a different legal character.

746. Firstly the right to demand a labour–management conference is not guaranteed by the Constitution. Both parties have only the duty of good faith which is inherent in the labour–management council system. However, the right to bargain collectively is recognized for workers by the Constitution together with the right to organize and the right to act collectively. This right is not recognized for employers. On the other hand the duty to bargain in good faith is imposed upon either an employer or an organization of employers.

747. Secondly, the labour–management council system has the purpose of promoting the common interests of labour and management by establishing joint consultation on matters concerning management and thereby securing industrial harmony and bringing about industrial democratization. However, the collective

670. Article 2.
671. Article 23.
672. Article 24.
673. Article 30, no. 2.
674. Article 5.

bargaining system has the purpose of improving the social and economic status of workers by maintaining and improving the working conditions of workers. The former may contribute to peace in industry as a result of concluding a collective agreement which puts an end to a dispute between employees and the employer, but this is only secondary and incidental to the original function of the collective bargaining system.

748. Thirdly, there are great differences between the subjects considered through collective bargaining (working conditions, etc.) and those pertinent to the deliberations of the labour–management council (the improvement of productivity, management policy, production plans and manpower policy, etc.)[675] Though it may be clear in theory, it is not easy to draw a sharp line between the areas of concern for the collective bargaining process and those overseen by the labour–management council.

749. Fourthly, if the labour–management council's discussions end in failure, workers cannot resort to the right to act collectively. However, when bargaining between management and labour is broken off, a labour dispute occurs.[676]

750. Fifthly, when the labour–management council's discussions result in success, both sides reach an agreement, but this does not have the character of a collective agreement. The collective agreement has a normative effect in addition to its obligatory effect. But the labour–management council result does not have a normative character.[677]

675. Working conditions, namely, wages, hours of work, ventilation, temperature, speed of work, and the like can be subjects of collective bargaining. Besides working conditions those matters which have a close relation to the living conditions of workers and are within an employer's discretion are generally regarded as subjects of collective bargaining. With respect to these matters we may find a conflict of interests between employees and employer. However, those matters concerning the management of an enterprise in which both employees and an employer have common interests can be the subjects of labour–management council. We may enumerate the improvement of productivity, management policy, production plans and manpower policy. These matters originally belonged to the employer's prerogative. Subjects of labour–management consultation differ among countries. Sometimes the same matters may be the subjects of both. In this case the issue undergo different processes because of the difference between these two systems (Chi Sun Kim, *op. cit.*, p. 145).
676. Then both sides may resort to force to accomplish their aims. The right to act collectively is constitutionally recognized to support the right to bargain collectively.
677. The collective agreement cannot be naturally extended to non-members of the trade union which is party to it. But a labour–management council applies to all employees whether or not they are members of a trade union (Chi Sun Kim, *op. cit.*, p. 145).

§2. The Establishment and Composition of Labour–Management Councils

I. The Establishment of Labour–Management Councils

751. A labour–management council shall be established, in each business or workplace, which is vested with the right to decide working conditions. However, this shall not apply to businesses or workplaces with fewer than 30 permanent workers. When one business has separately located workplaces, a Council may be established in each of these workplaces.[678]

A. *Composition*

1. Composition of the Council

752. A Council shall be composed of an equal number of members representing employers and members representing workers, which shall be at least three but not more than ten.

753. While members representing workers shall be elected by workers, and if there is a trade union composed of a majority of workers, the representatives of the trade union or the persons appointed by the trade union shall be workers' members.[679]

No employer shall intervene in or interfere with an election of workers' members. Members representing employers shall be the representatives of the business or workplace concerned, or the persons appointed by such representatives.[680]

2. Chairman and Secretary

754. There shall be a chairman of a Council and that chairman shall be elected by mutual vote from among the members. Alternatively one from workers' representatives and one of the members representing the employer may be co-chairman. The chairman shall represent the Council and oversee meetings thereof. Labour and management, shall each, have a secretary in charge of dealing with the clerical work of the council, such as the recording of meeting results, etc.[681] The term of office of members shall be three years and is renewable.[682] An employer shall not treat unfavourably workers' members in connection with the performance of their duties

678. Article 4.
679. Article 10.
680. Article 6.
681. Article 7.
682. Article 8.

as members of the council. The hours spent by a member to attend the council and engage in activities directly related thereto, and stipulated in the Council bylaws shall be regarded as hours worked.[683]

3. Orders of Correction

755. If an employer unfavourably treats workers' representatives or intervenes in or interferes with an election of workers' members in violation of the Act, the Minister of Employment and Labour may order him or her to correct such violations.[684]

B. The Operation of Councils

1. Calling of Meetings

756. A Council shall hold meetings once every three months.

757. A Council may hold an extraordinary meeting if it is deemed necessary.[685]

758. The chairman shall convene and preside over meetings of the Council. If the representatives of either labour or management requests a meeting to be held, specifying the purposes of the meeting in writing, the chairman shall accept the request. The chairman shall notify each member of the date, place, agenda, etc. of a meeting seven days prior to the meeting.[686]

759. A Council shall draw up and keep minutes of its meetings containing each of the following matters:

- date, time and place of each meeting;
- members present at each meeting;
- contents of consultations and matters decided at each meeting;
- other matters discussed at each meeting.

The meeting minutes taken shall be kept for three years from the date they are taken.[687]

683. Article 9.
684. Article 11.
685. Article 12.
686. Article 13.
687. Article 19.

2. Quorum

760. Meetings shall be held with the presence of a majority of workers' members and a majority of employers' members, and a decision shall be made with the approval of at least two-thirds of the members present.[688]

3. Opening of Meetings and Duty of Confidentiality

761. Council meetings shall be open to the public; however, they may be closed to the public upon a resolution of the council.[689] Members of a council shall not reveal any confidential matters which come to their knowledge at a meeting of the Council.[690]

4. Establishment of the Bylaws of a Council

762. A council shall establish bylaws ('council bylaws') governing the organization and operation of the council, and shall submit them to the Minister of Employment and Labour within 15 days from the date of the establishment of the council. The same shall apply where any part of the bylaws is amended.[691]

C. Functions of the Council

1. Introduction

763. The competence of the labour–management conference embraces those subjects in which labour and management usually have common interests. Formerly these subjects belonged exclusively to the prerogative of an employer. But to expect spontaneous cooperation from employees these subjects have been opened to employees through the workers' participation system. The forms of workers' participation differ form country to country.[692] In Korea according to the extent and degree of the workers' participation, subjects are divided into three groups,

688. Article 15.
689. Article 16.
690. Article 17.
691. Article 18.
692. Workers' participation may in theory be divided into various types. Depending on the extent to which workers participate in management in reality, labour–management joint consultation may take the form of information exchange, the exchange of advice, the exchange of ideas, or joint determination. Cooperation in information exchange means that both employees and the employer give and receive information that is useful to one another. How each evaluates and makes use of it is left solely to the decision of the other. When opinions and advice are shared with respect to pending problems, we call this the exchange of advice. In this case one side gives advice to the other side and defines its activities. Mutual understanding could be improved and lack of trust could be eliminated between employees and employer. But they still stick to and persist in their views.

- matters subject to consultation;
- matters subject to resolution; and
- matters subject to report and explanation.

2. Matters Subject to Consultation

764. Matters subject to consultation at meetings of a council shall be as follows:

- the improvement of productivity and the sharing of gain;
- the hiring, posting, education and training of workers;
- the handling of workers' grievances;
- the improvement of occupational safety and health and other matters pertaining to the working environment and the promotion of workers' health;
- institutional improvement for personnel and labour management;
- general rules of employment adjustment, such as reassignment and transfer, retraining, or dismissal for managerial or technological reasons;
- the administration of working hours and recess hours;
- institutional improvement of wage payment methods, wage structures, wage systems, etc.;
- the introduction of new machines and technologies or improvement of work processes;
- the establishment or revision of work rules;
- employees' stock ownership plans and other methods of support for the creation and enhancement of workers' wealth;
- matters concerning rewards given to workers for their work-related inventions, etc.;
- matter relating to the promotion of the welfare of workers;
- any installation of employee surveillance equipment within a workplace;
- matters concerning support the maternity rights of female workers and the balance between work and family life;
- other matters concerning labour–management cooperation.

765. A council may make a decision with regards to the above matters according to the quorum rules under the Act.[693] Then the council must promptly notify

However, in the exchange of ideas both parties take up a more open and positive attitude. Proposals and ideas concerning economy in expenditure, improvement in quality and production plans are put forward and the management side accepts them. Constructive cooperation can be established by sincere conferral. Though the final decision may be left to management. the management takes into consideration the results of joint consultation. Joint determination allows the most positive workers' participation. Here workers have the equal right to a voice and the equal right to a vote. This does not imply that all management questions should be decided by joint determination. Matters of common interest can be subjects of joint determination. This classification of workers' participation is made according to the degree and the extent of participation in management. These forms are only theoretical ones. Existing labour–management consultation may not exactly fall under any of these categories. It may involve any admixture of them (Chi Sun Kim, *op. cit.*, p. 143).

693. Article 20.

employees of the matters agreed upon.[694] Once an agreement is reached, the employer and employees must observe it in good faith.[695] On some matters the workers' representatives can require their opposite numbers to consult with them. The employers' members must consult with the workers' members side. In doing so they should take an open and positive attitude. Constructive proposals and ideas should be exchanged by both sides.

3. Matters Subject to a Resolution

766. An employer shall seek a resolution of the Council on any of the matters falling under the following criteria:

- the establishment of basic plans for the education and training and skills development of workers;
- the establishment and management of welfare facilities;
- the establishment of an employee welfare fund.

4. Matters Not Resolved by the Grievance Handling Committee

767. A council shall promptly notify workers of matters it has resolved.[696] Both workers and the employer shall implement in good faith resolutions made by the council.[697] When a representative of either labour or management has failed to comply in areas agreed upon without justifiable reason, a fine not exceeding 10 million won is to be imposed.[698]

5. Matters Subject to Report and Explanation

768. An employer shall report or explain any of the matters described in the following points in good faith at a regular meeting:

- matters concerning their general management plans and results;
- matters concerning the quarterly production plans and results;
- matters concerning manpower plans;
- the economic and financial conditions of the enterprise.

Workers' members may report and explain workers' demands. If an employer fails to make a report or give an explanation, workers' members may request the

694. Article 23.
695. Article 24.
696. Article 23.
697. Article 24.
698. Article 32, no. 2.

employer to submit documents relevant to the matters described, and the employer shall respond to such a request in good faith.[699]

D. *Voluntary Arbitration*

769. In cases falling under any of the following categories, a dispute may be settled by an arbitration organization set up within the council by agreement between the workers' members and the employers' members, or may be referred to arbitration by the labour relations commission or other third parties:

- where the council fails to make a resolution on matters subject to resolution;
- where there is any disagreement on the interpretation, implementation, etc., of resolutions made by the council.

770. If an arbitration decision is rendered, the matters concerned shall be deemed to have been decided by the council, and both workers and employer shall comply with the decision.[700]

E. *Grievance Handling*

1. Members of a Grievance-handling Committee

771. All businesses or workplaces shall have a grievance handling committee in order to hear and handle workers' grievances. However, this shall not apply to businesses or workplaces with fewer than 30 permanent workers.[701]

2. Composition and Terms of Grievance-handling Members

772. A grievance handling committee shall consist of not more than three members representing labour and management, and in the case of a business or workplace where a council is established, the council shall select such members from among its members and in the case of a business or a workplace where no council is established, the employer shall appoint them.[702]

3. Grievance Handling

773. If a member of a grievance handling committee hears from a worker about grievances, he or she shall inform the worker concerned of the measures taken and

699. Article 22.
700. Article 25.
701. Article 26.
702. Article 27.

results thereof within ten days. Matters deemed difficult for members of the grievance handling committee to deal with shall be brought before the council and dealt with through discussion at a following meeting.[703]

703. Article 28.

Chapter 3. Collective Bargaining

§1. The Concept and Functions of Collective Bargaining under Current law

774. Neither the Constitution nor the TULRAA contains a definition of collective bargaining. Collective bargaining entails negotiations about wages and other conditions of work between a trade union and an employer or an employers' organization. We may divide collective bargaining into two processes. One is the negotiating process which aims at the conclusion of a collective agreement and the other is the conclusion of the collective agreement itself. The former is one that has no legal effect, the latter is one that has a legally binding effect.

775. The principal aim of collective bargaining is to achieve an agreement between the parties through compromise and concession. Because collective bargaining is a process of dealing in a unified way, through representatives, with the labour relations of the parties and the formation of rules, those representatives must have the authority to bargain. Although collective bargaining is the act of forming rules through negotiations or by consent, both parties have complete freedom with regard to compromise.

776. Its core role is a collective transaction dealing with the purchase and sale of labour. An important role performed by collective bargaining currently is, by mutual consent, to formulate and put in practice rules governing both individual and collective labour relations.[704]

§2. The Right to Bargain and Duty to Bargain in Good Faith

777. Article 33 of Korea's Constitution guarantees the right of workers to bargain collectively. To improve working conditions, and thereby to enhance the economic and social status of workers, it is necessary for a favourable collective agreement to be concluded as a result of any process of collective bargaining. Although this is not the right of an individual worker but of an organization of workers, a trade union, of which the workers concerned are members. The right to

704. A worker, though the equal of the employer in law, is in fact subject to the employer in making a contract or in fulfilling the contract because of his or her lower social status and economic power. That is why workers should unite against an employer or an employers' organization. The term 'collective' does not mean that many workers really participate in bargaining but that an organization of workers, a trade union which represents the interests of workers, bargains as an equal party with an employer or employers' organization. Whether it is an individual employer or an employers' organization that participates in the bargaining with a trade union does not matter. The collective bargaining system has its significance in that working conditions are decided by mutual consent instead of by a unilateral decision of the employer (Chi Sun Kim, *op. cit.*, p. 95).

bargain, as with any other right, must be exercised fairly within intrinsic legal limits. If the right to bargain is exercised fairly, the trade union is exempted from criminal liability. Likewise, the employer cannot reject reasonable demands of the trade union.[705]

778. The TULRAA provides that 'a trade union and an employer or an employers' association have to bargain with each other in good faith and sincerity and make a collective agreement, and not abuse their authority. The TULRAA further provides that 'a trade union and an employer or an employers' association have not to refuse or delay, without just causes, negotiating or concluding collective agreements:[706] The obligation to bargain in good faith is mutual, that is, a trade union as well as an employer has the duty to bargain in good faith.[707]

779. This constitutional right to bargain is reinforced by the unfair labour practice system established in the TULRAA. An employer's refusal to, or delay in, conducting collective bargaining, without justifiable reasons,[708] with the representative of a trade union or a person who has been authorized by a trade union is considered an unfair labour practice.[709] The labour relations commission will issue a remedial order and order the employer to bargain with the union in good faith

§3. Subjects for Collective Bargaining

780. The TULRAA does not enumerate expressly the subjects that may the subject of collective bargaining. In principle, all matters can be discussed in a collective bargaining process as long as both parties agree to do so. However, the scope of matters about which an employer is required to bargain is limited. Judging from the purpose of collective bargaining system, we may conclude that besides working conditions those matters which relate to the living conditions of workers and at the same time are within an employer's control can be subjects of collective bargaining.

705. Chi Sun Kim, *op. cit.*, p. 96.
706. Article 30.
707. Article 84.
708. As the provision stipulates, an employer may refuse to bargain with justifiable reasons. These justifiable reasons exempt the employer from the duty to begin or continue bargaining. To decide whether the reasons are justifiable or not, the purpose of these provisions to facilitate and promote fair collective bargaining must be taken into consideration. First, consideration of the party involved in collective bargaining on the workers' side; secondly a consideration of the subjects being negotiated and, thirdly, a consideration of the procedural and circumstantial details, the elements may give an employer justifiable reasons. For example, issues concerning the labour policy or wage policy of the Government and those which clearly belong to management as a result of their prerogatives fall outside the scope of reasonable negotiating topics and an employer may refuse to negotiate about such issues. Likewise when representatives of a trade union assume a threatening attitude – using violence – a refusal to negotiate is justified (Chi Sun Kim, *op. cit.*, p. 97).
709. Article 81, sub-paragraph 4.

781. Mandatory subjects that fall under the purview of 'working conditions and other treatment' include wages, hours, holidays, health and safety, compensation for work related accidents, vocational training, and personnel matters (e.g. transfers, discipline, and dismissals). Matters concerning management and production policies, such as the introduction of new machines, the restructuring of production processes, relocation of plants, and subcontracting, are understood to be mandatory subjects only when they affect the working conditions or other treatment of union members.

782. Matters concerning the 'management of collective labour relations' include union shop agreements, rules governing union activities, grants aiding the convenience of the union's activities, rules and procedures for collective bargaining, labour–management consultations, rules and procedures for dispute acts, and so forth.[710]

783. 'Management rights' had often been asserted as a reason for limiting the scope of mandatory bargaining subjects, i.e. that a duty to bargain cannot exist with regard to personnel matters and production methods which are within the exclusive province of management. Under the statute, however, there is no special right based on 'management rights' to avoid the duty to bargain. There is no objection to labelling a host of matters that an employer is not required to bargain about "matters involving management rights.' It is inappropriate to determine at the start, however, whether a subject belongs in the 'management rights' category in order to decide whether it is a mandatory bargaining subject. Whether it is a mandatory bargaining subject should be determined from the goals of Article 33 of the Constitution and TULRAA to protect workers' rights to bargain collectively.[711]

784. The right of private ownership is guaranteed by the Constitution. As the owner, an employer has the management prerogative with regard to the enterprise. Therefore, matters concerning enterprise management fall outside the scope of collective bargaining in principle. For example, matters concerning appointment, discharge, promotion, and production schemes fall outside the scope of collective bargaining. However, we cannot draw a sharp line between matters concerning management prerogatives and matters concerning working conditions. This is because some matters concerning management prerogatives inevitably affect the working conditions of the workers. In this case, a trade union may also request an employer to negotiate on these matters.[712]

---

710. Takashi Araki, *op. cit.*, p. 172.
711. Kazuo Sugeno, *op. cit.*, p. 564.
712. Chi Sun Kim, *op. cit.*, p. 98.

§4. THE PARTIES TO COLLECTIVE BARGAINING

I. Union Parties to Collective Bargaining

785. The party to collective bargaining process on the labour side is a trade union. *Bona fide* trade unions, even though they do not meet all the legal requirements may be parties to collective bargaining.[713] The parties who practise bargaining are in practice the representatives of trade unions or a federation of trade unions which are entrusted with the authority to bargain by the member unions. Representatives have the authority to conduct negotiations with respect to all subjects of collective bargaining unless their authority is restricted by union constitutions or decisions of general conferences.

II. Employer Parties to Collective Bargaining

786. The parties involved in collective bargaining on the employer's side are either individual employers or an organization that represents them. An employers' organization means an organization of employers which has the authority to adjust and control its constituent members with regard to labour relations.[714] Employers' organizations practise bargaining sometimes as the subject of rights and duties resulting from a collective agreement, sometimes as the mandatory result of the authority to conduct bargaining.

III. Delegation of the Right to Bargain

787. Any person who has been authorized by a trade union or by an employer or an employers' association to bargain and to make a collective agreement may exercise his or her power within the scope of the authority which the trade union, employer or employers' association has granted. In cases where a trade union, or an employer or an employers' association delegates the authority to conduct negotiate or to conclude a collective agreement, it shall notify the other party of such a fact.[715]

713. In addition, there is no distinction between a majority union and a minority union. There is no trade union that monopolizes the right to bargain collectively. Even an agreement that a specific trade union has a unique bargaining right that gives it a monopoly in terms of collective bargaining cannot deprive other trade unions of that right. Such an agreement is deemed null and void (Chi Sun Kim, *op. cit.*, p. 98).
714. Article 2, sub-paragraph 3.
715. Article 29 paragraph 3–4.

§5. Plural Unionism and Collective Bargaining

788. Workers are free to organize a trade union or to join it.[716] Any union that meets the statutory requirements has the right to organize, bargain and act collectively. The representative of a trade union has the authority to bargain with employers or employers' associations, and to make collective agreements for the trade union and union members.

789. In Korea, multiple unions may exist within a single company. Therefore, in cases where a trade union exists in a business or workplace, a new trade union which has the same organizational jurisdiction as existing trade unions can be formed.[717] Plural unionism gives rise to various complex legal issues in relation to collective agreements and the establishment of union working conditions, the employer's neutrality towards unions, etc.

790. In relation to the collective agreements, in Korea, the TULRAA adopts a collective bargaining representation system. Under this system, a representative union, has the authority to bargain with employers or employers' associations, and to make collective agreements for the trade union and union members.[718]

791. Therefore, in cases where multiple unions coexist within a business or workplace, regardless of its form of organization, to bargain with employers collectively, unions have to decide upon a representative union on their own. Otherwise, the union that organizes the majority of all union members in a business or workplace may be deemed to be the representative union for bargaining purposes.[719]

792. In cases where unions have not reached a conclusion on the representative union, in the same way as stated above, plural unions have to organize joint bargaining representation units, and its union can bargain with employers.[720] In cases where unions did not reach a agreement on a joint bargaining representation union, the labour relations commission, at the unions' request, can decide the joint bargaining representative in the light of the ratio of union members.[721]

716. Article 6.
717. In fact, a large company occasionally may have multiple unions, one being the cooperative dominant union and a few radical minority unions, which organize only a few workers. It may also happen that an individual who is dissatisfied with the enterprise-based union's policy or activities belongs to a regional general union, which organizes workers in companies throughout the region (Takashi Araki, *op. cit.*, p. 162).
718. Article 29, paragraph 2.
719. Article 29-2, paragraph 1-2.
720. Article 29-2, paragraph 4.
721. Article 29-2, paragraph 5.

§6. Teachers' Unions: Collective Agreements

I. The Right to Bargain and Conclusion of Collective Agreements

793. The representative of a trade union shall have the authority to negotiate and conclude collective agreements on matters concerning the improvement of the economic and social status of teachers, such as wages, working conditions and welfare, with the Minister of Education, Science and Technology, the Superintendent of the Board of Education for the respective city or province, or the person who establishes and runs a private school. In the case of private schools, the persons who establishes and runs the schools shall participate in negotiations at the national level or at the city and provincial level.

794. The negotiating team of a trade union shall consist of the representative and members of the trade union concerned.

795. In the case that two or more trade unions are established, collective bargaining shall be conducted through only a unified bargaining channel of the trade unions concerned.

796. In the case of collective bargaining or agreements, the concerned parties shall negotiate in good faith, taking into consideration the opinion of the public and parents, and shall not abuse their rights.[722]

II. Procedure for Determining the Bargaining Representative Union, etc.

797. If there are two trade unions or more which are established or joined by workers in a business or workplace regardless of the type of organization, the trade unions shall determine the bargaining representative union (including the bargaining representative body composed of members of two different trade unions or more; hereinafter the same shall apply) and then demand bargaining. Provided, that this shall not apply where the employer consents not to undergo the procedure for determining the bargaining representative union channel prescribed in this Article within the period during which the bargaining representative union can be determined autonomously (paragraph 1).

All trade unions participating in the procedure for determining the bargaining representative union shall autonomously determine the bargaining representative union within the period prescribed by the Presidential Decree (paragraph 2).

Where the bargaining representative union is undetermined within the period referred to in paragraph (2) and the consent of the employer as referred to in paragraph (1) is not obtained from the employer, the trade union (including the case where two trade unions or more, between them, have a majority of the members of

722. Article 6.

all trade unions participating in the procedure for determining the bargaining representative union by delegating authority, uniting themselves together, etc.) composed of a majority of the members of all trade unions participating in the procedure for determining the bargaining representative union shall become the bargaining representative union (paragraph 3).

Where all trade unions participating in the procedure for determining the bargaining representative union, fails to determine such pursuant to paragraphs (2) and (3), shall jointly organize a bargaining representative team (hereinafter referred to as the joint bargaining representative team) and then conduct bargaining with the employer. In this case, a trade union eligible to participate in the joint bargaining representative team shall be the one whose members make up not less than 10/100 (tenth of a hundred) of the members of all trade unions participating in the procedure for determining the bargaining representative union (paragraph 4).

If no agreement is reached on the organization of the joint bargaining representative team, the Labor Relations Commission may decide in consideration of the proportions of union members at the request of the concerned trade union (paragraph 5).

Where an objection is raised to the demand for bargaining, the number of union members, etc., in relation to the determination of the bargaining representative union pursuant to paragraphs (1) through (4), the Labor Relations Commission may decide on such objection at the request of the trade union under the conditions prescribed by the Presidential Decree (paragraph 6).

Necessary matters concerning the procedure for determining the bargaining representative union, including the method by which a trade union demands and participates in bargaining and the standards for calculating the number of union members to determine the bargaining representative union, the prevention of an increase in bargaining costs, and so on shall be prescribed by the presidential decree (Article 29-1, paragraph 8).

III. The Effect of Collective Agreements

798. The contents of collective agreements concluded in accordance with the provisions of this Act shall not take effect as collective agreements, in case they are stipulated by the law, bylaws, and budget, or stipulated by the authority delegated by the law, bylaws and budget.

799. The Minister of Education, Science and Technology, the superintendents of the provincial education office, and those who establish and run private schools shall make efforts in good faith to implement the matters which do not take effect as collective agreements as prescribed above.[723]

723. Article 41.

IV. Mediation and Arbitration

A. *The Prohibition of Industrial Action and Political Activities*

800. A trade union and its members shall be prohibited from taking any industrial action, including strikes, work slowdowns and other activities hindering normal business operations.[724] Trade unions for teachers shall not be allowed to participate in any political activities.[725]

B. *Application for Mediation of Labour Disputes*

801. In the instance that collective bargaining breaks down, either or both parties concerned may apply for mediation to the National Labour Relations Commission. In the case that either or both parties apply for mediation, the National Labour Relations Commission shall commence mediation without delay, and the parties concerned shall participate in the mediation in good faith. A mediation process shall be completed within 30 days following the date of application.[726]

C. *Arbitration*

802. The National Labour Relations Commission shall conduct arbitration in the event of any of the following situations:

- when both parties concerned request arbitration after collective bargaining breaks down;
- when the mediation proposal of the national labour relations commission is rejected by either or both parties concerned;
- when the chairperson of the national labour relations commission determines to refer the case concerned to arbitration under his or her authority or at the request of the Minister of Employment and Labour.[727]

D. *Composition of the Labour Relations Adjustment Commission for Teachers*

803. The Labour Relations Adjustment Commission for Teachers shall be established under the National Labour Relations Commission to mediate and arbitrate in labour disputes involving teachers. The Commission shall consist of three mediating members of the National Labour Relations Commission representing the public interest who are nominated by the chairperson of the National Labour Relations Commission. However, a person, who is not a mediating member of the National

724. Article 8.
725. Article 43.
726. Article 9.
727. Article 10.

Labour Relations Commission representing the public interest, shall be recommended with the mutual consent of the parties concerned, and that person shall be nominated.

804. The chairperson of the Commission shall be elected mutually from among its members.[728]

E. Finality of an Award Following Arbitration

805. In the situation that a party concerned asserts that an arbitration award rendered by the National Labour Relations Commission violates the law or is an act beyond its authority, that party may file an administrative suit against the Chairperson of the National Labour Relations Commission within 15 days from the receipt of the arbitration decision.

806. If no administrative suit has been filed within the specified period, the arbitration award shall be finalized.

807. When the arbitration award is finalized, the parties concerned shall comply therewith.

808. The effect of an arbitration award rendered by the National Labour Relations Commission shall not be suspended by the institution of an administrative suit.

809. The arbitration award having been finalized, shall have the same effect as a collective agreement.[729]

§7. Public Officials: Collective Agreements

I. The Right to Negotiate and Conclusion of Collective Agreements

810. The representative of a trade union shall have the authority to negotiate and conclude collective agreements on matters concerning the improvement of the economic and social status of public officials, such as wages, welfare and other working conditions, with the Secretary-General of the National Assembly, the Secretary-General of the Court Administration Office, the Chairman of the Election Commissions, the Secretary-General of Constitutional Court, the Minister of Administration, the Mayors of Special Cities, the Mayors of Metropolitan Cities, the Governors of Provinces or Special Self-governing Provinces ('cities and provinces'), or the Superintendent of the Board of Education of their respective city or province.

728. Article 11.
729. Article 12.

811. The negotiating members of the trade union shall consist of the representative and members of the trade union concerned.

812. In the case that two or more trade unions are established, collective bargaining shall be conducted through only a unified bargaining channel of the trade unions concerned.

813. In the case of collective bargaining or agreements, the concerned parties shall negotiate in good faith, taking into consideration the opinions of the public and parents, and shall not abuse their rights.[730]

II. The Effect of Collective Agreements

814. The contents of collective agreements concluded in accordance with the provision of this Act shall not take effect as collective agreements, in cases that are stipulated by the law, bylaws, and budget, or stipulated by the authority delegated by the law, bylaws and budget.

815. The government's negotiating representative shall make efforts in good faith to implement the matters which do not take effect as collective agreements as prescribed above.[731]

III. Prohibition of Industrial Action and Political Activities

816. A trade union and its members shall be prohibited from taking any industrial action, including strikes, work slowdowns and other activities hindering normal business operation.[732] Trade unions for public officials shall not be allowed to participate in any political activities.[733]

IV. Application for the Mediation of Labour Disputes

817. If collective bargaining breaks down, either or both parties concerned may apply for mediation to the National Labour Relations Commission. If either or both parties apply for mediation, the National Labour Relations Commission shall commence mediation without delay, and the parties concerned shall participate in the mediation in good faith. The mediation process shall be completed within 30 days after the date of application.[734]

730. Article 9.
731. Article 10.
732. Article 11.
733. Article 4.
734. Article 12.

A. Arbitration

818. The National Labour Relations Commission shall conduct arbitration in any of the following situations:

- when both parties concerned request arbitration after collective bargaining breaks down;
- when the mediation proposal of the national labour relations commission is rejected by either or both parties concerned, When the Labour Relations Adjustment Commission for Public Officials at a plenary meeting determines to refer the case concerned to arbitration under its own authority.[735]

B. Composition of the Labour Relations Adjustment Commission for Public Officials

819. The Labour Relations Adjustment Commission for Public Officials shall be established under the National Labour Relations Commission to mediate and arbitrate labour disputes when collective bargaining breaks down. The Commission shall consist of within seven mediating members of the National Labour Relations Commission representing public interest who are nominated by the President with the National Labour Relations Commission's chairperson's and the Labour Minister's recommendation.[736]

C. Finality of an Award Following Arbitration

820. If a party concerned asserts that an arbitration award rendered by the National Labour Relations Commission violates the law or is an act beyond its authority, that party may file an administrative suit against the chairperson of the National Labour Relations Commission within 15 days from the receipt of the arbitration being awarded.

821. If no administrative suit has been filed within the specified period, the arbitration award shall be finalized.

822. When that the arbitration award is finalized, the parties concerned must comply therewith.

823. The effect of an arbitration award rendered by the National Labour Relations Commission shall not be suspended by the institution of an administrative suit.

735. Article 13.
736. Article 14.

824. The arbitration award, once finalized, shall have the same effect as a collective agreement.[737]

737. Article 16.

Chapter 4. Strikes, Lock-outs and the Settlement of Disputes

§1. Labour Disputes and the Law

I. Legal Protection of Acts of Disputation

825. The Korean Constitution guarantees the right to act collectively together with the right to organize and the right to bargain collectively (Article 33). This right is exercised by workers in an effort to accomplish their claims concerning working conditions when bargaining, undertaken in good faith, between workers and an employer cannot bring about a collective agreement. This right has been recognized in order to establish an essential equality between workers and employers. Acting to bolster this constitutional guarantee are the three legal protections provided by the TULRAA for 'proper' dispute acts: exemption from criminal liability (Article 4), exemption from civil liability or liability for damages caused by dispute acts (Article 3),[738] and prohibition of disadvantageous treatment, such as retaliatory discharge or disciplinary action (Article 81, no.1,5).

826. Although the right of workers to act collectively in pursuit of their claims is guaranteed by the Constitution, such collective activities are liable to cause irrecoverable economic loss to the parties engaged in labour disputes and to third parties not directly engaged in labour disputes. For this reason this right came to be regulated by law. As compared with the right to organize and the right to bargain collectively, this right is more rigidly restricted by law. To what extent this right should be guaranteed and restricted differs from one country to another depending upon the political and economic situation. To maintain a balance between the exercise of this right and the protection of third parties' interests and the national economy is an important goal of the law regulating the right to engage in collective activities.[739] The TULRAA declares that the purpose of this Act is to 'contribute to the maintenance of industrial peace and to the development of the national economy by preventing and resolving labour disputes through the fair adjustment of labour relations' (Article 1).

738. According to traditional civil and criminal law, these collective activities undertaken by workers constitute criminal and civil offences. When workers refuse to work, in other words when they go on strike, this amounts to non-performance of their obligations. Therefore, in theory, they must make compensation for all damages caused by such non-performance. The organization of the workers, namely a trade union, which does not nave any contractual relations with an employer must compensate such damages as are caused by having instigated and manipulated workers not to work. But since the constitution guarantees the right to engage in collective activities, these problems do not arise. The Korean TULRAA (Article 3) provides civil indemnity and provides for criminal indemnity (Article 4).

739. Chi Sun Kim, *op. cit.*, p. 120.

II. Definition of Labour Disputes and Dispute Activities

827. There is no other legal definition concerning labour disputes and dispute acts. 'Labour disputes' means any controversy or difference arising from a disagreement between a trade union and an employer or an employers' association (parties to labour relations) concerning the determination of terms and conditions of employment such as wages, working hours, welfare, dismissal, other treatment, etc. In this case, 'disagreement' is referred to as situations in which no agreement is likely to be reached by the parties even though they continue to attempt to make an agreement.[740]

828. A labour dispute takes place between an organization of workers and an employer or an organization of employers. Therefore, a controversy over claims concerning working conditions between an individual worker and an employer is not a labour dispute though it may be a cause for a labour dispute.

829. A controversy over claims results from the failure of collective bargaining between an organization of workers and an employer or an organization of employers. A labour dispute is a consequential state of the breakdown of negotiations between management and labour.[741] The Act defines a labour dispute as a controversy over claims concerning working conditions. Therefore, only working conditions are regarded as subjects of such a controversy.[742]

830. 'Dispute acts' means actions or counter-actions which obstruct the normal operation of a business, such as strikes, sabotages, lock-outs, or other activities through which the parties to labour relations intend to achieve their claims.[743]

831. The right to act collectively is granted only to workers, not to employers, by the Constitution. But in the TULRAA employers as well as workers are allowed to use methods such as a lock-out or other similar tactics though they are not subjects of this right.[744] Dispute acts are those which hamper the normal operation of

740. Article 2, no. 5.
741. Therefore a controversy over claims which has not passed through the procedure of collective bargaining cannot be regarded as a labour dispute to be regulated by the Act and in such a conflict a strike or a boycott cannot be inaugurated.
742. However, as in the case of collective bargaining, besides working conditions those matters related to the living conditions of workers and at the same time within an employer's disposal can be subjects of collective bargaining and a controversy concerning these matters may also be regarded as a labour dispute. Those matters concerning the management of an enterprise and belonging exclusively to the prerogative of an employer cannot be the subjects of a labour dispute. They can, however, be the subject of labour-management joint consultations. But matters pertaining to the managerial prerogative and at the same time inevitably affecting the working conditions of workers can be subjects of a labour dispute.
743. Article 2, no. 6.
744. As to whether the use of dispute tactics by management is the exercise of this right, opinions are divided. Some say that it is the exercise of this right based on property rights or based on the principle of equality between management and labour. But taking into consideration the fact that the Constitution guarantees the right to act collectively only for workers to secure an essential equality between workers and employers, who have much stronger economic power than the former, we

business. This normal operation of business does not mean the operation of the business in conformity with all the rules and regulations. Therefore a law-abiding labour struggle which hampers business is also a dispute act. Dispute acts are distinguished from the status of labour dispute itself in that the normal operation of business is hampered by them.

III. Categories of Dispute Acts

A. *Strikes*

832. A strike is the workers' collective and systematic refusal to offer their labour. As a result of their collective refusal to offer that labour an employer loses control of his or her workers. Therefore the strike is the most effective and strongest weapon of workers against an employer.

833. Strikes may be divided into many types; they could be divided into walk-out strikes and sit-down strikes, depending on whether or not the participating workers remain in their places of work.[745] According to the scale of a strike, they can be divided strikes into a general strike, an industry-wide strike and the partial strike.[746] A 'political strike' can be defined as a strike that is aimed at demonstrating or realizing workers' particular political opinions and is directly addressed at national or local governmental agencies. When dispute acts are understood as a means of making collective bargaining function, political strikes are improper, since they bear no relationship to collective bargaining.[747] But, as to the legality of the political strike against the economic or labour policy of a government, legal theories are divided. In Korea the major theory is the affirmative one which approves the legality of the political strike within certain limits.[748]

---

may safely say that an employer is allowed to resort to these tactics of dispute in an emergency situation in which an employer cannot be expected any longer to perform the obligations imposed upon them by a collective agreement or individual labour contracts.

745. A sit-down strike occurs in order to prevent an employer from employing scab labour to substitute for the former workers. Therefore, this is a very effective strike to frustrate the efforts of an employer to minimize the damage that may result from a strike.
746. A general strike extends over a province, state or country, involving workers engaged in many industries. It usually takes the form of a sympathetic strike or a political strike. An industry-wide strike is limited to a certain industry. In a partial strike workers of a certain part of an enterprise or part of a union participate.
747. Kazuo Sugeno, *op. cit.*, p. 626.
748. The affirmative theory is based on different points of view. Some say that a strike against economic or labour policies of a government which have a close relationship to workers' lives is the same as one against the management policy of an employer concerning working conditions. Others say that the right of workers to engage in collective activities historically has also meant the right to deal with government. This affirmative theory recognizes the legality of the so-called political strike under certain conditions. The most important condition is that it must have the purpose of maintaining and improving working conditions and thereby seek to enhance the economic and social status of workers. In Korea the major theory is the affirmative one which approves the legality of the political strike within certain limits.

B. Soldiering and Sabotage

834. The Act mentions sabotage as a dispute act.[749] But legal theorists are in accord that this means passive sabotage, not active sabotage or verbal sabotage. Active sabotage includes such practices as the breaking of machinery or the spoiling of raw materials or products. Verbal sabotage consists of revealing secrets to, or committing unlawful acts for, those who maintain business relations with an employer. Passive sabotage (soldiering) means inadequate performance on the job which causes a reduction in operational efficiency.[750]

C. Picketing and Boycotts

835. Picketing is defined as the 'conduct of workers on strike of watching, accosting, appealing to, or forcefully preventing workers from and the ingress and egress of persons siding with the employer or the employer's customers, to prevent the accomplishment of the employer's business, in order to maintain or reinforce their strike'.[751] Picketing is rarely used as an independent dispute act. It is commonly used as an ancillary dispute act in connection with a strike or a boycott. It is intended to frustrate the efforts of an employer to hamper the process of a strike and to prevent participants from withdrawing. Generally pickets hold placards at the entrance of a workshop or use megaphones. They often gather arm-in-arm in front of the gate. Picketing is generally used as a secondary dispute act.

836. A boycott is also used in connection with a strike. It signifies concerted activity to refuse to buy products or goods or to use facilities of an employer. A boycott may be either a primary boycott or a secondary boycott depending upon the positioning of the employer. When a boycott is aimed at the employer who is the party to a labour dispute, it is called a primary boycott. When a boycott is aimed at an employer who has business relations with the employer who is the party to a labour dispute, it is called a secondary boycott.[752]

749. TULRAA, Article 2, no. 5.
750. Therefore, sabotage is more favourable to workers than is a strike. First, although it may inflict economic loss on an employer, workers continuing in the job may still claim payment of their wages because the normal process of business goes on. Secondly, sabotage is protected from counter-tactics of an employer which are usually used to erode the dispute tactics of workers. Therefore it may inflict more damage and consequently be more efficient than a strike. Peaceful sabotage often occurs in those sectors where dispute acts are prohibited by Korean legislation. Because of the illegality of dispute acts in the public sector the slowdown is accompanied by working-to-rule. It is difficult to discern whether this is mere work-to-rule or a dispute act. Besides, in the public sector showdowns often occur in industries or enterprises where trade union are unions are not organized well enough to accomplish the aims of workers (Chi Sun Kim, *op. cit.*, p. 126).
751. Kazuo Sugeno, *op. cit.*, p. 632.
752. A secondary boycott is used after a secondary employer has refused the demands of the workers who are the party to a labour dispute, not to continue business relations with the primary employer. The trade union's strict control over its members and strong solidarity among them is needed for a boycott to be successful. In Korea the boycott has been rarely used and more rarely carried out successfully. This is because on the one hand it does not cause so much damage to an employer as

D. Lock-outs

837. The right of an employer to lock out is not guaranteed by the Korean Constitution. But the lock-out is recognized as an dispute act by the TULRAA (Article 2, no. 6).[753] In addition, the Supreme Court has repeatedly confirmed the ruling that recognizes the employers' right to initiate a lock-out.[754]

838. According to the Supreme Court, workers' constitutional right to engage in dispute acts is aimed at promoting and securing equality between labour and management and is thus ultimately based on the principle of fairness. Therefore, according to the Court, when the workers' dispute acts gives rise to a severe imbalance in the power relationship between labour and management and the employer is subject to extraordinary pressure, dispute acts by the employer may be justified in light of this same principle. If a lock-out is proper, an employer will not be required to pay wages to workers who offer to perform during the lock-out.[755]

839. The TULRAA provides that an employer may execute a lock-out of the workplace only after the trade union concerned commences a dispute act.[756] According to the Supreme Court, 'defensive lock-outs' in order to recover the balance of power lost by the workers' dispute acts are proper. In contrast, 'offensive lock-outs', whereby the employer pressures workers to achieve his own objectives are improper. The precedents suggest that the courts will recognize the propriety of lock-outs only in exceptional cases where the workers' dispute acts cause an immense hindrance to business.[757]

840. The TULRAA provides that in the case of a lock-out, an employer must report it in advance to the Administrative Authorities and to the Labour Relations Commission.[758] As to whether notification or pronouncement is sufficient or whether a genuine refusal by an employer to receive labour is needed for a lock-out to exist, opinions are divided.[759]

---

does a strike and on the other hand the solidarity among workers participating in a boycott has not been strong enough for the boycott to be maintained and continued successfully (Chi Sun Kim, *op. cit.*, p. 126).

753. Some say that it is the exercise of the employer's rights on the ground that the Act recognizes the lock-out as a dispute act. Others say that a lock-out is the exercise of rights derived from the employer's property rights. We may safely conclude that an employer, as a party to a labour dispute, is permitted to resort to this tactic, namely, a lock-out in an emergency situation in which he or she cannot perform and can no longer be expected to perform the obligations imposed by collective agreements and individual labour contracts (Chi Sun Kim, *op. cit.*, p. 127).
754. The *Marushima Suimon* case, Supreme Court (25 April 1975) 29 Minshu 481.
755. Takashi Araki, *op. cit.*, p. 187.
756. Article 46 paragraph 1.
757. This restrictive interpretation of the availability of lock-outs is generally supported by legal scholars because courts have provided employers with the ability to adjust working conditions through a reasonable modification of work rules (Takashi Araki, *op. cit.*, p. 187).
758. Artic841. e 46 paragraph 2.
759. Some say that a mere notification of the intention of an employer to close down a factory or an enterprise is sufficient. According to this view it does not matter if workers remain at work in spite of the employer's notification. On the contrary others say that a lock–out is a factual state when the

E. The Occupation of the Workplace and the Control of Operations and Management

841. The occupation of a workplace is the striking workers' act of occupying the workplace, i.e., the enterprise facilities, in support of their organization and/or to obstruct the employer's operation during the strike. In some advanced countries, such as the UK, the United States and Germany, this type of action is considered unlawful as an infringement of the employer's property (and other *in rem*) rights in its enterprise's facilities.[760]

842. Taking control of the management of an enterprise is clearly the most violent and radical measure which can be taken. When an economic situation is unstable and, consequently, the labour movement is violent or when an employer cannot manage an enterprise because of its bankruptcy, trade unions take over the management of enterprises.[761]

IV. Legal Effect of Dispute Acts

A. Exemption from Criminal and Civil Liability

843. Besides civil and criminal liability, dispute acts on the labour side may constitute disciplinary offences for having violated the disciplinary rules of an enterprise, namely, work rules.[762] But civil indemnity, criminal indemnity and disciplinary indemnity are to be deduced from the constitutional recognition of the right of workers to act collectively.[763]

---

offer of labour is rejected by an employer. This view insists that when necessary, the real act of an employer to close down a factory is required. But when the factual status is found without the real act of closure or even without notification of such an intention, this opinion recognizes the existence of a lock–out. This latter opinion is now the majority view (Chi Sun Kim, *op. cit.*, p. 187).

760. Kazuo Sugeno, *op. cit.*, p.634.
761. This management control (or operational control) may be divided into active control and passive control. In case of the former trade union shape[s] and carr[ies]out their own management policies. They adopt working conditions which have been demanded by workers. In case of the latter trade unions take over [but] follow the management policies of the enterprises. It is doubtful whether the control of management is recognized by Korean law. The major theory in Korea recognizes the legality of [the] passive control of management (Chi Sun Kim, *op. cit.*, p. 127).
762. From the standpoint of traditional civil law, a strike constitutes non-performance of the obligation of workers; the obligation to offer labour. Therefore, workers are liable for damages caused by this non-performance. The trade union which instigated and manipulated workers not to work is also liable for these damages. Such instigation and manipulation constitute a tort. From the standpoint of traditional criminal law, the strike constitutes a crime of interference in the execution of a business by having hampered the normal process of business. It also constitutes a crime of intimidation.
763. Since modern constitutions guarantee the right to engage in dispute acts as one of the essential human rights of workers, sanctions or punishments [can] not be taken against workers or their organizations for participating in dispute acts or having instigated workers to participate in dispute acts. Therefore, the provision of civil, criminal and disciplinary indemnity are a natural consequence of the constitutional recognition of the right to act collectively.

844. The TULRAA provides civil indemnity, criminal indemnity and disciplinary indemnity. Article 3 (TULRAA) stipulates that an employer may not be allowed to claim damages against a trade union or workers in cases where he or she has suffered damage because of collective bargaining or dispute acts undertaken under this Act. Article 4 (TULRAA) stipulates that the provisions of Article 20 of the Criminal Code shall apply to justifiable activities undertaken to achieve the purpose of Article 1 (TULRAA) as regards collective bargaining, dispute acts, or other activities by trade unions. However no act of violence or destruction shall be construed as being justifiable on any grounds. Article 20 of the Criminal Code recognizes the legality of those acts which are done either with the authorization of law or as business and other acts within the criterion of social appropriateness. Article 81 (TULRAA, no.1) prohibits the dismissal of or discrimination against a worker on the grounds that they have joined or intended to join a trade union, intended to establish a trade union, or performed a lawful act for the operation of a trade union. It is evident that these justifiable acts embrace dispute acts inaugurated by trade unions. And as long as the lock-out is permitted as a dispute act by the Act, we may safely say that an employer is not responsible for the results of the lock-out.[764]

B. Wages During Proper Dispute Acts

845. Although an employer cannot seek civil liability for proper acts of dispute or discipline workers for engaging in such acts, he or she can deduct wages during strikes based on the principle of 'no work, no pay'.[765]

846. The Act stipulates that an employers have no obligation to pay wages during a period of dispute activity to workers who did not provide labour because of their participation in the said actions. No trade unions shall take dispute activities in order to demand and achieve wage payment for the period of those actions.[766]

847. Wage deductions exceeding the proportional part of the work stoppage will be regarded as disadvantageous treatment violating workers' rights to engage in proper acts of dispute and thus can constitute an unfair labour practice. This makes it difficult for employers to deduct wages during slow-downs because it is almost impossible to measure the unperformed portion of work that results.

764. From the standpoint of traditional civil law, the lock–out on the management side also constitutes a non-fulfilment of the contractual obligation to receive the labour offered by workers.
765. In Japan, however, the 'no work, no pay' principle is a mere guideline for an interpretation of contractual rights and duties. Therefore, if there is an agreed provision that, for instance, no wage deduction is to be made for certain days of non-performance, wages should be paid according to the contractual agreement (Takashi Araki, *op. cit.*, p. 186).
766. TULRAA, Article 44.

C. Dispute Acts and a Third Party

848. Generally speaking, workers participating in dispute acts and their trade union are exempted from liability for damages caused to a third party by their acts. Though the Act provides civil immunity only against an employer, this must be interpreted as including civil immunity against a third party. When dispute acts are just, workers are not liable for damages.[767] When dispute acts are unjust, who is liable for the consequences of dispute acts; the workers or an employer?[768] It is not the workers but the employer who is the party to a contract. Therefore, we may rightly say that it is the employer who is liable for damages caused to a third party. However, there are exceptional cases when workers and trade unions are directly liable for these damages. When workers have directly caused damages to a third party by tort they share liability with their employer.

D. Effects of Unjustified Dispute Acts

849. Existing Korean labour law does not give a clear answer to the problem of the effect of unjustified dispute acts.[769] In Korea the major theory is that an unjust dispute act maintains its collective character. but it may also be dissected into individual acts.

767. Who is liable for these damages? Is an employer liable for damages caused to a third party? Those who think that the occurrence of dispute acts are beyond the control of an employer may reply in the negative. They consider the occurrence of dispute acts as tantamount to *force majeure* because the employer has already lost control over its workers. On the contrary, those who think that the occurrence of dispute acts does not amount to *force majeure* because if the employer had done his best to prevent their occurrence, then he could have done so, may reply in the affirmative. Taking into consideration the fact that the third party usually has close business relations with the employer, we too may reply in the affirmative, in Korea the affirmative theory prevails (Chi Sun Kim, *op. cit.*, p. 131).

768. Those who think that the occurrence of dispute acts amounts to *force majeure* against management say that it is the workers and their trade union who must make compensation for damages caused to a third party. Those who do not consider the occurrence of dispute acts as amounting to *force majeure* say that it is an employer who is liable for damages. They insist that workers are no more than assistants of an employer in the performance of obligations imposed on the employer in connection with the third party.

769. When dispute acts are not justified, who is liable for damages caused by them? This is a very difficult problem to resolve. It is closely related to the problem of the legal character of unjustified dispute act. Who is the real subject of the unjustified dispute act? There is a legal theory which insist that when dispute acts are not justified, they cannot be regarded as act of trade unions. This theory recognizes the collective character only of just dispute acts, not unjustified dispute acts. Therefore, an unjustified dispute act falls under the heading of individual acts by those workers participating in such unjustified dispute acts. As a natural consequence workers are jointly liable for damages caused by non-fulfilment of the obligation to offer labor and by tort. Furthermore they could be submitted to criminal or disciplinary punishment on the condition that such an act of individual workers constitutes a criminal and/or disciplinary offence. This theory is very unfavourable to workers. It is based on traditional civil law. However, those who regard collective labor law as having a special nature different from individual civil law attribute the collective character to both just and unjustified dispute acts. According to them an dispute act maintains its collective character regardless of whether it is justified. As to whether an unjustified dispute act has only a collective character or whether it could also be characterized as individual acts without losing its collective

850. Generally speaking, when a dispute act is deemed improper, the workers involved do not enjoy the three legal protections, and thus can be subject to civil liability for damages, any disciplinary actions by the employer, or criminal liability. A trade union cannot be the subject of a criminal offence. Therefore, only members of a trade union are subjects of criminal offence. An unjustified act becomes the constituent individual acts of those workers without maintaining a collective character. Though an dispute act may be justified as a whole, individual workers could be the subjects of civil compensation and criminal offences and be subject to disciplinary measures when they violate the orders of their union and when their behaviour can no longer be regarded as that of their trade union.[770]

V. Propriety of Dispute Acts

A. *General Principles of Dispute Acts*

1. Basic Principles

851. Dispute acts are protected by law as long as they are justified. Civil and criminal indemnity is given only to justified dispute acts, not to unjustified dispute acts. Therefore, it is very important to judge the propriety of dispute acts.

852. The Act provides that a dispute act, in its purposes, methods, and processes, must not violate 'legislation and public order' and that 'union members must not take part in any dispute act which is not led by a trade union'.[771]

853. The central legal issue concerning dispute acts is the determination of their propriety, since only 'proper' acts of dispute are provided legal protection. What are the criteria? Legal restrictions and prohibitions found in TULRAA, are not sufficient to judge the justifiability of dispute acts. Since the TULRAA remains silent on the criteria for determining propriety, judicial interpretation controls.

854. According to established interpretation, the following four elements are examined in a determination of propriety:

– the parties to the dispute acts;

---

nature, opinions are divided. Some say that workers participating in unjustified dispute acts are liable for damages by tort jointly with the trade union which has committed tort and that they are subject to disciplinary measures of their employer. Others say that it is the trade union, not the workers who are members of the trade union which is the subject of the dispute act. Therefore, it is the trade union rather than the workers which is liable for the unjustified dispute act. workers are no linger subject to the disciplinary measures of their employer. The above discussion makes sense only with respect to civil compensation for damages and to disciplinary measures (Chi Sun Kim, *op. cit.*, p. 131).

770. But in reality it is very difficult to decide whether or not the acts of workers are the acts of their trade union, or whether or not they fall within the orders of a trade union.

771. Article 37.

– their purposes;
– the procedures used to initiate the acts; and
– their means.

2. Guidance for and the Responsibility of Trade Unions

855. No dispute act shall be conducted in ways which obstruct or interrupt entry to premises, work and other normal services by individuals who are not related to the dispute or want to provide work, and no violence or threat shall be used to induce workers and individuals into participating in dispute act.

856. During the period of a dispute act, work to prevent damage to operational equipments, or to prevent impairment or deterioration of raw materials or manufactured goods, shall be conducted normally. A trade union shall have the responsibility to direct, manage, and supervise dispute acts so as to be conducted in compliance with the related laws.[772]

3. Restriction on the Detention of Workers

857. Except as a criminal caught in the act of committing a crime, no workers shall be detained for violation of this Act during a period of dispute act.[773]

B. Parties to the Dispute Act

858. The Act provides that 'union members must not take part in any dispute act which is not led by a trade union'.[774] The parties to the dispute act must be qualified to be parties to collective bargaining. Therefore, the propriety of wildcat strikes or strikes conducted by factions within a union without the approval of the union's competent organs will be denied.

C. The Purpose of Dispute Acts

859. The right to act collectively is guaranteed for workers in order to maintain and improve their working conditions and thereby to improve their economic status. Therefore, a dispute act must not exceed its purpose, namely, its economic purpose[775] and the purpose of the dispute act must be proper. Although scholarly

772. Article 38.
773. Article 39.
774. Article 37 paragraph 2.
775. But this does not mean that it has solely an economic purpose and that there is no scope for other purposes to be involved. This is because, nowadays, economic issues have a close relation to political and social issues.

opinions are divided,[776] the courts generally endorse the view that, since dispute acts are guaranteed in order to facilitate industrial autonomy through collective bargaining, the dispute act must be employed for the purpose of promoting collective bargaining. Adopting this view, the Supreme Court has held that political strikes, which cannot be settled by the parties to collective bargaining, lack propriety and warrant no legal protection.[777]

860. Similarly, sympathy strikes[778] and secondary strikes are understood to be improper in their purpose.[779]

861. The subjects of dispute acts are the same as subjects of collective bargaining. This is because a dispute act results from the failure of collective bargaining between labour and management. Therefore, besides working conditions those matters relating to the economic status of workers and at the same time within an employer's discretion can be subjects of dispute acts. Those matters belonging to the management's prerogative rest outside the scope of dispute acts.[780]

D. Procedural Requirements

862. No dispute act by a trade union shall be conducted unless a majority of union members have voted to take such a dispute act by a direct, secret, and unsigned ballot.[781] This provision is intended to encourage the democratic operation of trade unions. However, a dispute act which has not been ratified by a vote is not always illegitimate. In the case of an emergency or when justifiable causes may be found, the dispute act may be exempted from this procedure and may still be regarded as a justifiable one.

---

776. Because an economic or labour policy or a piece of legislation influences considerably the existing economic status of workers, some say that a strike against such policy or legislation may be allowed. Others say that it cannot be permitted because of its political character. The affirmative theory is based on the view that a strike against a government is the same as that against an employer on condition that it has the purpose of maintaining and improving the economic status of workers. The negative view insists that the right of workers to act collectively is recognized against their employer not against a government. In Korea the affirmative theory approving legality within certain limits is gaining support (Chi Sun Kim, *op. cit.*, p. 133).
777. The *Mitsubishi Junkogyo* case, Supreme Court (25 September 1992) 618 Rohan 14.
778. A strike to bring pressure to bear in favour of other workers involved in a strike against their employer is called a sympathetic strike. It has been generally denied legality on the grounds that a sympathetic strike has not passed though the process of collective bargaining. Recently some recognize, but narrowly, the legality of certain sympathetic strikes within certain limits. They say that if sympathetic strikers have the purpose of improving their own working conditions which have been observed without objection, it may be allowed. When workers go on strike in sympathy with other workers employed in enterprises of the same kind or within the same industry, they do so because they have common interests in the result of the strike of other workers. In Korea this theory is becoming more widely held (Chi Sun Kim, *op. cit.*, p. 133).
779. Takashi Araki, *op. cit.*, p. 185.
780. Chi Sun Kim, *op. cit.*, p. 133.
781. Article 41 paragraph 1.

863. Those strikes which fail to satisfy the procedural requirements can be considered to be improper. It is true that in Korea, unlike in Germany, dispute acts need not be the last resort (*ultima ratio*), and hence, dispute acts conducted prior to collective bargaining reaching an impasse can be deemed proper. However, dispute acts conducted without initiating collective bargaining are understood to be improper. In addition, when a collective agreement stipulates a peace obligation or requires certain procedures prior to initiating a dispute act (a so-called 'peace clause'), the violation of those clauses can lead to a finding that the dispute act is improper.[782]

E. Means of Dispute Acts

864. The means of a dispute act must be proper. As explicitly prescribed in the Act, no act of violence or destruction shall be construed as proper acts on any grounds.[783] Dispute acts must be justified in their means in order to be granted civil and criminal indemnity. Dispute acts are oppressive, coercive and threatening in their essence. They do not constitute the crime of intimidation or the crime of blackmail. But acts of violence and destructive action cannot be considered to be dispute acts. Thus, Article 4 (TULRAA) and Article 42 (TULRAA) prohibit these acts. Such practices as destroying machinery and facilities of an enterprise, in other words active sabotage, cannot be allowed.

865. In general, however, acts that are either a partial or complete withdrawal of work are broadly recognized to be proper. Accordingly, in contrast to American law, slow-downs, partial strikes or intermittent work stoppages can be proper acts of dispute.

866. Picketing, as long as it remains within the confines of peaceful, verbal persuasion is a proper act. When it exceeds such limitations and is accompanied by physical force or coercion, is be deemed improper.

867. Unlike Western countries' labour law, sit-downs or an occupation of the workplace is proper if the workers engaging in the sit-down merely stay on the employer's premises and do not hinder business operations.[784]

868. The propriety of dispute acts must be decided as a whole. Therefore, even though some workers resort to violence, destructive action and other acts prohibited

782. Takashi Araki, *op. cit.*, p. 185.
783. TULRAA, Article 4.
784. Although such sit-down strikes infringe on the employer's property interests, the predominant opinion among courts and academics seems to take into consideration the fact that, in the context of (Japan's) enterprise unionism, union offices are usually located on the employers' premises and that holding union meetings or engaging in other union activities on those premises is a common practice during peacetime (Takashi Araki, *op. cit.*, p. 186).

by law, this does not always divest the dispute act of its propriety as a whole. But when these acts are ordered by the executive members of a trade union, this is not so.

VI. Legal Restrictions and Prohibitions

A. *Restriction on and Prohibition of Dispute Acts*

869. Although workers' rights to engage in collective action is constitutionally guaranteed, there are certain restrictions and prohibitions. The Korean Constitution provides that 'only those public officials who are designated by Act, shall have the right to association, collective bargaining and collective action'.[785] Workers are free to organize a trade union or to join it, except for public servants or teachers, who are subject to other enactments (The Act on the Establishment, Operation etc., of Trade Unions for Teachers, The Act on the Establishment, Operation, etc., of Public Officials' Trade Unions).

870. No industrial action by a trade union shall be conducted unless a majority of its union members have decided in favor of taking industrial action by a direct, secret, and unsigned ballot. If the bargaining representative union has been determined, no industrial action shall be taken unless a majority of the members of all the trade unions (limited to union members belonging to the business or workplace concerned) involved in the process have decided in favor of taking industrial action by a direct, secret and unsigned ballot (Article 41).

871. In addition, the right to collective action by workers employed in important defence industries may be either restricted or denied under conditions as prescribed by Act.[786] Therefore, no dispute act shall be taken by those workers who are engaged in major defence businesses subject to the Defence Business Act, and by those who are involved in electricity, water or a business which produces mainly defence goods. The scope of workers who are engaged in a business which produces mainly defence goods shall be determined by presidential decree.[787]

B. *Prohibition of Acts of Violence, etc.*

872. No dispute act shall take the form of violence or destruction, or occupation of facilities related to production or other important businesses or such equivalent facilities as determined by the presidential decree.

873. No dispute act shall be conducted to stop, close, or interrupt the normal maintenance and operation of security facilities of a workplace.

785. Constitution, Article 33 paragraph 2.
786. Constitution, Article 33 paragraph 3.
787. Article 41.

874. If the administrative authorities determine that any dispute act falls under one of the matters prescribed above, it shall serve notice that such an action cease and desist, upon the resolution of the labour relations commission. If, however, there is not enough time to seek such resolution from the labour relations commission, it may serve notice to cease and desist such action immediately without waiting for the resolution of the labour relations commission. In the case of the proviso prescribed above, the administrative authorities shall obtain approval from the labour relations commission, *ex post facto*, without delay. If the administrative authorities fail to obtain such approval, the notice shall lose its effect from that moment.[788]

C. Propriety and Legal Protection of Union Activities

875. When labour unions are established on an enterprise basis, union activities often conflict with an employer's right to control the workplace. Therefore, whether union activities, such as the distribution of handbills, the pasting of posters, wearing ribbons, armbands or headbands, and holding union meetings, are protected activities is an important legal issue. The availability of legal protection turns on whether the activities are 'proper'.

876. The determination of the 'propriety' of union activities is made on the basis of four factors that are similar to those taken into consideration in dispute acts, namely the propriety as to the parties, purpose(s), procedures and means. However, the analysis of the purpose and means of union activities is notably different from that of dispute acts.[789]

877. Since union activities are not the vehicle for the promotion of collective bargaining, their purpose can be broader than those for dispute acts. One Supreme Court decision implies that political activities to promote or oppose legislation that directly relates to union members' interests can be deemed as proper.[790]

878. As for the means, union activities are, in principle, proper when they do not interfere with the performance of workers' contractual obligations. The following three points can be derived from this principle:[791]

– union activities during work hours will not be deemed as proper;[792]

---

788. Article 42.
789. Takashi Araki, *op. cit.*, p. 189.
790. The *Kokurou Hiroshima Chihon* case, Supreme Court (28 November 1975) 29 Minshu 1698 (Takashi Araki, *op. cit.*, p. 190).
791. Takashi Araki, *op. cit.*, p. 189.
792. Wearing ribbons, armbands, headbands or badges during work hours is problematic. The Supreme Court has held that wearing ribbons imprinted with slogans which read 'Meet our demands' and 'Hotel Union Alliance' at a first-class hotel during working hours was an improper union activity (the *Hotel Okura* case, Supreme Court 13 April 1982, 36 Minshu 659: Takashi Araki, *op. cit.*, p. 190). In a 1993 case, the Supreme Court further held that wearing a union badge while on duty was

- union activities on an employer's premises must comply with company regulations;[793]
- union activities outside of working hours and away from the employer's premises can be restricted by the contractual duty of loyalty.[794]

VII. Minimum Services to Be Maintained

A. The Meaning of 'Minimum Services to Be Maintained'

879. The 'minimum services to be maintained' in this Act refers to those services among essential public services, which, if suspended or discontinued, could remarkably endanger the lives, health, physical safety or daily life of the public and are prescribed by presidential decree.[795]

880. 'Essential public service' under this Act means any service described in the following sub-paragraphs, which falls within the category of public services (Article 71 paragraph 1) and whose stoppage and discontinuance may endanger the daily lives of the general public, or may undermine the national economy considerably, and whose replacement presents a hardship:[796]

- railroad services, inter-city railroad services, and aviation services;
- water, electricity, gas supply, oil refinery and supply services;
- hospital and blood supply services;
- the bank of korea; and – telecommunication services.

---

contrary to the worker's duty to devote oneself to work and the employer could therefore legally order its removal (the *Kokutetsu Kagoshima Jidosha Eigyo-sho* case, Supreme Court, 11 June 1993, 632 Rohan 10: Takashi Araki, *op. cit.*, p. 190).

793. According to the leading case on posting handbills on the company's premises, union activities conducted without obtaining the employer's permission are improper unless the employer's rejection of the union's request to so utilize the premises is an abuse of the employer's right to manage its premises (the *Kokutetsu Sappor Unten-ku* case, Supreme Court, 30 October 1979, 33 Minshu 647: Takashi Araki, *op. cit.*, p. 190). Prior to this decision, scholars contended that the propriety of union activities should be determined by weighing the necessity of conducting such union activities against the hindrance or inconvenience to the company's operation or control over its premises. However, this interpretation was explicitly rejected by the Supreme Court (the *Kokutetsu Sappor Unten-ku* case, Supreme Court, 30 October 1979, 33 Minshu 647: Takashi Araki, *op. cit.*, p. 190).

794. For instance, boycotts of the company's products violate the workers' duty of loyalty to their employer and therefore constitutes an improper union activity. This kind of activity can be conducted properly only as a dispute act.

795. Article 42-2 paragraph 1.

796. Article 71 paragraph 2.

B. Restrictions on Dispute Acts in Terms of Minimum Services to Be Maintained

881. No act of stopping, discontinuing or obstructing the proper maintenance and operation of minimum services to be maintained shall be carried out as legitimate dispute act.[797]

C. Agreement on Minimum Services to Be Maintained

882. The parties in labour relations shall conclude an agreement ('agreement on minimum services to be maintained') in writing that stipulates the levels of minimum services to be maintained and provided, the specific work designated as minimum services, the necessary number of workers, etc., in order to ensure the proper maintenance and operation of the minimum services during a period of dispute acts. In these cases, both parties shall sign or seal an agreement on the minimum services to be maintained.[798]

D. Decision on Maintenance and Levels of Operation of the Minimum Services to Be Maintained

883. If an agreement on the minimum services to be maintained is not concluded, both or either of the parties in terms of labour relations shall make an application to the Labour Relations Commission to decide the level of the minimum services to be maintained and operated, the specific work designated as minimum services, the necessary number of workers, etc.[799] The Labour Relations Commission, upon receiving the application, may decide the levels of minimum services to be maintained and operated, the specific work designated as minimum services, the necessary number of workers, etc., taking into account the characteristics, contents, etc., of the minimum services according to the business or workplace.[800] The special mediation committee (under Article 72) shall take charge of implementing the decision made by the Labour Relations Commission. If there is a difference of opinion between the parties concerned over interpretation or implementation of the decision made by the Labour Relations Commission, the parties shall follow the interpretation of the Special mediation committee. In this case, the interpretation of the Special mediation committee shall have the same effect as the decision made by the Labour Relations Commission pursuant to paragraph 2.[801]

797. Article 42-2 paragraph 2.
798. Article 42-3.
799. Article 42-4 paragraph 1.
800. Article 42-4 paragraph 2.
801. Article 42-4 paragraph 4.

VIII. Dispute Acts Resulting from a Decision of the Labour Relations Commission

884. If the Labour Relations Commission makes a decision and a dispute act is taken in accordance with that decision, the dispute act shall be deemed to have been taken while duly maintaining and operating the minimum services.[802]

IX. Designation of Workers for the Maintenance of Minimum Services

885. If an agreement on minimum services to be maintained is in place or a decision is made by the Labour Relations Commission, the trade union shall notify the employer of its members, among those engaged within those minimum services, who will work during the period of dispute act, and the employer shall designate workers accordingly and notify the trade union and the designated workers of this. However, if the case that the trade union in question fails to give such notification prior to the commencement of the dispute act, the employer shall designate workers who will work to provide minimum services to be maintained and shall notify the trade union and the workers of the same.[803] In making a notification and designation pursuant to paragraph (1), the trade union and employer, if there are two trade unions or more which are composed of workers engaged in minimum services to be maintained, shall give consideration to the proportion of members of each trade union who are engaged in such minimum services (Article 42-6).

X. Restrictions on Hiring by an Employer

886. In Korea, employers are free to continue operations by utilizing managerial staff, non-union members or temporary replacements during dispute acts. Unlike American employers, however, Korean employers can make the best use of strike replacement workers who are related to their business operations only during the strike, and striking workers have the right to return to their original posts afterward. The employer's refusal to reemploy the striking workers after the strike is regarded as a discriminatory treatment based on their participation in a legal act of disputation, and thus, constitutes an unfair labour practice.

887. However, no employer shall hire persons who are not related to their business operations, or use replacements during a period of dispute acts so as to continue works which have been stopped by those acts.[804] No employer shall, during the period of a dispute act, contract or subcontract out work which has been suspended because of the dispute act concerned.[805]

802. Article 42-5.
803. Article 42-6.
804. Article 43 paragraph 1.
805. Article 43 paragraph 2.

888. The provisions prescribed above shall not apply to an employer involved with essential public services who hires persons unrelated to the business concerned or uses replacements, or contracts or subcontracts out the work only during a period of a dispute act.[806] In this case, however, an employer may hire or use replacements or contract or subcontract out the work as long as the proportion of the replacement workers does not exceed 50/100 of the strike participants of the business or workplace concerned. In such cases, the method used to calculate the number of strike participants, etc., shall be prescribed by presidential decree.[807]

§2. Labour Committees and the Law

I. Introduction

A. The Purpose of the Labour Relations Commission Act

889. Korea has no courts specially designated for labour litigation. All labourand employment-related lawsuits must be filed in ordinary courts.[808] However, settlement by the courts is neither satisfactory nor efficient because of the special nature of labour problems. While other legal problems ordinarily settled by the Courts are in a static state, labour problems are in a state of flux because labour relations may enter a new phase as circumstances change. Therefore. the machinery to deal with labour relations needs be more flexible than the courts. To get remedies through the courts usually takes a great deal of time and money. Court procedures are too complicated for many workers to follow. Moreover, the remedies given by the courts are limited to the typical ones and some of these are meaningless and unimportant in regard to labour problems. Therefore, the machinery to deal with labour problems must be simpler and more informal and the remedies provided by this machinery must be more flexible and varied. The labour committee system provides a machinery that satisfies all the needs mentioned above. This is the *raison d'être* of the Labour Commission.[809]

890. The Labour Relations Commissions (the Central Labour Relations Commission, the Regional Labour Relations Commissions and the Special Labour Relations Commission) deal with the work of judging, deciding, resolving, approving, confirming or redressing discrimination, etc., in accordance with the TULRAA, the LSA, etc. These commissions are independent administrative committees comprised of an equal number of commissioners representing employers, workers and the public interest.

891. The Labour Relations Commission Act (LRCA) was enacted in 1997 to contribute to the security and development of labour relations by establishing the

806. Article 43 paragraph 3.
807. Article 43 paragraph 4.
808. Korea has a three-tiered court system: district courts, high courts and the Supreme Court.
809. Chi Sun Kim, *op. cit.*, p. 149.

Labour Relations Commission and regulating matters as to the operation of the commission in order to allow its performance, in a prompt and fair manner, of its functions of adjudication and necessary adjustments in terms of labour relations.

892. Under this Act, the Labour Relations Commissions are entrusted with the work of judging, deciding, resolving, approving, confirming or redressing discrimination, in addition they have responsibility for the conciliation, mediation and arbitration of labour disputes etc.,

B. The Status of the Labour Relations Commission

893. The Labour Relations Commission is an administrative body. But it operates independently of other administrative authorities. It is not regulated, controlled or governed by the government. In this sense it is an independent administrative body.

894. The Labour Relations Commission has discretion over the performance of functions and duties within its authority. The Chairman of the National Labour Relations Commission manages budgets, personnel affairs, education and training and other administrative matters of the National and Regional Labour Relations Commissions, and may direct and supervise their staff. The chairman of the National Labour Relations Commission may transfer some of his or her powers to direct and supervise administrative matters to the chairpersons of Regional Labour Relations Commissions, in accordance with presidential decree.[810]

II. Categories and Structures of the Labour Relations Commissions

895. The Labour Relations Commission shall be composed of the National Labour Relations Commission, the Regional Labour Relations Commissions and the Special Labour Relations Commission. The National and Regional Labour Relations Commissions shall be governed by the Minister of Employment and Labour, and the designation, location and jurisdictional areas of the Regional Labour Relations Commissions shall be prescribed by presidential decree. The Special Labour Relations Commission shall be attached to the Chief of the Central Administrative Authority which has jurisdiction over those specific matters, if necessary to deal with such matters according to legislation or decree.[811]

810. Article 4.
811. LRCA, Article 2.

III. Jurisdictions of the Labour Relations Commissions

A. *The National Labour Relations Commission*

896. The National Labour Relations Commission has jurisdiction over any cases falling within the following criteria:

- reviewing measures already taken by the Regional and Special Labour Relations Commissions;
- making adjustments in terms of industrial disputes which fall under the jurisdiction of two or more Regional Labour Relations Commissions;
- such cases as may fall under its jurisdiction as prescribed by other enactments.

B. *The Regional Labour Relations Commissions*

897. The Regional Labour Relations Commissions have jurisdiction over those cases which occur in their region; cases which span two or more Regional Labour Relations Commissions (excluding adjustment cases) shall be governed by the Regional Labour Relations Commission which has jurisdiction over the location of main workplace.

C. *The Special Labour Relations Commission*

898. The Special Labour Relations Commission has jurisdiction over the cases concerning specified matters which are prescribed by relevant enactments as an objective of its establishment.

899. Despite the above provision, the Chairman of the National Labour Relations Commission may designate a particular Regional Labour Relations Commission to deal with the case concerned, when it is deemed to be necessary to settle industrial disputes in an effective way.

900. When it is difficult to determine the main workplace relating to a dispute, or when the Regional Labour Relations Commission which has jurisdiction over the location of main workplace has difficulty in dealing with the case, the Chairman of the National Labour Relations Commission may, *ex officio* or upon an application submitted by either of the parties or the Chairman of the Regional Labour Relations commission, designate a particular Regional Labour Relations Commission to deal with the case concerned.[812]

812. Article 3.

IV. Composition of the Labour Committees

901. A labour committee is a tripartite body. It is composed of three categories of members, those representing workers, those representing employers and those representing the public interest. This three-way approach is the ideal of the labour committees. Members representing workers and those representing employers participate in the settlement of labour problems as the parties concerned.

902. For this reason a settlement made by a labour committee is regarded as more voluntary and autonomous than one made by courts or other labour administrative authorities. Through this process workers and employers can contribute to the development of labour relations and the national economy. Those members representing the public interest do not control or interfere with the members representing workers or those members representing employers. Settlements reached by labour committees represent the result of cooperation from all three categories of members.[813]

V. The Organization of the Labour Relations Commission

A. *The Composition of the Labour Relations Commission*

903. The Labour Relations Commission shall be composed of members representing employees (hereinafter referred to as 'employee members'), members representing employers (hereinafter, 'employer members') and members representing the public interest ('public interest members').

904. The number of members of the Labour Relations Commission shall be prescribed by presidential decree, in the light of of the work load of each commission, within the limit of at least 10 but not more than 50 for employee members and employer members and at least 10 but not more than 70 for public interest members. In any case, the number of members representing employees and employers shall be equal.

905. Employee members shall be appointed from among those recommended by the relevant trade union, and the employer members shall be appointed from among those recommended by the relevant employers' association, the public interest members of the National Labour Relations Commission shall be appointed by the President upon the nomination of the Minister of Employment and Labour, and those of the Regional Labour Relations Commissions shall be appointed by the chairman of the National Labour Relations Commission upon the nomination of the chairman of the Regional Labour Relations Commission.

906. Those who are recommended by the Chairman of the Labour Relations Commission, the relevant trade union and the employers' association concerned,

813. Chi Sun Kim, *op. cit.*, pp. 149–150.

and those who survive exclusion by trade unions and the employers, by turns, shall be candidates for public interest members who can be appointed. From among those candidates, the public interest members of the National Labour Relations Commission shall be appointed by the President upon the nomination of the Minister of Employment and Labour and the public interest members of the Regional Labour Relations Commissions shall be appointed by the Chairman of the National Labour Relations Commission upon the nomination of the Chairman of the Regional Labour Relations Commission.

907. Notwithstanding the provision of paragraph (4), if the relevant trade union or the concerned employers' association refuses to follow the procedures for recommending public interest members or, by turns, those to exclude the recommended public interest members one by one, the chairman of the Labour Relations Commission concerned may select candidates to represent the public interest who may be appointed.

908. The public interest members shall be classified and appointed as follows:

- public interest members in charge of adjudication cases;
- public interest members in charge of cases redressing discrimination;
- public interest members in charge of adjustment cases.

909. Procedures for the recommendation of the members of the Labour Relations Commissions, methods of excluding candidates for public interest members one by one and other necessary matters as to the designation of the members shall be prescribed by presidential decree.[814]

B. Terms of Office of Members

910. The term of office of the members of the Labour Relations Commission shall be three years and may be renewed.

911. In the case of a vacancy, the term of office for a member elected to fill that vacancy shall be the remainder of the term of their predecessor: provided that if the successor in question is appointed to fill the vacant post for the chairman or that of a permanent member, the term of office of the successor shall start a new.

912. When a member's term of office expires, that member shall continue to perform his/her duties until a successor is appointed.

913. The remuneration, rights and duties of members shall be prescribed by presidential decree.[815]

814. Article 6.
815. Article 7.

C. Qualifications Required for Public Interest Members

914. The public interest members of the National Labour Relations Commission and the Regional Labour Relations Commissions shall be appointed from among those who fall under any of the categories prescribed by the Act, and have knowledge and experience in labour issues (professors, judges, prosecutors, military judicial officers, defence lawyers, certified public labour attorney, senior civil servants, etc).

D. Chairpersons

915. 915, There shall be a chairperson of all Labour Relations Commissions. In the case of the National Labour Relations Commission, the chairperson shall be appointed by the President, upon the nomination of the Minister of Employment and Labour, from among the public interest members of the National Labour Relations Commission, and in the case of the Regional Labour Relations Commissions, on the recommendation of the Chair of the National Labour Relations Commission and with the nomination of the Minister of Employment and Labour, from among those qualified as public interest members of a Regional Labour Relations Commission. The Chairman of the National Labour Relations Commission shall be a public servant as determined by political decision. The Chairperson of the Labour Relations Commission shall be a public interest member, and may take charge of cases of adjudication, redressing discrimination and adjustment.[816]

916. The chairperson shall represent the Labour Relations Commission concerned, and control the affairs of the commission.[817] There shall be permanent members of the Labour Relations Commissions, and they shall be appointed by the President, on the recommendation of the chairman of the National Labour Relations Commission and Minister of Employment and Labour, from among the public interest members of the Commission concerned.

917. The permanent members shall be public interest members, and may take charge of cases of adjudication, redressing discrimination and adjustment.[818]

E. Code of Conduct for Members

918. The members of the Labour Relations Commission shall carry out their work in accordance with the law and in good conscience and in a manner of fairness and good-faith. The National Labour Relations Commission may set up the rules of conduct the members of the Labour Relations Commission should follow to carry out their work and matters concerning the operation of the commission

816. Article 9.
817. Article 10.
818. Article 11.

through a resolution of the Labour Relations Commission at a plenary session. The rules of conduct shall be set for matters falling under any of the following categories:

- matters concerning the prohibition of the members of the Labour Relations Commission from accepting entertainment, money, valuable goods, etc., in relation to the work they carry out;
- matters concerning the prohibition and restriction of the members of the Labour Relations Commission from undermining fairness and neutrality such as by interfering with the handling of a case or being biased in favour of one of the parties;
- matters concerning the carrying out of work in good faith, including their attendance at a divisional committee;
- other matters necessary to ensure the decency of the members of the Labour Relations Commission.[819]

F. Disqualification and Guarantee of Status of Members

919. Any one who is subject to Article 33 of the State Public Officials Act shall not be appointed as a member of the Labour Relations Commission.[820] Any member of the Labour Relations Commission shall not be dismissed or discharged from office against his or her intention. Only when he or she falls under any of the following categories, shall he or she be dismissed or discharged from office:[821]

- if he/she falls under Article 33 of the State Public Officials Act;
- if he/she becomes incapable of performing his/her duties due to a prolonged period of mental or physical weakness;
- where there is proven corruption relating to their performance of their role, or proven corruption making it inappropriate for them to continue in that role;
- where he/she has violated the rules of conduct as prescribed in Article 11-2 so that he/she cannot perform his/her duties as a Commission member.

G. Secretariat Office and Secretariat Bureau

920. The National Labour Relations Commission shall have a secretariat office and Regional Labour Relations commissions shall have secretariat bureau.[822] The secretariat office and secretariat bureau, shall each have investigative officers.

819. Article 11-2.
820. Article 12.
821. Article 13.
822. Article 14.

921. These officers may conduct such investigations as are necessary under the direction of the chairman, the chairman of a divisional committee or the chief member, and attend a divisional committee to report back their findings and opinions.[823]

VI. Meetings

A. *The Structure of Meetings*

1. Types of Meeting

922. The Labour Relations Commission shall have, unless otherwise prescribed in other laws, an adjudication committee, a discrimination redress committee, a mediation committee, a special mediation committee, an arbitration committee, an adjustment committee for teachers' labour relations and an adjustment committee for public officials' labour relations (hereinafter referred to as the 'divisional committee'), in addition to plenary sessions, to handle businesses under its own jurisdiction by each division.

a. Plenary sessions

923. The plenary session shall be composed of all of the members of the Labour Relations Commission concerned, and deal with matters which fall into the following sub-paragraphs:

- decisions on general matters such as the operations of the Labour Relations Commission;
- recommendations regarding the improvement of working conditions;
- formulation of instructions and rules (only in the case of the National Labour Relations Commission).

b. The adjudication committee

924. The adjudication committee shall be composed of three people designated by the chairman, from among public interest members in charge of adjudication (including the Chairman or one permanent member), and shall deal with matters which require judgment, resolution, approval, confirmation, etc., of the labour relations commission in accordance with the TULRAA, the LSA, the Act on the Promotion of Employee Participation and Cooperation and other laws.

c. The discrimination redress committee

925. The discrimination redress committee shall be composed of three people designated by the chairman from among the pubic interest members in charge of

823. Article 14-3.

redressing discrimination (including the chairman or one permanent member) and shall deal with matters concerning redress for discrimination in accordance with the Act on the Protection, etc., of Fixed-term and Part-time employees or the Act on the Protection, etc., of Dispatched employees.

d. The mediation committee, the special mediation committee and the arbitration committee

926. The mediation committee, the special mediation committee and the arbitration committee shall be established by the TULRAA, and deal with mediation, arbitration and other matters related thereto, provided by that act respectively. in this case, the public interest members shall be selected from among public interest members in charge of adjustment (including the chairman or permanent members).

e. The adjustment committee for teachers' labour relations

927. The adjustment committee for teachers' labour relations shall be established and composed of members, pursuant to the Act on the Establishment, Operation, etc., of Trade Unions for Teachers, and handle mediation, arbitration and other related matters under the Act.

f. The adjustment committee for public officials' labour relations

928. The adjustment committee for public officials' labour relations shall be established and composed of members, pursuant to the Act on the Establishment, Operation, etc., of Public Officials' Trade Unions, and handle mediation, arbitration and other related matters under the Act.[824]

2. Calling of Meetings

929. The chairman shall preside over plenary sessions. The chairman of the divisional committees shall be elected by mutual vote among the members and shall preside over the divisional committee concerned unless there are particular provisions in other enactments.

930. The chairman or a chairman of a divisional committee shall convene an entire membership meeting or a divisional committee meeting. However, the chairman, if he/she deems it necessary, may convene a divisional committee meeting.

931. The chairman of the labour relations commission or the divisional committee shall convene a meeting when a majority of the members of the labour relations commission or the divisional committee call for a meeting.[825]

824. Article 15.
825. Article 16.

3. Chief Members

932. The Chairman of a divisional committee, if it is deemed necessary for the smooth operation of that divisional committee, may designate a chief member and have that chief member handle the case.[826]

B. Recommendations of Conciliation

933. The Labour Relations Commission may recommend conciliation or present a conciliation proposal at the request of the parties concerned or by virtue of its own authority before making a judgment, issuing an order or rendering a decision pursuant to Article 84 of the TULRAA or Article 28 of the LSA. When preparing the conciliation proposal, the Labour Relations Commission shall hear sufficient opinions from the parties concerned. If the parties concerned accept the conciliation proposal, the Labour Relations Commission shall draw up a conciliation statement.

934. The conciliation statement shall be signed or sealed by the parties concerned and all members involved in the conciliation. The conciliation statement prepared shall have the same effect as the conciliation imposed by the courts in accordance with the Civil Procedure Act.[827]

C. Resolutions

935. A plenary session shall be held when a majority of the members registered are present, and pass a resolution with a majority approval of the members present.

936. Meetings of any divisional committee shall be held when all the members are present, and pass a resolution with a majority approval of the members present.

937. A plenary session of the adjustment committee for public officials' labour relations shall be held when a majority of the members registered are present and pass a resolution with a majority approval of the members present.

938. A member who attends a plenary session or a meeting of a divisional committee shall sign or place a seal on the resolution.[828]

939. The Labour Relations Commission shall notify the parties concerned of the results of the resolution made by a divisional committee without delay.

826. Article 16-2.
827. Article 16-3.
828. Article 17.

940. The Labour Relations Commission shall notify the parties concerned of the consequent measures in writing and the measures shall take effect on the date they receive a letter of order, a letter of decision or a letter of re-examination of a decision.[829]

D. *Reporting and the Hearing of Opinions*

941. The chairman of the Labour Relations Commission or the divisional committee may call the members or the investigation officers concerned to report on subjects which have been referred to the meetings.

942. The adjudication committee and the discrimination redress committee shall hear the opinions of one or more employee and employer members of the Labour Relations Commission concerned before passing a resolution, provided that this understanding does not apply when the employee or employer members have failed to appear without reasonable grounds after being notified to appear.[830]

E. *The Opening of Meetings and the Maintenance of Order During the Meetings*

943. Meetings of the Labour Relations Commission shall be open to the public, provided that a meeting may not be open to the public if there is an *in camera* resolution made by a commission.[831] The chairman of the Labour Relations Commission or the divisional committee may order the withdrawal of any person who obstructs fair procedures or disturbs the order of the meeting concerned and take other necessary measures to maintain order.[832]

F. *Exclusion, Challenge, etc., of Members*

944. If a member falls under any of the following categories, he/she shall be excluded from carrying out duties concerning the case in question:

- if the member, or his or her spouse or ex-spouse, is a party to the case or is related to a person who has a right or duty jointly with a party in the case;
- if the member is or was a relative of a party to the case under Article 777 of the Civil Act;
- if the member made a statement or gave an expert opinion about the case;
- if the member is or was involved in the case on behalf of a party;
- if the member is involved in any measure or non-action which becomes the cause of the case.

829. Article 17-2.
830. Article 18.
831. Article 19.
832. Article 20.

945. If there is a reason as described above, the chairman shall decide to exclude the member by virtue of his or her authority or at the request of the parties. If there is a member from whom fairness is hard to be expected during deliberations, resolutions or adjustments, the Chairman may write down the reason and apply to challenge him or her. If the application for challenge as described above is deemed reasonable, the Chairman shall replace the member with another member. As soon as a case is filed, the Chairman shall notify the parties concerned that they can apply for such exclusions and challenges.[833]

§3. The Authority of the Labour Committees

I. The Work of the Labour Relations Commission

946. The work of the Labour Relations Commission is described in the following manner:

1. the work of judging, deciding, making a resolution, approving, confirming, redressing discrimination, etc., in accordance with the TULRAA, the LSA, the WPCA, the Act on the Establishment, Operation, etc., of Trade Unions for Teachers, the Act on the Establishment, Operation, etc., of Public Officials' Trade Unions, the FPWPA and the DWPA;
2. the work of mediating or arbitrating a labour dispute or providing support for the interested parties to autonomously settle their labour disputes in accordance with the TULRAA, the Act on the Establishment, Operation, etc., of Trade Unions for Teachers and the Act on the Establishment, Operation, etc., of Public Officials' Trade Unions;
3. the work of conducting surveys, research, education, publicity activities, etc., in relation to performing the work prescribed in sub-paragraphs (1) and (2);
4. other work, as stipulated by other laws, as being within the jurisdiction of the Labour Relations Commission.[834]

II. Functions of Labour Committees

947. In the process of resolving labour problems, whether disputes of rights or disputes of interests, a labour committee sometimes adjudicates them as a quasi-judicial body or sometimes adjusts them as an administrative body. To make an adjudication or an adjustment, it investigates documents and requests the parties or anyone concerned to be present and to explain their views.

833. Article 21.
834. Article 2-2.

948. Besides these subsidiary functions a labour committee gives advice and suggestions concerning the improvement of labour conditions,[835] stipulates regulations concerning their operation; and the NLC gives instructions necessary for the interpretation of the law to an LLC and the SLC. So, the functions of a labour committee could be divided into two main groups, namely, those of adjudication and adjustment, and other functions[836] such as deciding, making a resolution, approving, confirming, redressing discrimination.

III. Adjudications under the LSA

A. *Application for Remedy for Unfair Dismissal, and Related Acts*

949. No employer shall dismiss, lay off, suspend, or transfer a worker, nor reduce their wages, nor take other punitive measures ('unfair dismissal, etc.') against a worker without justifiable reasons.[837]

950. If an employer takes such unfair action against a worker, the worker may apply for remedy to the Labour Relations Commission. The application for remedy shall be made within three months of the date on which the unfair dismissal or related acts took place.[838]

951. From the standpoint of traditional civil law, an employer is liable only for *mens rea*, intention and negligence. But we may identify many cases in which no *mens rea* whether of an employer or of an employee who suffers injury from an accident may be found. Applying the traditional principle would be severe to the employee and clearly contrary to the principles of justice. However, it would seem right that the one who benefits from an enterprise should suffer from a loss occurring within the enterprise. So, in modern labour law an employer assumes absolute liability for any accident occurring within the enterprise with several exceptions, for example *force majeure* and intention or gross negligence on the employee's part. It may be difficult to determine whether an accident is caused by intent or gross negligence on the employee's part or by *force majeure*, and this problem is closely related to the interests of the parties concerned. It needs to be decided objectively and impartially. The LSA leaves this decision to a labour committee.[839]

952. First, if business is suspended for reasons attributable to an employer, the employer shall pay a worker an allowance equivalent to 70 per cent or more of their average wages during the period of suspension. However, an employer who is unable to continue business for unavoidable reasons may, upon approval of the labour relations commission, pay allowances during the suspension of business at

835. Article 22 paragraph 2.
836. Chi Sun Kim, *op. cit.*, p. 151.
837. LSA, Article 23.
838. LSA, Article 28.
839. Chi Sun Kim, *op. cit.*, p. 153.

an amount lower than the standard stipulated above.[840] In this case a labour committee decides whether or not the continuation of business is impossible due to unavoidable circumstances or *force majeure*. Secondly, if a worker suffers from an occupational injury or disease due to his own gross negligence, and the employer obtains the acknowledgment of the labour relations commission recognizing that negligence, the employer shall not be liable to provide compensation for the suspension of work nor compensation for disability.[841]

953. If any of the working conditions set forth in accordance with a statement of working conditions is found to be inconsistent with the actual conditions, the worker concerned shall be entitled to claim damages resulting from the breach of the working conditions or may terminate the labour contract forthwith. Any worker who intends to claim for damages may do so through the labour relations commission.[842]

954. The employee may bring a civil suit against the employer, but this usually takes a great deal of time and money. In addition court procedures are too complex for many employees to follow. For these reasons the LSA allows an employee suffering damages resulting from a breach of the labour contract by his or her employer to file a request with the labour committee in addition to the right recognized by the Constitution to take legal action.[843]

B. Adjudication under the TULRAA

955. Organizations of workers should meet the requirements provided in the TULRAA to be legally recognized and accordingly to be protected as legal trade unions. These requirements should be met and satisfied not only in the formation but also in the operation and administration of trade unions. In such cases trade unions should not be operated dictatorially or arbitrarily by a small number of executive members but democratically and autonomously in accordance with the views of the majority of union members.[844]

956. The TULRAA invests the Labour Relations Commission with the authority to see to it that trade unions operate legally in conformity with the purpose of this Act. First, the administrative authorities may, with a resolution of the Labour Relations Commission, order the correction of union bylaws which are in conflict with labour-related laws.[845] Secondly, the administrative authorities may, with a resolution of the Labour Relations Commission, order the correction of resolutions or

840. LSA, Article 46.
841. LSA, Article 81.
842. Article 19 paragraph 2.
843. Chi Sun Kim, *op. cit.*, p. 154.
844. *Ibid.* p. 151.
845. TULRAA, Article 20 paragraph 1.

measures made by a trade union, which are determined to be in conflict with labour-related laws or union bylaws. An order for the correction of bylaws shall be made only on the application of an interested party.[846] In the case of orders for correction, a trade union shall implement such orders within 30 days, unless that the period is extended for a reasonable cause. Thirdly, when the trade union has no officials and has not carried out any activity for more than one year, the pertinent administrative authority may, with a resolution of the Labour Relations Commission, order dissolution.[847] Fourthly, where a representative of a trade union deliberately neglects or avoids the convening of the general meeting, and a request is made by one third or more of the union members to appoint a convener of the meeting, the administrative authorities shall ask the Labour Relations Commission to adopt a resolution within 15 days, and upon adoption of such resolution by the Labour Relations Commission, immediately appoint a person to convene the meeting.[848]

957. Where more than two-thirds of the workers performing the same kind of job and employed in the same area are subject to the application of one collective agreement, the administrative authorities may, with the resolution of the labour relations commission, and upon the request of one or both parties to the collective agreement or by its own authority, make a decision that such a collective agreement shall apply to other workers performing the same kind of job and employed in the same area, as well as to their employers.[849] This is an exception to the principle that a collective agreement has binding force only on the trade union (including its members) and the employer who are the parties to it.[850]

958. A worker or trade union whose rights have been infringed by unfair labour practices may make an application for remedy to the Labour Relations Commission.[851] The Labour Relations Commission, after completing their inquiry, should they find that the employer has committed unfair labour practices, shall issue an order for remedy to the employer. However if the Commission determines that unfair labour practices have not been committed, it shall enter a decision to dismiss the application for remedy.[852]

959. As already mentioned, the procedure of a labour committee is more informal, simpler and shorter and takes less time and money than that of the courts. The remedies offered by a labour committee are more efficient and flexible than the typical remedies provided by courts. A labour committee may order the employer to

846. TULRAA, Article 20 paragraph 2.
847. TULRAA, Article 28 no. 4.
848. Article 18 paragraph 3.
849. TULRAA, Article 36 paragraph 1.
850. The working conditions of organized workers are usually better than those of non-organized workers. So, the employer of organized workers is driven by the impulse to replace organized employees with non-organized employees. If so, the status of organized employees becomes endangered and accordingly the collective agreement that covers them cannot be expected to be faithfully observed by the employer. That is why an exception is made to the principle of the effect of a collective agreement (Chi Sun Kim, *op. cit.*, p. 152).
851. TULRAA, Article 82 paragraph 1.
852. TULRAA, Article 84 paragraph 1.

reinstate a dismissed employee and compensate them for lost wages or revoke a yellow-dog contract or to bargain in good faith and, if necessary, to conclude a collective agreement or to refrain from any act affecting the operation of a trade union. Besides these orders the labour committee may issue any kind of order that is proper as a remedy for unfair labour practices.[853]

960. In cases where the parties do not reach an agreement on the interpretation or implementation of the collective agreement, one or both of the parties to the collective agreement may ask the Labour Relations Commission for its opinion about the disputed interpretation or implementation. The labour relations commission shall give its clear view on the requested matter within 30 days of the receipt of such request. The opinions of the Labour Relations Commission regarding the interpretation or implementation rendered by the commission shall have the same effect as that of an arbitrated judgment.[854]

C. *Redress of Discriminatory Treatment under the FPWPA and DWPA*

961. If a fixed-term or part-time employee receives discriminatory treatment, he or she can apply for redress to the Labour Relations Commission under the LRCA. However, this does not apply if three months or more have passed since the day when the discriminatory treatment occurred (or since the last day of the treatment in the case of continuous discriminatory treatment).[855]

962. The Labour Relations Commission, if it judges that the treatment in question is discriminatory after concluding an investigation and inquiry, shall issue a redress order to the employer. If it judges that the treatment in questions is not discriminatory, it shall make a decision to dismiss the application for redress.[856]

963. Neither the sending employer nor the using employer shall treat a dispatched worker in a discriminatory manner in comparison to a worker who performs the same work in the business of the using employer. If a dispatched worker is discriminated against, he or she may apply for redress to the labour relations commission. The FPWPA shall apply *mutatis mutandis* to the application for redress and other redress procedures relating to the dispatched worker.[857]

853. Chi Sun Kim, *op. cit.*, pp. 152–153.
854. Article 34.
855. FPWPA, Article 9.
856. *Ibid.*, Article 12
857. *Ibid.*, Article 21.

§4. The Function of Adjustment (Mediation and Arbitration)

I. Adjustments under the TULRAA

964. A labour committee mediates and arbitrates labour disputes. While a NLLC and the SLC undertake ordinary mediation and arbitration, only the NLC undertakes emergency mediation and arbitration according to a decision for emergency adjustment by the Minister of Employment and Labour.[858] Arbitration is a stricter procedure which permits more positive intervention by a labour committee than mediation. It is generally admitted that the settlement of labour disputes by a labour committee is more voluntary and autonomous than that by the courts and other administrative authorities.

II. Adjustments under the LSA

965. If a person has an objection to the determination of occupational injury, disease or death, methods of medical care, determination of compensation or any other matters regarding compensation, the person concerned may request the Minister of Employment and Labour to reappraise or arbitrate the case. If a request is filed, the Minister of Employment and Labour shall reappraise or arbitrate the case within one month.[859] If reappraisal or arbitration has not been made by the Minister of Employment and Labour within the specified period, or if a person is dissatisfied with the result of that reappraisal or arbitration, a request may be filed with the labour relations commission for reappraisal or arbitration. If a request is filed, the Labour Relations Commission shall reappraise or arbitrate the case within one month.[860]

III. Mediation and Arbitration under the FPWPA

966. The Labour Relations Commission can commence mediation procedures at the request of both or either of the parties concerned or by virtue of its own authority during an inquiry. If the parties concerned file for arbitration under an agreement to follow an arbitration decision taken by the labour relations commission, the commission may conduct such an arbitration. Mediation or arbitration shall be filed for within 14 days of the date on which an application was made to redress discriminatory treatment pursuant to Article 9. However, if there is approval from the labour relations commission, the mediation or arbitration can be filed for after the 14-day period.[861]

858. TULRAA, Article 77.
859. LSA, Article 88.
860. LSA, Article 89.
861. FPWPA, Article 11.

IV. Voluntary Arbitration under the Act on the Promotion of Worker Participation and Cooperation

967. In cases falling under any of the following sub-paragraphs, a dispute may be settled by an arbitration organization set up within the Labour–Management Council by agreement between workers' members and employers' members, or may be referred to arbitration by the labour relations commission or other third parties:

- where the Council fails to make a resolution on matters subject to resolution;
- where there is any disagreement on the interpretation, implementation, etc., of resolutions made by the Council.[862]

V. Mediation or Arbitration under the Act on the Establishment, Operation, etc., of Trade Unions for Teachers and the Act on the Establishment, Operation, etc., of Public Officials' Trade Unions

968. If collective bargaining breaks down, either or both parties concerned may apply for mediation to the National Labour Relations Commission. In the case either or both parties apply for mediation, the National Labour Relations Commission shall commence mediation without delay, and the parties concerned shall participate in the mediation in good faith.

969. This mediation process shall be completed within 30 days from the date of application.[863]

970. The National Labour Relations Commission shall conduct arbitration in any of the following situations:

- when both parties concerned request arbitration after collective bargaining breaks down;
- if the mediation proposal of the National Labour Relations Commission is rejected by either or both parties concerned, or when the Labour Relations Adjustment Commission for public officials determines to refer the case concerned to arbitration at a plenary meeting.[864]

VI. Remedial Procedures

971. With a few notable exceptions, general remedial procedures for application and complaint, etc., are divided into: (1) initial examination procedures at the local

862. Act on the Promotion of Worker Participation and Cooperation, Article 25.
863. Act on the Establishment, Operation, etc., of Trade Unions for Teachers, Article 9; Act on the Establishment, Operation, etc., of Public Officials' Trade Unions, Article 12.
864. Act on the Establishment, Operation, etc., of Trade Unions for Teachers, Article 10; Act on the Establishment, Operation, etc., of Public Officials' Trade Unions, Article 13.

labour relations commission; (2) administrative review procedures at the National Labour Relations Commission; and (3) judicial review procedures.

A. *Initial Examination Procedures by the Local Labour Relations Commission*

1. Applications for Remedy for Unfair Dismissal, and Related Acts

972. If an employer dismisses a worker unfairly, the worker may apply for remedy to the Regional Labour Relations Commission. The application for remedy shall be made within three months from the date on which the unfair dismissal or related acts took place.[865] Upon receiving the application for remedy, the labour relations commission shall conduct the necessary investigations and question the related parties without delay.[866] When conducting an inquiry, the Labour Relations Commission may, at the request of the parties concerned or by virtue of its own authority, have witnesses appear before the commission and question them regarding necessary matters. When conducting an inquiry, the Labour Relations Commission shall give sufficient opportunities for the parties concerned to present evidence and to cross-examine the witnesses.

973. The Labour Relations Commission shall issue a remedy order to the employer, if the case is determined to constitute an unfair dismissal, etc., after the completion of the inquiry, and shall dismiss the application for remedy if the case is determined not to constitute an unfair dismissal, etc.[867]

2. Unfair Labour Practice

974. A worker or trade union whose rights have been infringed by unfair labour practices may make an application for remedy to the local labour relations commission.[868] The application for remedy shall be made within three months from the date when such unfair labour practices had been committed (or from the date of termination in cases where such activities continue).[869]

975. The Labour Relations Commission shall, without delay, conduct the necessary investigation and make inquiries of the parties concerned, upon receipt of an application for remedy. When conducting the inquiry, the Labour Relations Commission may, at the request of the parties or by its own authority, have witnesses appear before the commission, and conduct examinations of the pertinent matters.

865. LSA, Article 28 paragraph 1.
866. LSA, Article 29.
867. LSA, Article 30.
868. TULRAA, Article 82 paragraph 1.
869. TULRAA, Article 84 paragraph 1.

When conducting the inquiry, the Labour Relations Commission shall provide sufficient opportunities for the parties concerned to present evidence and to cross-examine witnesses.[870]

976. The Labour Relations Commission, after completing the inquiry, if it is found that the employer has performed unfair labour practices, shall issue an order for remedy to the employer. When the Commission determines that unfair labour practices have not been committed, it shall enter a decision to dismiss the application for remedy.

977. Judgments, orders and decisions shall be made in writing, and shall be issued to the pertinent employer and the applicant. Each of the parties shall comply with the order issued.[871]

B. Administrative Review Procedures for the National Labour Relations Commission

1. Application for Remedy for Unfair Dismissal, and Related Acts

978. If an employer or a worker is aggrieved by a remedy order or dismissal decision rendered by a Regional Labour Relations Commission in accordance with the Labour Relations Commission Act, he or she may apply for reexamination to the National Labour Relations Commission within 10 days of the date on which he or she received the notice of the remedy order or dismissal decision.[872]

2. Unfair Labour Practice Cases

979. Where one of the parties disagrees with any remedy order or dismissal decision by the Regional Labour Relations Commission or by the Special Labour Relations Commission, he or she may make an application for review of such an order to the National Labour Relations Commission within 10 days of the date of receiving the notice of the order or decision.[873]

980. When the Labour Relations Commission makes its findings relating to the facts and determines that the facts alleged in the complaint constitute a commission of an unfair labour practice, it issues a remedial order, the contents of which are at its discretion. Typical remedial orders for each type of unfair labour practice are: (1) In disadvantageous treatment cases, to reinstate the discharged or transferred workers with or without backpay; (2) in refusal to bargain cases, to order the employer to bargain with the union in good faith on the subject concerned; and (3)

870. TULRAA, Article 83.
871. TULRAA, Article 84.
872. LSA.
873. TULRAA, Article 85 paragraph. 1.

in domination and interference cases, to cease and desist the actions at issue and/ or the posting of notices that the employer will not engage in those actions in the future.[874] As an independent administrative organ with expertise concerning labour relations, the Labour Relations Commissions have the discretionary power to determine the remedial order's content. Therefore, the Commission may order measures that it sees as most likely, in the context of the circumstances concerned, to eliminate the harm caused by the unfair labour practices and restore harmonious labour relations. The Supreme Court has recognized this discretionary authority of the Labour Relations Commissions with regard to the content of their remedial orders and has held that they should be treated with deference when under judicial review.[875]

C. Judicial Review of the Order

1. Application for Remedy for Unfair Dismissal, and Related Acts

981. An employer or a worker may file a lawsuit in accordance with the Administrative Litigation Act against a decision made by the National Labour Relations Commission after the reexamination within 15 days from the date on which he or she received the notice of the decision regarding the reexamination.[876] If no application for reexamination is made or no administrative lawsuit is filed within the specified period, the remedy order, dismissal decision or decision on reexamination shall be finally confirmed.

2. Unfair Labour Practice Cases

982. The party concerned may bring an administrative suit in accordance with the Administrative Litigation Act against a decision on a review made by the National Labour Relations Commission within 15 days of the date of receiving the notice of the decision on the review.[877]

983. It is possible for an employer to file with a court and appeal for cancellation of the order without seeking an administrative review by the National Labour Relations Commission.

D. The Effect of Orders

984. The effect of remedy order, dismissal decisions or decisions on reexamination rendered by the labour relations commission shall not be suspended by an

874. Takashi Araki, *op. cit.*, p. 201.
875. *Ibid.* p. 202.
876. LSA, Article 31 paragraph 2.
877. TULRAA, Article 85 paragraph 2.

application for reexamination to the National Labour Relations Commission or by the initiation of an administrative lawsuit.[878]

§5. REQUESTS FOR ASSISTANCE AND RIGHT TO INVESTIGATE

I. The Labour Relations Commission's Requests for Assistance

985. The Labour Relations Commission may request the relevant administrative authorities for assistance if it is deemed to be necessary to perform its functions and duties, and such authorities shall respond to that request unless there are particular reasons. The Labour Relations Commission may recommend the relevant administrative authorities to take the necessary measures to improve working conditions.[879]

II. The Labour Relations Commission's Right to Investigate

986. The Labour Relations Commission may request the employers, the employers' organization, the trade union or other relevant persons to show up and report or to submit necessary documents, and may authorize the members or investigative officers designated by the chairman of the Labour Relations Commission or a divisional committee to investigate the status of a business or a workplace, its documents or other items, if it is deemed necessary to carry out its business, such as fact-finding, with regard to the work within its jurisdiction (work of the Labour Relations Commission), prescribed in the Act. The member or investigative officer of the Commission authorized for an investigation as stated above shall present an identification card which indicates his or her authority to the relevant person.[880]

III. The National Labour Relations Commission's Rights

A. The Right to Give Instruction

987. The National Labour Relations Commission may give necessary instructions concerning the basic policies on the performance of functions and the duties of the Labour Relations Commission and the interpretation of laws and regulations to a regional Labour Relations Commission and Special Labour Relations Commission.[881]

878. LSA, Article 32 TULRAA, Article 86.
879. LSA, Article 22.
880. Article 23.
881. Article 24.

B. The Right to Stipulate Regulations

988. The National Labour Relations Commission may formulate rules for the operation and other necessary matters for the National Labour Relations Commission, the Regional Labour Relations Commissions or the Special Labour Relations Commission.[882]

C. The Right to Review

989. The National Labour Relations Commission may review measures taken by the Regional Labour Relations Commissions or the Special Labour Relations Commission, and may confirm, revoke or modify such measures, if a request is made by the parties concerned. The request for review shall be made, except otherwise stipulated in laws or decrees, within 10 days after notice is given to the parties concerned of the measures taken by the Regional Labour Relations Commission or the Special Labour Relations Commission. The period (10 days) shall be an unchangeable one.[883]

D. Appealing Against the Measures of the National Labour Relations Commission

990. Appeals against the measures of the National Labour Relations commission must be submitted within 15 days following notice of the measures with the chairman of the National Labour Relations Commission to be defendant. The effects of the measures shall not be suspended because of appealing under this Act. The period (15 days) shall be shall be an unchangeable term.[884]

E. The Duty of Confidentiality and Presumption as Being Public Servants

991. Anyone who is or used to be a member or staff of the Labour Relations Commissions shall not divulge any secrets learned in connection with his or her duties.

992. A member or staff of the Labour Relations Commission who is involved in handling a case or a defence lawyer, certified labour affairs consultant, etc., who was a member or staff of the Labour Relations Commission shall not perform his or her duties concerning the case.[885]

882. Article 25.
883. Article 26.
884. Article 27.
885. Article 28.

993. The members of the Labour Relations Commissions who are not public servants shall be construed as public servants in relation to the application of the penal provisions in the Criminal Act or other enactments.

IV. Mediation before Dispute Acts

994. Upon the occurrence of a labour dispute, one of the parties to labour relations shall notify the fact to the other in writing. No dispute act shall be taken without first undergoing mediation procedures (excluding mediation procedures that come after the decision to end the mediation is made pursuant to Article 61-2) under this Act (the provisions of Sections 2-4 of Chapter V). This paragraph shall not apply when mediation procedures do not finish within the period prescribed (in Article 54), or when the arbitration ruling is not made within the period prescribed (in Article 63).[886]

§6. Adjustment of a Labour Dispute

I. Introduction

995. If a dispute act extends over a whole industry, province, state or country, not only the parties concerned suffer great damage, but also the public suffer inconvenience with respect to their daily life. The economic and social systems within a certain district or of a whole nation may be paralysed or be rendered damaged irrecoverably. So, the machinery of collective bargaining needs to be put into a practical context to prevent the occurrence of labour disputes and, if a labour disputes do occur, this is the best way to settle this labour dispute peacefully without the parties concerned resorting to tactics of dispute such as strikes, sabotage, etc.[887]

996. The TULRAA provides for adjustment procedures for labour disputes. The labour relations commission, a tripartite body instituted in each prefecture, is entrusted with the adjustment of labour disputes under the law by means of mediation and arbitration. Since private dispute resolution systems, private mediation or arbitration, do not function actively in Korea, the role of the commissions are very important.

997. The basic principle of the adjustment of a labour dispute is voluntary settlement. Thus, the Labour Relations Commission defers to the parties' own volition to resolve the dispute in the process of its adjustment procedures, namely conciliation, mediation and arbitration. In both conciliation and mediation, the commission may propose a settlement plan, but the parties remain free to reject it. In arbitration, the

886. Article 45.
887. Chi Sun Kim, *op. cit.*, p. 136.

Commission final decision is binding. However, either party to the dispute can refuse to participate in arbitration procedures, and thus there can be no compulsory arbitration.

II. General Provisions

A. *Efforts for Voluntary Adjustment*

998. The settlement of a labour dispute must be reached by the parties' own accord. As collective labour relations between labour and management are established and maintained on the basis of the autonomy of the parties, labour disputes must be settled voluntarily and autonomously without outside interference. The autonomy of the parties concerned is the foremost principle in the settlement of labour disputes.

999. The TULRAA provides that 'no provisions of this Act may be construed to prevent the parties to labour relations from taking part in deciding labour related matters including, but not limited to, working conditions, or from making every effort to resolve disputes or differences arising from labour relations, through labour–management consultations or by collective bargaining'.[888]

B. *The Obligations of the Parties*

1000. The parties to labour relations shall stipulate in their collective agreement the procedures and methods for labour–management consultation or other collective bargaining methods to maintain reasonable labour relations, and shall make every effort to resolve labour disputes by themselves when such disputes arise.[889]

C. *Obligations of the Government, etc.*

1001. The government and local self-governing bodies, when the parties are unable to reach an agreement with regard to their labour relations, shall make every effort to prevent acts of dispute from taking place and to resolve labour disputes rapidly and fairly by helping the relevant parties to those industrial relations settle differences on their own.[890]

888. Article 47.
889. Article 48.
890. Article 49.

D. Expedient Proceedings and the Priority Given to Public Services, etc.

1002. The parties to labour relations in the Labour Relations Commission and other relevant institutions shall make their best efforts to provide expeditious means for settlement when labour disputes need to be mediated pursuant to this Act.[891]

1003. Labour disputes related to the government, local self-governing bodies, state or public corporations, defence industries, and public services shall be given a priority and dealt with expeditiously.[892]

E. Private Mediation or Arbitration

1004. The provisions relating to mediation (Section 2) and arbitration (Section 3) shall not be construed as to prevent the parties to labour relations from settling labour disputes through other means of mediation or arbitration ('private mediation, etc.') pursuant to mutual agreements or collective agreements.[893] When the parties to labour relations have agreed to resolve labour disputes pursuant to private mediation or arbitration, they shall notify this to the Labour Relations Commission.[894]

1005. When labour disputes are to be resolved in accordance with private mediation or arbitration, each of the following sub-paragraphs shall apply:[895]

- With respect to resolutions reached by means of mediation, the provisions of the Mediation Before a Dispute Act (Article 45 paragraph 2) and the period of mediation (Article 54) shall apply. In these cases, a deemed period of mediation shall begin with the date of the commencement of such mediation.
- With respect to resolutions by means of arbitration, the provisions of the Prohibition of a Dispute During a Period of Arbitration Act (Article 63) shall apply. In this case, a prohibition period of dispute acts shall begin with the date of commencement of arbitration.

1006. An agreement made by means of mediation or arbitration shall have the same effect as that of a collective agreement.[896]

1007. Persons who conduct private mediation, etc., shall be those who meet the qualification requirements described in the LRCA (each item of Article 8, 22). In these cases, the person who conducts private mediation, etc., may receive service fees, allowances and travel expenses from the parties concerned.[897]

891. Article 50.
892. Article 51.
893. Article 52 paragraph 1.
894. Article 52 paragraph 2.
895. Article 52 paragraph 3.
896. Article 52 paragraph 4.
897. Article 52 paragraph 5.

III. Categories of Adjustment

1008. The autonomous and independent settlement of labour disputes is an ideal but this ideal cannot be always expected to be realized. We may imagine cases in which negotiations between labour and management fall through, conversation is broken off and the voluntary settlement of labour dispute cannot be pursued. To make things worse, suppose that this is a case which involves a public utility, the shutdown of which has a severe impact upon the daily life of the public. Here we may rightly anticipate external intervention, namely by the legislature or the government.[898]

1009. The TULRAA recognizes two procedures to be used in an ordinary situation and one procedure to be used in an emergency situation. The ordinary procedures are mediation and arbitration and the emergency procedure is emergency adjustment.

IV. Mediation

A. *The Meaning of Mediation*

1010. Mediation permits more positive intervention than conciliation[899] by the mediators. They hear the opinions of the parties concerned, prepare a draft mediation and recommend that the parties concerned accept it. When this draft mediation is accepted by the parties it has the same legal effect as a collective agreement.

B. *Commencement and Period of Mediation*

1011. The labour relations commission shall conduct the proceedings of any mediation, without any delay, when one of the parties engaged in labour relations submits a request for mediation to the labour relations commission. The parties concerned shall undertake, in good faith, the proceedings of mediation.[900]

1012. The Labour Relations Commission may assist the parties concerned to settle their dispute autonomously and efficiently by, among other things, arranging negotiation prior to the request for mediation.[901]

1013. Mediation shall be completed within ten days in the case of general businesses, and 15 days in the case of public services, after the request is made for

898. Chi Sun Kim, *op. cit.*, p. 137.
899. Conciliation is the simplest procedure which least binds the parties concerned. It is carried out by a public officer appointed by the relevant administrative authority. He or she confirms and clarifies the conflicting claims of the parties concerned and thereby helps them to reach an agreement.
900. Article 53 paragraph 1.
901. Article 53 paragraph 2.

mediation. The parties concerned may agree to extend a period of mediation by up to ten days in the case of general businesses, and 15 days in the case of public services.[902]

C. *The Composition of a Mediation Committee*

1014. A mediation committee shall be established within the Labour Relations Commission for purpose of the mediation of labour disputes. The mediation committee shall be composed of three mediating members.

1015. The mediating members shall be designated by the chairman of the Labour Relations Commission from among members of the Labour Relations Commission concerned so that one member can represent employers, another the workers, and the third the public interest. The member representing workers shall be designated from among the members recommended by the employer, and the member representing employers shall be designated from the members recommended by the trade union. However, in cases where a list of members who have been recommended by the parties concerned is not submitted within three days prior to a meeting of the mediation committee, the chairman may designate the members.

1016. If it presents an undue hardship to organize a mediation committee due to the fact that either the member representing the workers or the member representing employers fails to participate, the chairman of the Labour Relations Commission may designate three members, from among members of the commission who represent the public interest, as the mediation members, except where there is a member of the labour relations commission, selected based on an agreement between both parties, the member shall be designated as a mediation member.[903]

1017. There shall be a chairman in the mediation committee. The chairman shall be the mediation member representing the public interest, excepting that the chairman of the mediation committee shall be elected by a mutual vote of the mediation committee.[904]

D. *Mediation by a Single Mediator*

1018. The Labour Relations Commission may authorize a single mediator to conduct mediation proceedings in lieu of a mediation committee at the request, or with the agreement, of both of the parties concerned. The single mediator shall be

902. Article 54.
903. Article 55 paragraph 4.
904. Article 56.

designated by the Chairman of the Labour Relations Commission from among the members of the Labour Relations Commission who have been agreed upon by the parties involved.[905]

E. *Verification of Claims to, and Restriction on, Attendance*

1019. The mediation committee or the single mediator, as the case may be, shall designate a specific date for the parties concerned to appear so as to verify the main points of their respective claims.[906]

1020. The chairman of the mediation committee or the single mediator, as the case may be, may restrict the attendance of persons other than the parties concerned and witnesses for the hearing.[907]

F. *Preparation of a Mediation Proposal*

1021. The mediation committee or the single mediator, as the case may be, shall prepare a mediation proposal to be presented to the parties concerned, with a recommendation for their acceptance, and may simultaneously publish it along with their reasons, and, if necessary, may request the cooperation of the press or broadcast media for its dissemination.[908] If the mediation committee or the single mediator, as the case may be, determines that further proceedings of the mediation process is not warranted due to the parties' refusal to accept the mediation proposal, it/he/she shall decide to terminate the mediation procedure and notify that decision to the parties concerned.[909]

1022. If the parties concerned, after accepting the mediation proposal, do not agree on any of the interpretations or implementation measures of the proposal, they shall request that the mediation committee or the single mediator, as the case may be, provide a clear opinion on the interpretation or implementation measures.[910] Upon receiving the request, the mediation committee or the single mediator, as the case may be, shall render a clear opinion within seven days of the date of receipt of such request.[911]

1023. No parties concerned shall conduct dispute acts with regard to the interpretation or implementation of the mediation proposal concerned, until the opinion on the interpretation or implementation measures is rendered.[912]

---

905. Article 57.
906. Article 58.
907. Article 59.
908. Article 60 paragraph 1.
909. Article 60 paragraph 2.
910. Article 60 paragraph 3.
911. Article 60 paragraph 4.
912. Article 61-2.

G. The Effect of Mediation

1024. If the parties have accepted the mediation proposal, all members of the mediation committee or the single mediator, as the case may be, shall prepare a mediated agreement in writing, and sign or seal it together with the parties concerned.[913] The contents of the mediated agreement shall have the same effect as a collective agreement.[914] The opinion relating to the interpretation and implementation measures which have been rendered by the mediation committee or the single mediator, as the case may be, shall have the same effect as an arbitration ruling.[915]

1025. The Labour Relations Commission may conduct mediation to settle a labour dispute even after the decision to end mediation is made.[916]

V. Arbitration

A. The Concept of Arbitration

1026. Arbitration is a procedure which permits the most active intervention by the arbitrators. An arbitration award issued by an arbitration committee has legal binding force on the parties concerned whether they accept it or not. The content of the final award has the same effect as a collective agreement. Arbitration is an adjustment procedure in which external intervention is most clearly evident. It is carried out by an arbitration committee which is composed of three arbitrators appointed by the chairman of the labour relations committee.

B. Commencement of Arbitration and the Prohibition of Dispute Acts During a Period of Arbitration

1027. The Labour Relations Commission shall conduct arbitration in any of the following cases:[917]

- where a request for arbitration is made by both of the parties concerned; or
- where a request for arbitration is made by one of the parties in accordance with the provisions of a collective agreement.

1028. Dispute acts shall not be conducted for 15 days from the date when those labour disputes have been referred to arbitration.[918]

913. Article paragraph 1.
914. Article 60 paragraph 1
915. Article 61 paragraph 3.
916. Article 62-1.
917. Article 62.
918. Article 63.

C. *Composition and the Chairmanship of an Arbitration Committee*

1029. An arbitration committee shall be established within the Labour Relations Commission for the arbitration or review of labour disputes. The arbitration committee shall be composed of three members. The arbitration members shall be designated by the Chairman of the Labour Relations Commission from among those who represent the public interest in the labour relations commission and are mutually agreed upon by both parties. In cases where the parties do not reach an agreement, the arbitration members shall be designated from members of the Labour Relations Commission who represent the public interest.[919]

1030. There shall be a chairman of the arbitration committee. The Chairman shall be elected by a mutual vote among members of the arbitration committee.[920]

D. *The Verification of Claims and Restriction on Attendance*

1031. The arbitration committee shall designate a specific date for one or both of the parties concerned to appear so as to verify the main points of their respective claims. With the consent of the arbitration committee, members of the Labour Relations Commission representing employers or workers who are designated by the parties concerned may attend an arbitration meeting to testify as to their opinion.[921] The Chairman of the arbitration committee may restrict the attendance of persons other than the parties concerned and witnesses for the hearing.[922]

E. *Arbitration Rulings*

1032. An arbitration ruling shall be made in writing and the date upon which it comes into effect shall be clearly stated therein. If the parties concerned do not agree on the interpretation or the implementation measures of the arbitration ruling, the interpretation by the arbitration committee concerned shall prevail and have the same effect as that of an arbitration ruling.[923]

F. *The Finalization of an Arbitration Ruling, etc.*

1033. If the party concerned considers that an arbitration ruling rendered by the Regional Labour Relations Commission or the Special Labour Relations Commission violates the law or is an act beyond its authority, he or she may apply for a

919. Article 64.
920. Article 65.
921. Article 66.
922. Article 67.
923. Article 68.

review of the case to the National Labour Relations Commission within 10 days of the date of receipt of the arbitration ruling.[924]

1034. If the party concerned considers that an arbitration ruling rendered by the National Labour Relations Commission or a decision on review violates law or is an act beyond its authority, he or she may bring an administrative suit within 15 days of the date of receipt of an arbitration ruling or a decision on review.[925] When a request for review has not been made, or an administrative suit has not been brought within the designated period, the arbitration ruling or decision on review shall be final.[926] When an arbitration ruling or a decision on review has been finalized, the parties concerned shall comply therewith.[927]

G. *The Effect of an Arbitration Ruling*

1035. The contents of an arbitration ruling shall have the same effect as a collective agreement. The effect of the arbitration ruling or review decision rendered by the Labour Relations Commission shall not be suspended by any application for review or any administrative lawsuit filed with the National Labour Relations Commission.[928]

VI. Special Provisions for the Mediation of Labour Disputes in Public Services

A. *The Scope of Public Services, etc.*

1036. The 'public service' means a service described in any of the following sub-paragraphs, namely those that are indispensable to the daily lives of the general public or have a great influence on the national economy:[929]

- regular public transportation services;
- water, electricity or gas supply; oil refinery and supply services;
- public health and medical services and blood supply services;
- banking and minting services; and – broadcasting and telecommunication services.

1037. The notion of an essential public service means each of the services described in the following sub-paragraphs, which falls within the category of 'public services' and whose stoppage or discontinuance may endanger the daily lives of

924. Article 69 paragraph 1.
925. Article 69 paragraph 2.
926. Article 69 paragraph 3.
927. Article 69 paragraph 4.
928. Article 70.
929. Article 71 paragraph 1.

the general public, or may undermine the national economy considerably, and whose replacement presents a hardship:[930]

- railroad services, inter-city railroad services, and aviation services;
- water, electricity and gas supply; oil refinery and supply services;
- hospital and blood supply services;
- the Bank of Korea; and
- telecommunication services.

B. The Composition of a Special Mediation Committee

1038. A special mediation committee shall be established within the Labour Relations Commission for the mediation of labour disputes in public services. The special mediation committee shall be composed of three members.[931] The members of the special mediation committee, under paragraph (2), shall be designated by the chairman of the Labour Relations Commission from among four to six members of the Labour Relations Commission who represent the public interest and have not been excluded by either the trade union or by the employer in question, after the completion of rounds of selection by exclusion. However, in cases where the parties concerned agree to recommend those who are not the members of the Labour Relations Commission concerned, those non-members shall be designated.[932]

C. The Chairman of a Special Mediation Committee

1039. There shall be a chairman of a special mediation committee.

1040. The chairman shall be elected by mutual voting among the members of the special mediation committee who are members of the Labour Relations Commission representing public interest. If the special mediation committee is composed solely of only members not from the Labour Relations Commission, then the chairman shall elected by mutual voting among the members. However, in cases where there is only one member representing public interest in the special mediation committee, that member shall be the chairman.[933]

1041. When a dispute act affects the public interest or is of such a large scale or a specific nature as to threaten damage to the national economy or endanger the daily life of the public, the Minister of Employment and Labour may issue a decision, he should hear the views of the Central Committee (LDAA, Article 40, Section 2). This does not mean that he is restricted by their views but that he should respect them.

930. Article 71 paragraph 2.
931. Article 72 paragraph 2.
932. Article 72 paragraph 3.
933. Article 73 paragraph 3.

1042. When the Minister of Employment and Labour has made a decision, he shall, without delay, announce it along with the reasons therefore and shall simultaneously notify it to the central labour committee and the parties concerned (LDAA, Article 40, Section 3). When a decision has been announced, the dispute act is thereby suspended and no dispute act may be commenced until 30 days have elapsed from the date of the announcement (LDAA, Article 41). Upon receipt of such a notice the Central Labour Committee shall undertake mediation (LDAA, Article 42); when it considers that conciliation is not likely to be successful, it must decide whether or not to refer the case to arbitration within 10 days of the date of receipt of the notice (LDAA, Article 43). When a draft mediation proposal is accepted by the parties concerned or an award of arbitration is made, the text of mediation and award have the same effect as that of a collective agreement.

VII. Emergency Adjustment

A. *The Concept of an Emergency Adjustment*

1043. Emergency adjustment is made in cases when a dispute act is commenced in a public utility or when it is so large-scale or of such a specific character that it may impair the national economy or endanger the daily life of the public. While the above two procedures are prior ones to prevent the occurrence of dispute acts, this procedure is a subsequent one to stop an dispute act.

B. *The Decisions of an Emergency Adjustment*

1044. The Minister of Employment and Labour may make a decision to conduct an emergency adjustment when a labour dispute is related to public services, widespread, or of a specific character; and there is a danger of impairing the national economy or the daily lives of the general public.[934] The Minister of Employment and Labour shall consult with the chairman of the National Labour Relations Commission prior to making a decision for an emergency adjustment.[935]

1045. When the Minister of Employment and Labour decides to conduct the emergency adjustment, he or she shall publicize, without any delay, his or her decision along with his of her reasons and shall simultaneously notify the decision to each of the parties concerned as well as the National Labour Relations Commission.[936]

934. Article 76 paragraph 1.
935. Article 76 paragraph 2.
936. Article 76 paragraph 3.

C. The Suspension of Dispute Acts and Mediation by Commission

1046. The parties concerned shall suspend any dispute act immediately when a decision of emergency adjustment is publicized, and shall not resume such a dispute act within 30 days of the date of publication of the decision.[937]

1047. The National Labour Relations Commission shall commence, without delay, the process of mediation, when it has been notified.[938]

D. The Commission's Right to Refer Disputes to Arbitration and Arbitration by the Commission

1048. The Chairman of the National Labour Relations Commission shall, in consultation with its members representing the public interest, determine whether a case shall be referred to arbitration, if mediation is not likely to be concluded. The decision shall be made within 15 days of the date of the receipt of the notification (made in accordance with paragraph 3 of Article 76).[939]

1049. The National Labour Relations Commission shall conduct, without delay, an arbitration if one or both of the parties concerned have made a request for arbitration, or if it has made a decision to refer the case to arbitration in accordance with Article 79.[940]

937. Article 77.
938. Article 78.
939. Article 79.
940. Article 80.

Chapter 5. Unfair Labour Practices and the Law

§1. An Overview of the Unfair Labour Practices System

1050. The TULRAA prohibits four types of anti-union acts by employers:[941] disadvantageous treatment of union members, yellow-dog contracts, a refusal to, or a delay in, bargaining, and the domination or interference in the union's administration. The unfair labour practices system is a device worked out to protect three workers' rights guaranteed by the Constitution – the right to organize, the right to bargain and the right to act collectively – from infringement by employers or their organizations.[942] The three workers' rights ultimately aim at the organization, existence and operation of trade unions. So, the unfair labour practices system, which has the purpose of protecting the three workers' rights, amounts to a system which protects the existence and operation of trade unions.

1051. The Labour Relations Commissions provide administrative remedies for unfair labour practices. The remedial procedures of the the Labour Relations Commissions are prescribed in Articles 82–86 of the TULRAA.

1052. The Korean unfair labour practices system is modelled on that of the Wagner Act of 1935 enacted in the United States of America. The 1949 revision also added several new prohibitions, such as barring employers from refusing to bargain and from dominating or interfering with the union's administration,[943] while the Taft–Hartley Act which amended the Wagner Act equally prohibits certain practices of

941. Article 81.

942. Formerly the state or the government was always faced with the temptation of placing workers and trade unions under its control or at least under its influence to promote the nation's welfare or its economic development. In practice at the beginning of the history of the labour movement, governments prohibited the organization of workers and arrested workers participating in the labour movement. In modern times, even though the constitutions of states guarantee their workers' rights, there still remains the danger of infringement by governments and, in practice, many governments infringe these rights by craftily evading the law. But nowadays the infringement(s) of workers' rights by employers or their associations has become more frequent and damaging than that by states, and their influence over workers and trade unions has become more direct. For example, sometimes employers disturb the combination of workers by splitting them up or dismissing the chief initiator and they control the operation or administration of trade unions by exercising their social and economic power. Sometimes they dismiss or threaten workers because of their attempts to join a trade union or because of their participation in the labour movement for the purpose of exercising their influence indirectly over the trade unions. In the cases stated above guaranteeing workers' rights by constitutional provision is fruitless. So, it has become necessary to work out a device to practically protect those workers' rights as guaranteed by the constitutional formulation against infringement by their employers'. This is the unfair labour practices system (Chi Sun Kim, *op. cit.*, pp. 108–109).

943. This Act was promulgated to promote the flow of commerce within and between states by eliminating substantial obstructions to the free flow of commerce. Experience demonstrated that the inequality of bargaining power between employers and workers served as both a burden and a hindrance to the flow of commerce and deepened industrial strife and unrest. In other words, the inequality in bargaining power between employers and workers was a substantial obstruction to the free flow of commerce. So, this Act protects the rights of workers to unite and to bargain collectively by prohibiting certain practices of employers which infringe upon these rights as unfair

a trade union or its agents which obstruct the free flow of commerce as unfair labour practices, the Korean Trade Union Act prohibits only the practices of employers which infringe workers' rights as unfair labour practices. In Korea unfair labour practices of a trade union or its agents do not exist.

I. An Employer Liable for Unfair Labour Practices

1053. The employer shall not commit unfair labour practices. Therefore, only an employer can be the subject of unfair labour practices. An employer, as defined in Article 2 paragraph 2 (TULRAA), includes any person who is in charge of the operation of an enterprise, or a person who acts as an agent in the interests of the owner of the enterprise with regard to matters concerning workers employed in the enterprise. In actual labour relations, however, persons other than the party to an employment contract can commit anti-union acts which have harmful effects on labour relations. Thus, scholars and courts have extended the definition of employer in two ways for the purposes of unfair labour practice regulations.

A. *Internal Extensions*

1054. Acts of supervisors or others who represent the employer's interests may give rise to the question of whether they can be regarded as the employer's acts. Generally, the acts of executive board members or upper level supervisors are attributable to the employer, whereas acts of lower level supervisors or rank-and-file workers are only attributable to the employer when there is evidence that the employer directed or authorized the acts.[944]

B. *External Extensions*

1055. Under certain conditions, an outside entity can be deemed the employer, especially for the purposes of collective bargaining. The first situation where such an extension is recognized is where there is a relationship between the client company (the receiving company) and workers sent from the subcontractor or worker dispatching company (supplying company) working at and for the client company. In this context, the client company has a duty to bargain with the dispatched workers' union although there is no direct contractual relationship between the client company and the dispatched workers.

1056. In cases where a subcontracting company is a mere shell and its workers are incorporated into the recipient company's operational organization and subject to the recipient employer's direction, the Supreme Court has held that the client

labour practices, thereby to strengthen the bargaining power on the workers' side. The Korean unfair labour practices system is modelled on that of the Wagner Act.

944. Takashi Araki, *op. cit.*, p. 193.

company is deemed to be the employer with regard to the workers of the supplying company for the purposes of collective bargaining.[945] In these cases, an implied employment contract was deemed to exist between the workers and the client company. The second type is the relationship between a parent company and its subsidiary's workers. Unlike the first instance, the relationship between workers engaged by the subsidiary in the premises of the subsidiary and thus within the parent company's control is not as direct as in the first type.[946]

II. Types of Unfair Labour Practices

1057. The TULRAA prescribes that an employer shall not commit an act falling under the following categories:[947]

1. dismissal of, or discrimination against, a worker on the grounds that the worker has joined or intends to join a trade union, intends to establish a trade union, or performs a lawful act for the operation of a trade union;
2. making it a condition of employment that the worker abstain from joining or withdraw from a trade union, or join a particular trade union. However, in cases where a trade union represents more than two-thirds of workers employed in the same business, the conclusion of a collective agreement under which a person is employed on condition that he/she becomes a member of the trade union shall be allowed as an exception. In this case, the employer shall not put the worker in any disadvantageous position in terms of status, on the grounds that the worker has been expelled from the trade union, or has withdrawn from the trade union to organize a new trade union or to join another trade union;
3. refusal or delay in concluding a collective agreement or conducting collective bargaining, without justifiable reasons, with the representative of a trade union or a person who has been authorized by a trade union;
4. domination of or interference with the formation or operation of a trade union by workers and wage payment for full-time officials of a trade union or financial support for the operation of a trade union. However, the employers may allow the workers to take part in consultation or bargaining with the employers during the working hours, may provide subsidies for the welfare of the workers, or for the prevention and relief of financial difficulties and other disasters, and may provide union office space of minimal size; or
5. the dismissal of or discrimination against a worker on the grounds that the worker has taken part in lawful collective activities, has reported the violation of the provisions of this article by the employer to the Labour Relations Commission, or has testified about such violations or presented evidence to the administrative authorities.

945. The *Yuken Kogyo* case, Supreme Court (5 May 1976) 30 Minshu 409; the *Hanshin Kanko* case, Supreme Court (26 February 1987) 492 Rohan 6 (Takashi Araki, *op. cit.*, p. 194).
946. Takashi Araki, *op. cit.*, pp. 194–195.
947. Article 81.

1058. These five acts could be categorized into four groups under the headings of disadvantageous treatment of union members (items (1) and (5)), yellow-dog contract (item (2)), refusal to bargain (item (3)) and domination and interference (item 4) according to the content of these actions.

III. Disadvantageous Treatment of Union Members

A. *Significance*

1059. Discharges or other disadvantageous treatment of workers on the grounds that they have joined,[948] tried to join, or attempted to organize a trade union;[949] or have carried out a justifiable act for the operation of a trade union;[950] or have reported a violation by an employer; or have given testimony or presented evidence at the labour relations commission, are prohibited as unfair labour practices.[951] The same applies to making it a condition of employment that the worker must not join or must withdraw from a trade union (yellow-dog contracts).

1060. In this case trade union includes not only the trade union qualified by the TULRAA but also one designated as a *bona fide* trade union.

B. *Forms of Disadvantageous Treatment*

1061. Disadvantageous treatment embraces any kind of unfavourable treatment: making a contract with unfavourable working conditions, dismissal, reducing a worker to a lower rank, transferring a worker to a more inconvenient workplace or to an inferior job, delaying a promotion, reducing salary, refusing to grant privileges allowed to other workers or suspending workers' attendance. 'Unfavourable' treatment is any such treatment which generates inconvenience, causes a handicap, inflicts a disadvantage or economic damage in regard to membership of a trade union or in their pursuing a social life. In judging whether the treatment is unfavourable or not, all factors must be taken together. A treatment which may even be considered to be favourable in one aspect could be an unfair labour practice in other regards. For example, transferring an worker to a higher position which interferes with his or her union activities or inflicts disadvantages on their family life is an unfair labour practice.[952]

948. The term 'joining a trade union' means becoming a member of a trade union or a specific trade union.
949. The term 'attempting to organize a trade union' means arranging or assisting the organization of a trade union.
950. The term 'operation of a trade union' means, chiefly, collective bargaining, strikes and lock–outs. So, we may consider the 'collective action' prescribed in the sixth item of Article 2 of the TULRAA as being included in the operation of a trade union.
951. Presenting evidence' means participating in an unfair labour practice case as a party concerned.
952. Chi Sun Kim, *op. cit.*, p. 111.

C. Subjective Requisites

1062. Generally speaking the burden of proof for the existence of intention, in terms of committing an unfair labour practice, rests with the worker. But it is very difficult, or nearly impossible, to prove the private intention of an employer. If direct and perfect proof of intention by the worker concerned were required, the unfair labour practices system would become a nominal system for workers. To make the unfair labour practices system an efficient one, it is necessary to lighten the burden of proof. Therefore, the proof introduced by a worker need not be directly or perfectly based on direct or perfect evidence. If a worker points to facts from which the existence of intention may be inferred or presumed indirectly, this is considered sufficient to prove the intention of an employer to discriminate.[953]

D. Intention of and Justifiable Reasons for Disadvantageous Treatment

1063. When an employer, in spite of proof of the existence of an unfair labour practice provided by a worker, contends that there is justifiable cause for such disadvantageous treatment and also proves the justifiability of his or her cause, it is very difficult to decide whether or not an unfair labour practice exists. One requirement for a finding that disadvantageous treatment represents unfair labour practices is that the treatment was 'by reason' of anti-union animus (the intent to commit an unfair labour practices). Because of the difficulties in ascertaining the intent of the employer in particular conduct, it is generally accepted that the inferred intent of the employer from indirect facts or circumstantial evidence surrounding the disadvantageous treatment satisfies this requirement.

1064. More complex is the mixed motive case where, for instance, a union leader is discharged for serious misconduct while, at the same time, the employer has been wanting to expel him from the company. At present, at both the labour relations commissions and in the courts, such cases turn on whether the anti-union animus is the decisive factor motivating the disadvantageous treatment in question.[954]

IV. Yellow-dog Contracts

1065. A contract including a condition that a worker may not join or must withdraw from a specific trade union, or must become a member of a specific trade union is generally called a 'yellow-dog contract'.[955]

953. *Ibid.*, p. 112.
954. Takashi Araki, *op. cit.*, p. 196.
955. A worker may accept such conditions as to remain in employment, i.e. to retain his or her job. The employer attaches such conditions in order to weaken the vigorous activities of the existing union and to strengthen the organization and activities of the company union. Though such a contract is made under the pretext of the liberty of contract, it is in reality an unfair contract which infringes upon the worker's right to organize as guaranteed by the Constitution (Article 33). That is why the TULRAA (Article 81 sub-paragraph 2) prohibits it as an unfair labour practice. In addition to the

1066. Attaching a condition not to join or to withdraw from a specific union or not to organize a trade union is an explicit infringement of fundamental labour rights. There can be no excuse for affixing such a condition. In cases of yellow-dog contracts, the intention of malicious or unfair labour practices is so manifest and explicit that a worker need not prove the existence of such intention and there is no scope for the employer to offer evidence in disproof. If a worker proves that a contract with such a condition was concluded between him or her and the employer, that is enough to prove the existence of an unfair labour practice.[956]

1067. As stated above, making it a condition of employment that a worker abstain from joining, or withdraw from a trade union, or join a particular trade union is generally called a 'yellow-dog contract'. However, in cases where a trade union represents more than two-thirds of the workers employed in the same business, the conclusion of a collective agreement under which a person is employed on condition that he or she becomes a member of the trade union shall be allowed as an exception. In this case, the employer shall not put the worker at any disadvantageous position in terms of status, on the grounds that the worker has been expelled from the trade union, or has withdrawn from the trade union to organize a new trade union or to join another trade union.[957]

V. Refusal to Bargain

1068. Trade unions which represent the interests of workers have, as their *raison d'être*, acquiring favourable working conditions by bargaining with employers.[958] If an employer refuses to negotiate with a trade union, the refusal is no less than a denial of the existence of the trade union. That is why the TULRAA charges employers with the obligation to bargain with representatives of trade unions (Article 29) and why this Act prohibits the refusal to negotiate on the part of an

conditions stated above, a condition that a worker shall not organize any trade union, nor shall not participate in any trade union activity; for example, collective bargaining or strike action; may also be attached. A contract with the former condition also infringes the workers' right to organize, and a contract with the latter condition infringes upon the workers; rights to bargain collectively and to act collectively. Therefore, from a constitutional viewpoint such a contract may also be regarded as being included in the so-called yellow-dog category and be prohibited as an unfair labour practice. If the employer dismisses or gives disadvantageous treatment to a worker on the grounds that the worker did not abide by such a condition, such an act falls under the first category of unfair labour practice, namely, disadvantageous treatment.

956. Attaching a condition not to participate in any trade union activity being also an explicit and manifest infringement of the right to bargain and the right to act collectively, an worker is also exempted from the duty to prove the existence of intention to commit an unfair labour practice.

957. Article 81 paragraph 2.

958. It is only when a favourable collective agreement is concluded between an employer and workers as a result of collective bargaining that the purpose of labour legislation to improve working conditions and thereby to enhance the economic and social status of workers is attained. The right to bargain is a fundamental and important activity of trade unions. The mutual relations among the workers generate three rights as follows; the right to organize without the right to bargain is meaningless, just as the right to organize aims at the right to bargain; the right to act collectively serves as a means to facilitate and expedite collective bargaining (Chi Sun Kim, *op. cit.*, p. 114).

employer as an unfair labour practice (Article 81 no.3). The parties to such collective bargaining are trade unions on the workers' side and employers or employers' organizations on the employers' side.[959]

1069. Article 30, sub-paragraph 1 (TULRAA) stipulates that a trade union and an employer or an employers' association shall bargain with each other in good faith and with sincerity when making a collective agreement, and shall not abuse their authority. To satisfy this duty to bargain in good faith, most scholars hold that the employer must not only listen to the union's requests but also provide a substantive response that corresponds to the degree of concreteness of the request. Depending upon the circumstances, an employer may be required to show the basis for his or her response and present supporting data.[960] A duty to bargain in good faith does not translate into a duty to agree or compromise with the union.

1070. Article 30 sub-paragraph 2 (TULRAA) stipulates that a trade union and an employer or an employers' association shall not refuse or delay, without just cause(s), negotiations or the conclusion of collective agreements. Therefore, an employer is under an obligation to negotiate with trade unions. This obligation does not mean that the employer must accept all subjects offered for negotiation or that he or she must reach a collective agreement. If an employer has justifiable reasons for their refusal to do so, he is not liable for failing to fulfil this obligation. However, whether or not the obligation has been fulfilled is a difficult problem to assess. All factors must be taken into consideration, and above all the purpose of this unfair labour practice system must be taken into account.[961]

---

959. It is not necessary that a trade union be one qualified in accordance with the TULRAA. Even an unqualified trade union which falls under Section 4 of Article 3, unless it is a company union, is entitled to ask to negotiate with an employer. The notion of a single trade union monopolizing collective bargaining rights does not exist. Both a majority trade union and a minority trade union have the right to request the right to collective bargaining. Even an agreement between an employer and a trade union that a specific trade union is a unique bargaining unit that may request the right to bargain with the employer could not be a justifiable cause for a refusal to bargain with another. Such an agreement could not deprive other trade unions of the right to bargain as guaranteed by the Constitution. It is the representatives of a trade union who have the actual authority to bargain.

960. To express it concretely, the employer has the obligation to meet at reasonable times, in appropriate places, and to confer in good faith with respect to working conditions and any problems incidental to the negotiations. To fulfil this obligation, the employer must sometimes disclose information which needs to be given to trade unions, and must sometimes explain sincerely and with precision such troubles and problems that may exist within the enterprise, further they must sometimes offer counter-proposals or make concessions to a trade union.

961. Let us make some of these points clear. First concerning the party to collective bargaining on the workers' side, when qualification as a representative is doubtful or when their authority to conduct negotiations is limited to certain subjects, an employer may refuse to negotiate or may ask to put off the negotiation until the issue in doubt has been resolved. Secondly, concerning the subjects of collective bargaining, certain subjects are outside the scope of negotiation. An employer may refuse to negotiate on political issues, for example the labour policy of the government or the wage guidelines adopted by the government; likewise the issues which are beyond the power or control of an employer, for example those that belong to the management of another enterprise, rest outside the scope of collective bargaining. Furthermore, issues which belong to the management prerogative of an employer are beyond the scope of collective bargaining. Thirdly, with regard to procedural

1071. When collective bargaining is interrupted, a trade union may request assistance from the labour relations committee. Then a trade union has only to point out the fact that the collective bargaining process ended in failure. An employer must disprove existence of unfair labour practices. Because an employer has the obligation to bargain in good faith, he or she must prove that he has fulfilled that obligation, in other words, that he or she has refused to bargain with justifiable cause. In the case of the breakdown of collective bargaining an intention to engage in unfair labour practices on the employer's side is presumed and the employer's side must offer evidence in disproof.[962]

VI. Domination and Interference

1072. In principle employers are outsiders with regard to the organization and the operation of trade unions, notably concerning the internal affairs of those unions. They must refrain from exercising influence over trade unions.

1073. Trade unions must be organized and operated independently of the influence of employers so that they may represent the interests of workers. If they are controlled or dominated by employers or their organizations, they effectively company unions. The TULRAA guarantees the independence of trade unions from the influence of, or interference by, employers. Control or interference with the formation or management of a trade union, the provision of financial support in defraying the trade union's operational expenditures or wage payment for full-time officials of a trade union is third category of prohibited unfair labour practices (TULRAA Article 81 r.4).

1074. The proviso being, however, the employers may allow workers to take part in consultation or bargaining with their employers during their working hours, may provide subsidies for the welfare of their workers, or for the prevention and relief of financial difficulties and other disasters, and may provide a union office of minimal size.[963]

1075. To speak theoretically, domination differs from interference in terms of the degree of influence over a trade union. However, in practice it is very difficult to draw a sharp line between the two. There are various types of conduct on behalf of the employer, throughout the labour–management relationship, which can be

---

and circumstantial details, an employer's refusal to bargain can be justified in certain circumstances. When the length of the time spent on collective bargaining is excessive or such bargaining goes on until late at night, an employer may refuse to bargain. When the representatives of a trade union assume a threatening attitude, using violence or harsh language, the employer may also refuse to bargain. But if the parties have not come to an agreement about the place, date, time and the number of the representatives participating in the negotiations, the refusal to bargain on the grounds that the representatives do not accept the proposals offered unilaterally by the employer amounts to unfair labor practice (Chi Sun Kim, *op. cit.*, p. 115).

962. *Ibid.*, p. 116.

963. TULRAA, Article 81 no. 4.

deemed to be either domination or interference. For example, if an employer criticizes a union or its activities, implies that disadvantageous treatment will ensue for workers who join a union, discharges or transfers active union members, or establishes a company-dominated organization to counteract the organization of a labour union, a finding of an unfair labour practice may result.[964]

1076. Speaking generally, assisting with expenses, namely, giving financial support to a trade union, is a typical means by which an employer can efficiently dominate or control a trade union. That is why Article 81, Section 4 specifically prohibits assisting with expenses as an act of domination and interference. However, this does not mean that a trade union cannot receive any financial assistance from an employer. Whether giving financial support is an unfair labour practice or not must be decided after having taken into consideration the existing practices between the employer and the trade union. As Article 2 (TULRAA) provides that when a trade union receives assistance primarily from an employer in the disbursement of the expenses thereof, the definition of a trade union shall not be applied, we may conclude that receiving minimal financial assistance that does not infringe their independence may be acceptable. For example, a trade union may receive financial aid which is the result of collective bargaining.[965] To the same effect, as in the case of minimal financial assistance, Article 81, Section 4 makes exceptions as follows: an employer may allow workers to take part in consultation or bargaining with their employers during working hours, may provide subsidies for the welfare of workers, or for the prevention and relief of financial difficulties and other disasters, and may provide a union office of minimal size.

1077. The most controversial issues concerning domination and interference involve the conflict between an employer's right to control its facilities and the protection of union activities. The Supreme Court established a distinct ruling called the 'permission theory'.[966] The Court held that the prohibition of the use of the employer's premises was not tantamount to domination or interference unless special circumstances were involved, whereby a denial of permission was regarded as

964. And we may enumerate the enactment and change of the trade union constitution, the election of executive members, merger, division and dissolution of a trade union, collective bargaining and acts of dispute as the operation of a trade union. Domination and interference would include persuading or forcing a worker to join a company union; preventing workers from attending an inaugural meeting; dismissing important promoters of the organization; or criticizing the organization or the operation of a trade union which stands against an employer. Forcing a worker who is a member of a trade union to withdraw from it, or ordering an worker to work on rest day when a general meeting of a trade union is to be held on that day also constitutes control or interference with a trade union. In the above cases, if the employer dismisses the worker on the grounds that she or he has joined or has not withdrawn from the trade union, this constitutes both domination and interference with a trade union and disadvantageous treatment against the worker. 'Organization' includes any activities affecting the organization itself.

965. Chi Sun Kim, *op. cit.*, p. 117.

966. The *Kukutesta Sapporo Unten-ku* case in 1979 concerning the validity of disciplinary action against workers involved in union activities (posting handbills within a company's facilities).

an abuse of the employer's right to control their facilities.[967] The Supreme Court rarely recognizes the existence of special circumstances.[968]

1078. In addition, the most controversial issues concerning domination and interference involve the problem of conflict between the employer's freedom of speech or use of the press on the one hand and the workers' right to organize, to bargain and to act collectively on the other. For example, when an employer expresses views in writing or verbally against the organization or operation of a trade union, it is difficult to decide whether this expression is a justifiable one based on the freedom of speech or access to the press or whether it is an interference in the affairs of a trade union. In the USA a principle has been developed with respect to this problem. As Article 8 (c) of the Wagner Act provides, the expression of any views, arguments, opinions or the dissemination thereof, whether in written, printed, graphic or visual form, shall not constitute or be evidence of an unfair labour practice if such expression contains no threat of reprisal of force or promise of benefit.[969] However, unlike the USA, in Korea where only the workers rights to bargain and to act collectively are guaranteed by the Constitution (Article 33), the principle stated above could not be accepted as it stands. If this principle were accepted, the workers' rights could not be protected sufficiently and the unfair labour practice system would become nothing more than a mere nominal one, losing its reason for being. Whether the expression of views against a trade union contains a threat of reprisal of force or promises of benefits is not the only evidence; it serves only as decisive and positive evidence. All factors and the situation attendant upon the expression of the employer's opinion should be taken into account. Even though the expression may not contain any direct and certain threat of reprisal or force, it can be a threatening one judging from the situation on that day, at that place, at that time and all other factors and it would consequently constitute an unfair labour practice.[970]

1079. When it is referred to the labour relations committee, it is the employer who has to prove the non-existence of such an intention. However, in the case that the exceptions made by this provision of presumption cannot be permitted, then it is the trade union which must prove that in spite of the provisory clause, such as exceptional acts, were also intended in order to dominate or interfere with a trade union.

967. The *Oriental Motor* case, Supreme Court (8 September 1995) 679 Rohan11 (Takashi Araki, *op. cit.*, p. 198).
968. Takashi Araki, *op. cit.*, p. 198.
969. C. Werne, *The Law of Labour Relations*, 1951, pp. 191 and 202f.
970. Chi Sun Kim, *op. cit.*, p. 118.

§2. RELIEF FOR UNFAIR LABOUR PRACTICES

I. Remedial Procedures for Unfair Labour Practices

1080. Remedial procedures for unfair labour practice cases are divided into:

- initial examination procedures by the labour relations commission;
- administrative review procedures by the Central Labour Relations Commission; and
- judicial review procedures through the courts.

1081. The process for undertaking remedial procedures is labourious but not complex. It begins with the local Labour Relations Commission, where an application or complaint leads to an investigation followed by a hearing, which, in turn allows the commission to deliberate and, ultimately issue an order. If either side has a problem with such a decision they may appeal to the Central Labour Relations Commission. At this point the process is, essentially the same, leading from an original complaint to a final decision. If one or both parties are still unsatisfied, they may then move on to:

- the High Court; and finally,
- the Supreme Court.

II. Application for Remedy

1082. A worker or trade union whose rights have been infringed by unfair labour practices may make an application for remedy to the Labour Relations Commission.

1083. In seeking a remedial order, the complainant, namely a worker or a union, must file a complaint alleging that an employer has violated the provisions prohibiting unfair labour practices. The complaint must be filed with the local labour relations commission in the district in which the parties reside, where the party's main office is located, or where the alleged unfair labour practice was committed. Application for remedy must be filed within three months from the date when such unfair labour practices have been committed (or from the date of termination in cases where such activities continue).[971]

III. Remedial Procedures

1084. Remedial procedures shall follow these methods;

- examination procedures by the local Labour Relations Commission;

971. Article 82.

- upon receiving the complaint, the Labour Relations Commission shall, without delay, conduct the necessary investigations and inquiries of the parties concerned;
- while conducting the inquiry, the Labour Relations Commission may, at the request of the parties or by its own authority, have witnesses appear before the Commission, and conduct an examination with relation to the pertinent matters;
- when conducting such an inquiry, the Labour Relations Commission shall provide sufficient opportunities for the parties concerned to present evidence and to cross-examine witnesses. The procedures concerning both the investigation and inquiry by the Labour Relations Commission shall be specified by separate rules promulgated by the National Labour Relations Commission.[972]

A. *Orders of Remedy*

1085. The Labour Relations Commission, after completing an inquiry under Article 83 and finding that an employer has perpetrated labour practices considered to be unfair, shall issue an order for remedy to the employer. The contents of such a remedial order are at its own discretion. As an independent administrative organ with expertise concerning labour relations, the Labour Relations Commission has the discretionary power to determine the remedial order's content. Therefore, the commission may order measures that it sees as most likely, in the context of the circumstances concerned, to eliminate the harm caused by the unfair labour practices and restore harmonious labour relations. The Supreme Court has recognized this discretionary authority of the Labour Relations Commissions with regard to the content of the remedial orders and has held that they should be treated with deference when under judicial review.[973]

1086. When the commission determines that an unfair labour practice has not been committed, it shall enter a decision to dismiss the application for remedy.[974]

1087. Typical remedial orders for each type of unfair labour practice are:

- in disadvantageous treatment cases, to reinstate the discharged or transferred workers with or without back pay;
- in instances of a refusal to bargain, to order the employer to bargain with the union in good faith on the subject concerned; and
- in cases of domination and interference, to cease and desist the acts at issue and/or the posting of notices;
- that the employer will not engage in those acts in the future.[975]

972. Article 83.
973. The *Daii Hato Taxi* case, Supreme Court (23 February 1977) 31 Minshu 93 (Takashi Araki, *op. cit.*, p. 202).
974. Article 84.
975. Takashi Araki, *op. cit.*, p. 201.

1088. Judgments, orders and decisions shall be made in writing, and shall be issued to the pertinent employer and the applicant. Each of the parties must comply with the order issued.[976]

B. Finalization of Remedy Orders

1089. Where one of the parties disagrees with any remedy order or dismissal decision made by the Regional Labour Relations Commission or by the Special Labour Relations Commission, he or she may make an application for review of such an order to the National Labour Relations Commission within ten days of the date of receiving the notice of the order or decision.[977]

1090. The party concerned may bring an administrative suit in accordance with the Administrative Litigation Act against a decision of review made by the National Labour Relations Commission within 15 days of the date of receiving notice of the decision regarding a review.[978]

1091. Unless an application for review or an administrative suit has been made within the period specified, remedy orders, dismissal decisions or review decisions shall be final.[979] When dismissal decisions or review decisions have been finalized, the parties concerned must comply with those decisions.[980] When an employer has initiated an administrative suit, the competent court may, at the request of the National Labour Relations Commission, order the enforcement of the whole or part of the remedy order made by the Central Labour Relations Commission until the judgment of the court is rendered, and may, at the request of the parties or by its own authority, revoke such a decision.[981]

C. Effect of Remedy Order, etc.

1092. The effect of remedy orders, dismissal decisions or review decisions made by the Labour Relations Commission shall not be suspended by an application for review to the National Labour Relations Commission or by the initiation of an administrative suit.[982]

1093. Violators of the Labour Relations Commission's finalized orders face sanctions including both administrative and criminal penalties.[983]

976. Article 84.
977. Article 85 paragraph 1.
978. Article 85 paragraph 2.
979. Article 85 paragraph 3.
980. Article 85 paragraph 4.
981. Article 85 paragraph 5.
982. Article 86.
983. Articles 89–90

Selected Bibliography

BOOKS

Araki, Takashi, *Labour and Employment Law in Japan*, The Japan Institute of Labour, 2002.

Blanpain, Roger *European Labour Law*, Kluwer Law International, The Hague London Boston, 2002.

Brox, *Arbeitsrecht*, 10th edn, 1991.

Coleman, Charles J., *Managing Labour Relations in the Public Sector*, 1990.

Edwards, Clark and Craver, *Labour Relations Law in the Public Sector*, 1991.

Gould, William B., *Strikes, Disputes Procedures, and Arbitration*, 1985.

Gould IV, William B., *A Primer on American Labour Law* 4th edn, The MIT Press, Cambridge, Massachusetts, and London, 2003.

Ha, Kap-rea, *Labour Standards Act*, Joongangkyungje, 2008.

Ha, Kap-rea, *Collective Labour Relations Law*, Joongangkyungje, 2010.

Ha, Kyung-hyo, *Case Study on Labour Law*, Parkyoungsa, 2017.

Hanau and Adomeit, *Arbeitsrecht*, 11th edn 1994.

Hepple, Bob and Sandra Fredman, *Labour Law and Industrial Relations in Great Britain*, 1992.

Jung, Bongsoo, *The Korean Labour Law Bible*, Joongangkyungje, 2015.

Jung, Bongsoo, *Korean Labour Law: Disputes and Resolutions*, Joongangkyungje, 2014.

Kazuo, Sugeno, *Japanese Employment and Labour Law*, Carolina Academic Press/ University of Tokyo Press, 2002.

Kim, Chi Sun, Kluwer Law International, The Hague, London, Boston, 1994.

Kim, Chi-sun, *Lecture on Labour Law*, Parkyoungsa, 1992.

Kim, Hyung-bea, *Labour Law*, Parkyoungsa, 2018.

Kim, Hyung-bea, *Labour Standards Act*, Parkyoungsa, 2001.

Kim, Soo-bok, *Industrial Accident Compensation Insurance Act*, Chungangkyungje, 2008.

Kim, You-sung, *Labour Law I*, Bummunsa, 2005.

Kim, You-sung, *Labour Law II*, Bummunsa, 2001.

Ko, Zoon-ki, *Labour Law*, Goshigye, 2010.

Lee, Byung-tea, *Labour Law*, Joongangkyungjesa, 2008

Lee, Chul-soo, *Labour Law Dictionary*, Bummunsa, 1994.

Lee, Eul-hyung, *Labour Law*, Deawangsa,1995.

Lee, Eul-hyung, *International Labour Law*, Soongsildeachulpanboo, 1996.

Lee, Hak-chun, *Labour Law*, Deamyungchulpansa, 2003.
Lim, Jong-ryul, *Labour Law*, Parkyoungsa, 2019.
Lee, Jung, *Japanese Labour Law*, Bummunsa, 2015.
Lee, Sang-deak, *Labour Law*, Goshigye, 1995.
Lee, Sang-deak, *Case Study on the Labour Law*, Deamyungchulpansa, 2010.
Lee, Sang-kuk, *Industrial Accident Compensation Insurance Act*, Deamyongchulpansa, 2019.
Lee, Sang-youn, *Labour Law*, Bummunsa, 2019.
Lee, Sang-youn, *Trade Union Act*, Parkyoungsa, 1996.
Lee, Young-hee, *Labour Law*, Bummunsa, 2001.
Lowisch, *Arbeitsrecht*, 3rd edn, 1991.
Park, Hong-kyu, *Labour Law*, Samyoungsa, 2002.
Park, Sang-pil, *Korean Labour Law*, Deawangsa, 1995.
Park, Sung-dea, *Outline of Labour Law*, Joongangkyungjesa, 1995.
Rideout, R.W., *Rideout's Principles of Labour Law*, Sweet & Maxwell (London),1989.
Schaub, *Arbeitsrechtshandbuch*, 8th edn, 1996.
Shin, Hong, *Explanation of Labour Relations Adjustment Act*, Korean Nodongkyoyoukwon, 1996.
Shin, In-ryung, *Study on the Basic Legal Rights of Labour*, Mireasa, 1989.
Smith & Wood, *Industrial Law*, 4th edn, 1989.
Sollner, *Grundriβ des Arbeitsrecht*, 10th edn, 1990.
Song, Gang-jik, *Legal Principles of Collective Labour Relations Law,* Samjiwon, 1999
Wallington, Peter *Butterworths Employment Law Handbook*, 1990.
You, Sung-jea, *Case Study on the Labour Law*, Bummunsa, 2008.
Zollner and Loritz, *Arbeitsrecht*, 4th edn, 1992.

SOURCES OF KOREAN LABOUR LAW

The Basic Employment Policy Act (2017)
The Employment Security Act (2019)
The Workers Vocational Skills Development Act (2019)
The Act on Equal Employment and Support for Work Family Reconciliation amended from the Act on Equal Employment) (2019)
The Act on Employment Promotion and Vocational Rehabilitation for Disabled Persons (2018)
The Act on Age Discrimination Prohibition in Employment and Aged Employment Promotion (2016)
The Employment Insurance Act (2019)
The Act on Foreign Workers' Employment, etc. (2017)
The Labour Standards Act (2019)
The Minimum Wage Act (2018)
The Occupational Safety and Health Act (2018)
The Industrial Accident Compensation Insurance Act (2017)
The Act on the Protection, etc., of Dispatched Workers (2019)
The Act on the Prevention of Pneumoconiosis and Protection, etc., of Pneumoconiosis Workers (2017)

The Wage Age Claim Guarantee Act (2018)
The Employee Retirement Benefit Security Act (2018)
The Act on the Protection, etc., of Fixed-term and Part-time Employees (2018)
The Act on the Protection, etc., of Dispatched Workers (2019)
The Act on the Employment Improvement, etc., for Construction Workers (2016)
The TULRAA (2018)
The Labour Relations Commission Act (2019)
The Act on the Promotion of Worker Participation and Cooperation (2016)
The Act on the Tripartite Commission for Economic and Social Development (2018)
The Act on the Establishment, Operation, etc., of Public Officials' Trade Unions (2014)

Selected Bibliography

Index

The numbers here given refer to paragraph numbers.

Made in the USA
Monee, IL
13 September 2026

62974273R00177